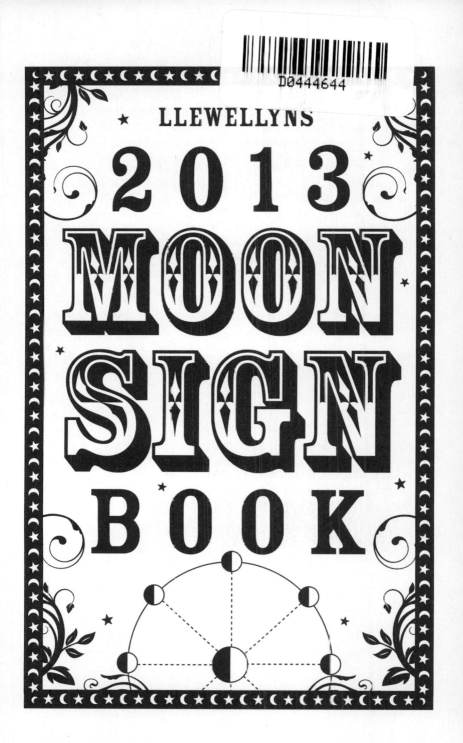

LLEWELLYNS

2013

MOON SIGN BOOK

Llewellyn's 2013 Moon Sign Book®

ISBN 978-0-7387-1513-1

Cover design by Kevin R. Brown
Cover illustrations: Floral elements: iStockphoto.com/Heidi Kristensen;
  Moon: iStockphoto.com/Magnilion
Editing by Nicole Edman
Stock photography models used for illustrative purposes only and may not endorse or represent the book's subject.

Any Internet references contained in this work are current at publication time, but the publisher cannot guarantee that a specific location will continue to be maintained.

Astrological data compiled and programmed by Rique Pottenger. Based on the earlier work of Neil F. Michelsen.

You can order Llewellyn annuals and books from *New Worlds*, Llewellyn's catalog. To request a free copy of the catalog, call toll-free 1-877-NEW-WRLD, or visit our Web site at www.llewellyn.com.

Llewellyn Publications
A Division of Llewellyn Worldwide Ltd.
2143 Wooddale Drive
Woodbury, MN 55125-3989
www.llewellyn.com

Printed in the United States of America

Table of Contents

What's Different About the Moon Sign Book?

Readers have asked why *Llewellyn's Moon Sign Book* says that the Moon is in Taurus when some almanacs indicate that the Moon is in the previous sign of Aries on the same date. It's because there are two different zodiac systems in use today: the tropical and the sidereal. *Llewellyn's Moon Sign Book* is based on the tropical zodiac.

The tropical zodiac takes 0 degrees of Aries to be the Spring Equinox in the Northern Hemisphere. This is the time and date when the Sun is directly overhead at noon along the equator, usually about March 20–21. The rest of the signs are positioned at 30-degree intervals from this point.

The sidereal zodiac, which is based on the location of fixed stars, uses the positions of the fixed stars to determine the starting point of

0 degrees of Aries. In the sidereal system, 0 degrees of Aries always begins at the same point. This does create a problem though, because the positions of the fixed stars, as seen from Earth, have changed since the constellations were named. The term "precession of the equinoxes" is used to describe the change.

Precession of the equinoxes describes an astronomical phenomenon brought about by the Earth's wobble as it rotates and orbits the Sun. The Earth's axis is inclined toward the Sun at an angle of about 23½ degrees, which creates our seasonal weather changes. Although the change is slight, because one complete circle of the Earth's axis takes 25,800 years to complete, we can actually see that the positions of the fixed stars seem to shift. The result is that each year, in the tropical system, the Spring Equinox occurs at a slightly different time.

Does Precession Matter?

There is an accumulative difference of about 23 degrees between the Spring Equinox (0 degrees Aries in the tropical zodiac and 0 degrees Aries in the sidereal zodiac) so that 0 degrees Aries at Spring Equinox in the tropical zodiac actually occurs at about 7 degrees Pisces in the sidereal zodiac system. You can readily see that those who use the other almanacs may be planting seeds (in the garden and in their individual lives) based on the belief that it is occurring in a fruitful sign, such as Taurus, when in fact it would be occurring in Gemini, one of the most barren signs of the zodiac. So, if you wish to plant and plan activities by the Moon, it is helpful to follow *Llewellyn's Moon Sign Book*. Before we go on, there are important things to understand about the Moon, her cycles, and their correlation with everyday living. For more information about gardening by the Moon, see page 61.

Weekly Almanac

Your Guide to Lunar Gardening
& Good Timing for Activities

When one tugs at a single thing in nature,
he finds it attached to the rest of the world.
~JOHN MUIR

♑ January

December 30–January 5

Wouldn't it be great if people could get to live as suddenly as they die suddenly.   ~KATHARINE HEPBURN

Date	Qtr.	Sign	Activity
Dec 30, 2:45 am– Jan 1, 12:35 pm	3rd	Leo	Cultivate. Destroy weeds and pests. Harvest fruits and root crops for food. Trim to retard growth.
Jan 6, 1:09 am– Jan 8, 3:28 am	4th	Scorpio	Plant biennials, perennials, bulbs and roots. Prune. Irrigate. Fertilize (organic).

Try growing your own lettuce this winter. Put seeds in soil and just barely cover them over. Place the pot or flat in cool (not cold) place. Once the plants sprout, keep them in a moderately cool and sunny place. You will be able to continuously harvest leaves as long as you leave small, growing leaves intact to recover.

_____

_____

_____

◐
January 4
10:58 pm EST

JANUARY

S	M	T	W	T	F	S
		1	2	3	4	5
6	7	8	9	10	11	12
13	14	15	16	17	18	19
20	21	22	23	24	25	26
27	28	29	30	31		

January 6–12 ♑

*At the center of your being you have the answer; you know
who you are, and you know what you want.*   ~Lao Tzu

Date	Qtr.	Sign	Activity
Jan 6, 1:09 am– Jan 8, 3:28 am	4th	Scorpio	Plant biennials, perennials, bulbs and roots. Prune. Irrigate. Fertilize (organic).
Jan 8, 3:28 am– Jan 10, 3:54 am	4th	Sagittarius	Cultivate. Destroy weeds and pests. Harvest fruits and root crops for food. Trim to retard growth.
Jan 10, 3:54 am– Jan 11, 2:44 pm	4th	Capricorn	Plant potatoes and tubers. Trim to retard growth.
Jan 11, 2:44 pm– Jan 12, 4:01 am	1st	Capricorn	Graft or bud plants. Trim to increase growth.

Herbs de Provence is an herb blend used in many savory French dishes. The name comes from the Provence region of France, where the mixture was made popular. You can easily make your own at home. Combine 2 dried tablespoons each of savory, rosemary, thyme, basil, oregano, marjoram, and fennel seeds. Use on vegetables or meats you plan to roast.

●
January 11
2:44 pm EST

			JANUARY			
S	M	T	W	T	F	S
		1	2	3	4	5
6	7	8	9	10	11	12
13	14	15	16	17	18	19
20	21	22	23	24	25	26
27	28	29	30	31		

January 13–19

For all our insight, obstinant habits do not disappear until replaced by other habits.   ~CARL JUNG

Date	Qtr.	Sign	Activity
Jan 14, 5:49 am– Jan 16, 11:07 am	1st	Pisces	Plant grains, leafy annuals. Fertilize (chemical). Graft or bud plants. Irrigate. Trim to increase growth.
Jan 18, 8:36 pm– Jan 21, 9:04 am	2nd	Taurus	Plant annuals for hardiness. Trim to increase growth.

Save yourself needless headaches each year by keeping a detailed gardening journal. Record your hits and misses, weather patterns, tricks, and thoughts on plant performance and placement. Not only will you enjoy reading over your successes, but you might be able to pinpoint trouble areas or species for future years. Don't have a journal? Use the lines on these weekly pages! Then you'll have your garden notes and lunar data all in one place for easy reference.

_____

_____

_____

_____

January 18
6:45 pm EST

	JANUARY					
S	M	T	W	T	F	S
		1	2	3	4	5
6	7	8	9	10	11	12
13	14	15	16	17	18	19
20	21	22	23	24	25	26
27	28	29	30	31		

2012 © Maria Adelaide Silva. Image from BigStockPhoto.com

January 20–26 〜〜

Talent hits a target no one else can hit; genius hits a target no one else can see.   ~Arthur Schopenhauer

Date	Qtr.	Sign	Activity
Jan 18, 8:36 pm– Jan 21, 9:04 am	2nd	Taurus	Plant annuals for hardiness. Trim to increase growth.
Jan 23, 10:00 pm– Jan 26, 9:20 am	2nd	Cancer	Plant grains, leafy annuals. Fertilize (chemical). Graft or bud plants. Irrigate. Trim to increase growth.
Jan 26, 11:38 pm– Jan 28, 6:27 pm	3rd	Leo	Cultivate. Destroy weeds and pests. Harvest fruits and root crops for food. Trim to retard growth.

To keep various pests out of the garden, many are deterred by human scent, so collecting hair from your hairbrush or clippings when you get your hair cut and sprinkling them around your garden and on your plants can keep creatures away. The same could be said of your dog's fur, whether it comes from a brush or the groomer's floor. —Aili, Minnesota

○
January 26
11:38 pm EST

JANUARY

S	M	T	W	T	F	S
		1	2	3	4	5
6	7	8	9	10	11	12
13	14	15	16	17	18	19
20	21	22	23	24	25	26
27	28	29	30	31		

~~~ February

January 27–February 2

I conceive that the great part of the miseries of mankind are brought upon them by the false estimates they have made of the value of things.   ~BENJAMIN FRANKLIN

Date	Qtr.	Sign	Activity
Jan 26, 11:38 pm– Jan 28, 6:27 pm	3rd	Leo	Cultivate. Destroy weeds and pests. Harvest fruits and root crops for food. Trim to retard growth.
Jan 28, 6:27 pm– Jan 31, 1:36 am	3rd	Virgo	Cultivate, especially medicinal plants. Destroy weeds and pests. Trim to retard growth.
Feb 2, 7:02 am– Feb 3, 8:56 am	3rd	Scorpio	Plant biennials, perennials, bulbs and roots. Prune. Irrigate. Fertilize (organic).

Birds that lay eggs will benefit from the calcium in your broken eggshells. Rinse the shells and break into two. Microwave the halves on a sheet of paper towel for 2–3 minutes. Crush the sterilized shells and sprinkle the small pieces on a walkway or large rock in the early spring.

_____

_____

_____

FEBRUARY

S	M	T	W	T	F	S
					1	2
3	4	5	6	7	8	9
10	11	12	13	14	15	16
17	18	19	20	21	22	23
24	25	26	27	28		

2012 © Emilia Stasiak. Image from BigStockPhoto.com

February 3–9 〜〜

Love, and a cough, cannot be hid.

~GEORGE HERBERT

Date	Qtr.	Sign	Activity
Feb 2, 7:02 am– Feb 3, 8:56 am	3rd	Scorpio	Plant biennials, perennials, bulbs and roots. Prune. Irrigate. Fertilize (organic).
Feb 3, 8:56 am– Feb 4, 10:45 am	4th	Scorpio	Plant biennials, perennials, bulbs and roots. Prune. Irrigate. Fertilize (organic).
Feb 4, 10:45 am– Feb 6, 12:55 pm	4th	Sagittarius	Cultivate. Destroy weeds and pests. Harvest fruits and root crops for food. Trim to retard growth.
Feb 6, 12:55 pm– Feb 8, 2:16 pm	4th	Capricorn	Plant potatoes and tubers. Trim to retard growth.
Feb 8, 2:16 pm– Feb 10, 2:20 am	4th	Aquarius	Cultivate. Destroy weeds and pests. Harvest fruits and root crops for food. Trim to retard growth.

Beyond baths and seed, birds can be attracted to your yard if you provide nesting materials. When cleaning up your yard, leave a pile of twigs and long-stem grasses available. You can add straw, natural yarn or string, short lengths of hair, feathers, moss, pine needles, and thin strips of cloth. Use a suet cage to hold materials that would otherwise blow away.

2012 © Duncan Noakes. Image from BigStockPhoto.com

◑

February 3
8:56 am EST

FEBRUARY

S	M	T	W	T	F	S
					1	2
3	4	5	6	7	8	9
10	11	12	13	14	15	16
17	18	19	20	21	22	23
24	25	26	27	28		

〜〜 February 10–16

There is a wisdom of the head, and … a wisdom of the heart.

〜CHARLES DICKENS

Date	Qtr.	Sign	Activity
Feb 8, 2:16 pm– Feb 10, 2:20 am	4th	Aquarius	Cultivate. Destroy weeds and pests. Harvest fruits and root crops for food. Trim to retard growth.
Feb 10, 4:20 pm– Feb 12, 8:51 pm	1st	Pisces	Plant grains, leafy annuals. Fertilize (chemical). Graft or bud plants. Irrigate. Trim to increase growth.
Feb 15, 5:08 am– Feb 17, 3:31 pm	1st	Taurus	Plant annuals for hardiness. Trim to increase growth.

A rain barrel can help you make use of rainfall to water your garden. A 1000-sq-ft roof will shed 625 gallons of water from a 1-inch rainfall, though most rain barrels hold around 50 gallons. Choose a barrel with a covered top (to prevent contamination) and a low outlet that will accept a hose (to make emptying easier). Position the barrel near your gutter's downspout or your garden's edge.

February 10
2:20 am EST

FEBRUARY

S	M	T	W	T	F	S
					1	2
3	4	5	6	7	8	9
10	11	12	13	14	15	16
17	18	19	20	21	22	23
24	25	26	27	28		

2012 © Denise Lett. Image from BigStockPhoto.com

February 17–23 ✲

He who knows others is wise; he who knows himself
is enlightened.   ~Lao Tzu

Date	Qtr.	Sign	Activity
Feb 15, 5:08 am– Feb 17, 3:31 pm	1st	Taurus	Plant annuals for hardiness. Trim to increase growth.
Feb 17, 3:31 pm– Feb 17, 4:50 pm	2nd	Taurus	Plant annuals for hardiness. Trim to increase growth.
Feb 20, 5:45 am– Feb 22, 5:12 pm	2nd	Cancer	Plant grains, leafy annuals. Fertilize (chemical). Graft or bud plants. Irrigate. Trim to increase growth.

We all know that more than two-thirds of Earth is covered in water—71 percent of the surface, to be precise—but do you know how much water that really is? The answer is 1.3 billion cubic kilometers, or 310 million cubic miles. Imagine the immense power of the Moon's gravitational pull when moving that much water for the oceanic tides.

February 17
3:31 pm EST

FEBRUARY

S	M	T	W	T	F	S
					1	2
3	4	5	6	7	8	9
10	11	12	13	14	15	16
17	18	19	20	21	22	23
24	25	26	27	28		

2012 © Cheryl Casey. Image from BigStockPhoto.com

✼ March

February 24–March 2

The season has shed its mantle of wind and chill and rain.

~CHARLES D'ORLEANS

Date	Qtr.	Sign	Activity
Feb 25, 3:26 pm– Feb 27, 8:02 am	3rd	Virgo	Cultivate, especially medicinal plants. Destroy weeds and pests. Trim to retard growth.
Mar 1, 12:33 pm– Mar 3, 4:11 pm	3rd	Scorpio	Plant biennials, perennials, bulbs and roots. Prune. Irrigate. Fertilize (organic).

Correctly measuring rainfall is key in determining your watering needs. An inch of rain means that a solid inch of water would cover the entire surface if it weren't allowed to run off or drain. In general, vegetables need 1–2 inches of water per week. Consider how much volume it takes to cover a 10x10-foot garden (100 square feet) with 1 inch of water: around 62 gallons.

○

February 25
3:26 pm EST

MARCH

S	M	T	W	T	F	S
					1	2
3	4	5	6	7	8	9
10	11	12	13	14	15	16
17	18	19	20	21	22	23
24	25	26	27	28	29	30
31						

2012 © Stanislav Perov. Image from BigStockPhoto.com

March 3–9 ✄

*Some books are to be tasted, others to be swallowed, and
some few to be chewed and digested.*

~FRANCIS BACON

Date	Qtr.	Sign	Activity
Mar 1, 12:33 pm– Mar 3, 4:11 pm	3rd	Scorpio	Plant biennials, perennials, bulbs and roots. Prune. Irrigate. Fertilize (organic).
Mar 3, 4:11 pm– Mar 4, 4:53 pm	3rd	Sagittarius	Cultivate. Destroy weeds and pests. Harvest fruits and root crops for food. Trim to retard growth.
Mar 4, 4:53 pm– Mar 5, 7:14 pm	4th	Sagittarius	Cultivate. Destroy weeds and pests. Harvest fruits and root crops for food. Trim to retard growth.
Mar 5, 7:14 pm– Mar 7, 10:01 pm	4th	Capricorn	Plant potatoes and tubers. Trim to retard growth.
Mar 7, 10:01 pm– Mar 10, 1:19 am	4th	Aquarius	Cultivate. Destroy weeds and pests. Harvest fruits and root crops for food. Trim to retard growth.

Buy a rain gauge that has a wide top and narrow bottom to get more accurate readings of small rainfall events, and place the gauge in the middle of your garden. It's best to water in the morning or late afternoon, in 1-inch increments. Stop watering if the water starts to pool or run off and resume after it's all soaked in.

◑

March 4
4:53 pm EST

MARCH

S	M	T	W	T	F	S
					1	2
3	4	5	6	7	8	9
10	11	12	13	14	15	16
17	18	19	20	21	22	23
24	25	26	27	28	29	30
31						

March 10–16

True happiness consists not in the multitude of friends, but in the worth and choice.   ~BEN JONSON

Date	Qtr.	Sign	Activity
Mar 7, 10:01 pm– Mar 10, 1:19 am	4th	Aquarius	Cultivate. Destroy weeds and pests. Harvest fruits and root crops for food. Trim to retard growth.
Mar 10, 1:19 am– Mar 11, 3:51 pm	4th	Pisces	Plant biennials, perennials, bulbs and roots. Prune. Irrigate. Fertilize (organic).
Mar 11, 3:51 pm– Mar 12, 7:17 am	1st	Pisces	Plant grains, leafy annuals. Fertilize (chemical). Graft or bud plants. Irrigate. Trim to increase growth.
Mar 14, 3:08 pm– Mar 17, 2:09 am	1st	Taurus	Plant annuals for hardiness. Trim to increase growth.

You can add more energy to your plants and flowers by using crystal charged water. Make sure crystals are cleansed first, place in water and state the intention of what it is you are adding to the plant and your own growth. For instance, if you are growing roses, you could make a love elixir that would have rose quartz in it. Growing mint? Water it with citrine for added luck or money. —Lisa, New Jersey

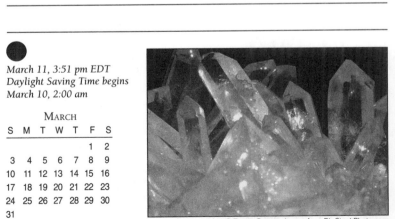

March 11, 3:51 pm EDT
Daylight Saving Time begins
March 10, 2:00 am

MARCH

S	M	T	W	T	F	S
					1	2
3	4	5	6	7	8	9
10	11	12	13	14	15	16
17	18	19	20	21	22	23
24	25	26	27	28	29	30
31						

2012 © Emma Gosney. Image from BigStockPhoto.com

March 17–23 ✂

*Plants of great vigor will almost always struggle into blossom,
despite impediments.*   ~MARGARET FULLER

Date	Qtr.	Sign	Activity
Mar 14, 3:08 pm– Mar 17, 2:09 am	1st	Taurus	Plant annuals for hardiness. Trim to increase growth.
Mar 19, 2:55 pm– Mar 22, 2:50 am	2nd	Cancer	Plant grains, leafy annuals. Fertilize (chemical). Graft or bud plants. Irrigate. Trim to increase growth.

Nothing can ruin a nice side yard or back patio like an ugly air conditioning unit. These units need freely circulating air, so try cutting wood trellising into squares to build a loose "box" that slips over the top of the unit. Don't allow plants to climb these trellises, but you could cluster potted plants along its base. You might even choose to paint the wood trellising to match your house color.

2012 © Tim Grover. Image from BigStockPhoto.com

◐

*March 19
1:27 pm EDT*

MARCH

S	M	T	W	T	F	S
					1	2
3	4	5	6	7	8	9
10	11	12	13	14	15	16
17	18	19	20	21	22	23
24	25	26	27	28	29	30
31						

♈ March 24–30

Let us give Nature a chance; she knows her business better
than we do.   ∼Michel Eyquem de Montaigne

Date	Qtr.	Sign	Activity
Mar 26, 5:32 pm– Mar 27, 5:27 am	2nd	Libra	Plant annuals for fragrance and beauty. Trim to increase growth.
Mar 28, 8:53 pm– Mar 30, 11:13 pm	3rd	Scorpio	Plant biennials, perennials bulbs and roots. Prune. Irrigate. Fertilize (organic).
Mar 30, 11:13 pm– Apr 2, 1:35 am	3rd	Sagittarius	Cultivate. Destroy weeds and pests. Harvest fruits and root crops for food. Trim to retard growth.

Add some visual interest to your garden and plate by planting unusually colored varieties of standby crops. Most oddly colored produce tastes and cooks just like the regular version. Try blue potatoes, purple basil, yellow carrots, orange/yellow watermelon, or purple or orange cauliflower. There are even beets with concentric circles of red and white when you slice them—what kid could resist?

_____

_____

_____

_____

○
March 27
5:27 am EDT

MARCH

S	M	T	W	T	F	S
					1	2
3	4	5	6	7	8	9
10	11	12	13	14	15	16
17	18	19	20	21	22	23
24	25	26	27	28	29	30
31						

2012 © Pauline Wessel. Image from BigStockPhoto.com

April ♈

March 31–April 6

The goal in life is living in agreement with nature.

~ZENO

Date	Qtr.	Sign	Activity
Mar 30, 11:13 pm–Apr 2, 1:35 am	3rd	Sagittarius	Cultivate. Destroy weeds and pests. Harvest fruits and root crops for food. Trim to retard growth.
Apr 2, 1:35 am–Apr 3, 12:37 am	3rd	Capricorn	Plant potatoes and tubers. Trim to retard growth.
Apr 3, 12:37 am–Apr 4, 4:41 am	4th	Capricorn	Plant potatoes and tubers. Trim to retard growth.
Apr 4, 4:41 am–Apr 6, 9:00 am	4th	Aquarius	Cultivate. Destroy weeds and pests. Harvest fruits and root crops for food. Trim to retard growth.
Apr 6, 9:00 am–Apr 8, 3:02 pm	4th	Pisces	Plant biennials, perennials, bulbs and roots. Prune. Irrigate. Fertilize (organic).

One of the most useful tips I've received was the use of Epsom Salts in the garden. A quarter cup applied to the base of any nightshade (tomatoes, peppers, eggplant, etc.) will help it grow beautifully. —Tracci, Ohio

2012 © Mcfields. Image from BigStockPhoto.com

◑

April 3
12:37 am EDT

APRIL

S	M	T	W	T	F	S
	1	2	3	4	5	6
7	8	9	10	11	12	13
14	15	16	17	18	19	20
21	22	23	24	25	26	27
28	29	30				

♈ April 7–13

The greatest things ever done on Earth have been done little by little.   ~WILLIAM JENNINGS BRYAN

Date	Qtr.	Sign	Activity
Apr 6, 9:00 am– Apr 8, 3:02 pm	4th	Pisces	Plant biennials, perennials, bulbs and roots. Prune. Irrigate. Fertilize (organic).
Apr 8, 3:02 pm– Apr 10, 5:35 am	4th	Aries	Cultivate. Destroy weeds and pests. Harvest fruits and root crops for food. Trim to retard growth.
Apr 10, 11:22 pm– Apr 13, 10:13 am	1st	Taurus	Plant annuals for hardiness. Trim to increase growth.

Most commercial honey has been pasteurized (heated) to kill yeast cells and strained to remove any bits of honeycomb wax. Raw honey, however, is making a resurgence, as folks don't mind having to mix their honey a bit before use. Raw local honey is also used an alternative allergy treatment, the theory being that the local pollens contained within will desensitize a person against seasonal allergies to those local plants. If your honey has crystallized, simply give its container a hot water bath to return it to a liquid state.

April 10
5:35 am EDT

APRIL

S	M	T	W	T	F	S
	1	2	3	4	5	6
7	8	9	10	11	12	13
14	15	16	17	18	19	20
21	22	23	24	25	26	27
28	29	30				

2012 © Joanna Wnuk. Image from BigStockPhoto.com

April 14–20 ♈

Astronomy compels the soul to look upwards and leads us
from this world to another.   ~Plato

Date	Qtr.	Sign	Activity
Apr 15, 10:49 pm– Apr 18, 8:31 am	1st	Cancer	Plant grains, leafy annuals. Fertilize (chemical). Graft or bud plants. Irrigate. Trim to increase growth.
Apr 18, 8:31 am– Apr 18, 11:13 am	2nd	Cancer	Plant grains, leafy annuals. Fertilize (chemical). Graft or bud plants. Irrigate. Trim to increase growth.

Roasting peppers yourself will elevate you to master chef status in all your friends' eyes. Wash, seed, and quarter sweet bell peppers, then flatten the sections by pressing down on them. Broil 4–6 inches from heat for 5–10 minutes, until they are blackened but not on fire—this takes a watchful eye! Remove peppers and cover them while they cool. Then simply peel off the blackened skins and use the roasted peppers in your recipe. You may also store these in plastic bags in the fridge for several days.

2012 © Dušan Zidar. Image from BigStockPhoto.com

◑
April 18
8:31 am EDT

APRIL

S	M	T	W	T	F	S
		1	2	3	4	5	6
7	3	9	10	11	12	13
14	15	16	17	18	19	20
21	22	23	24	25	26	27
28	29	30				

April 21–27

Love the animals, love the plants, love everything.

~FYODOR DOSTOYEVSKY

Date	Qtr.	Sign	Activity
Apr 23, 3:25 am– Apr 25, 6:25 am	2nd	Libra	Plant annuals for fragrance and beauty. Trim to increase growth.
Apr 25, 6:25 am– Apr 25, 3:57 pm	2nd	Scorpio	Plant grains, leafy annuals. Fertilize (chemical). Graft or bud plants. Irrigate. Trim to increase growth.
Apr 25, 3:57 pm– Apr 27, 7:32 am	3rd	Scorpio	Plant biennials, perennials, bulbs and roots. Prune. Irrigate. Fertilize (organic).
Apr 27, 7:32 am– Apr 29, 8:21 am	3rd	Sagittarius	Cultivate. Destroy weeds and pests. Harvest fruits and root crops for food. Trim to retard growth.

Most of us don't yet have outdoor flowers to fill May Day baskets, so make paper flowers. Kids can trace a spiral onto paper and then roughly cut along the line. Roll up the strip of paper and glue the bottom to a circle of paper or staple to a pipe cleaner stem. Roll a large piece of paper into a cone and add a handle. Tradition says we should hang the flower-filled cone on someone's door knob, then ring the bell and run away to hide and watch them enjoy the colorful surprise.

○
April 25
3:57 pm EDT

APRIL

S	M	T	W	T	F	S
	1	2	3	4	5	6
7	8	9	10	11	12	13
14	15	16	17	18	19	20
21	22	23	24	25	26	27
28	29	30				

2012 © Jurgita Genyte. Image from BigStockPhoto.com

May ♉
April 28–May 4

Ask the plants of the earth and they will teach you.

~JOB 12: 7–8

Date	Qtr.	Sign	Activity
Apr 27, 7:32 am– Apr 29, 8:21 am	3rd	Sagittarius	Cultivate. Destroy weeds and pests. Harvest fruits and root crops for food. Trim to retard growth.
Apr 29, 8:21 am– May 1, 10:20 am	3rd	Capricorn	Plant potatoes and tubers. Trim to retard growth.
May 1, 10:20 am– May 2, 7:14 am	3rd	Aquarius	Cultivate. Destroy weeds and pests. Harvest fruits and root crops for food. Trim to retard growth.
May 2, 7:14 am– May 3, 2:25 pm	4th	Aquarius	Cultivate. Destroy weeds and pests. Harvest fruits and root crops for food. Trim to retard growth.
May 3, 2:25 pm– May 5, 9:03 pm	4th	Pisces	Plant biennials, perennials, bulbs and roots. Prune. Irrigate. Fertilize (organic).

If deer are eating the new growth on young trees or bushes, tie one handle of a plastic bag to a branch. The bags are easily moved by the slightest breeze and the movement/noise keeps the deer away. Be sure to check the bags after rain because they will collect water and that hinders their movement and their effectiveness. —Aili, Minnesota

2012 © Keith Hughes. Image from BigStockPhoto.com

◑

May 2
7:14 am EDT

MAY

S	M	T	W	T	F	S
			1	2	3	4
5	6	7	8	9	10	11
12	13	14	15	16	17	18
19	20	21	22	23	24	25
26	27	28	29	30	31	

May 5–11

This month is a kiss, which heaven gives the earth, that now she becomes a bride, and then a future mother.
~Friedrich von Logau, "Characteristics of May"

Date	Qtr.	Sign	Activity
May 3, 2:25 pm– May 5, 9:03 pm	4th	Pisces	Plant biennials, perennials, bulbs and roots. Prune. Irrigate. Fertilize (organic).
May 5, 9:03 pm– May 8, 6:09 am	4th	Aries	Cultivate. Destroy weeds and pests. Harvest fruits and root crops for food. Trim to retard growth.
May 8, 6:09 am– May 9, 8:28 pm	4th	Taurus	Plant potatoes and tubers. Trim to retard growth.
May 9, 8:28 pm– May 10, 5:21 pm	1st	Taurus	Plant annuals for hardiness. Trim to increase growth.

The super-nutritious and decorative plant kale is easy to grow. Direct seed in a full-sun location after the last frost. Plants will appear in about a week. Most types will grow 1–3 feet wide and 1–2 feet tall. Tender leaves can be eaten after about two months; mature leaves are best when harvested after a light frost and cooked before eaten.

●
May 9
8:28 pm EDT

MAY

S	M	T	W	T	F	S
			1	2	3	4
5	6	7	8	9	10	11
12	13	14	15	16	17	18
19	20	21	22	23	24	25
26	27	28	29	30	31	

2012 © Zeljko Radojko. Image from BigStockPhoto.com

May 12–18 ♉

The cure for anything is salt water—sweat, tears, or the sea.

~Isak Dinesen

Date	Qtr.	Sign	Activity
May 13, 5:57 am– May 15, 6:38 pm	1st	Cancer	Plant grains, leafy annuals. Fertilize (chemical). Graft or bud plants. Irrigate. Trim to increase growth.

When planting a vegetable garden, consider including a few marigolds around the border. Not only are they a pretty splash of color, they'll guard against a slew of plant destroyers such as aphids, bean bugs, and even those hard-to-see white worms that destroy roots. If your whole plot is infested, turn marigolds into the soil at the end of the season. When they decay, they'll release a chemical that will ensure the area is ready for planting next spring.—Laura, Minnesota

_____

_____

_____

2012 © Cheryl Casey. Image from BigStockPhoto.com

◐
May 18
12:35 am EDT

May

S	M	T	W	T	F	S
			1	2	3	4
5	6	7	8	9	10	11
12	13	14	15	16	17	18
19	20	21	22	23	24	25
26	27	28	29	30	31	

♊ May 19–25

This is the kind of night whose perfume teases boys out of their warm cages. They forsake their beds for brighter stars than these.   ~PHYLLIS K. COLLIER, "MAY NIGHT"

Date	Qtr.	Sign	Activity
May 20, 1:07 pm– May 22, 4:55 pm	2nd	Libra	Plant annuals for fragrance and beauty. Trim to increase growth.
May 22, 4:55 pm– May 24, 5:49 pm	2nd	Scorpio	Plant grains, leafy annuals. Fertilize (chemical). Graft or bud plants. Irrigate. Trim to increase growth.
May 25, 12:25 am– May 26, 5:28 pm	3rd	Sagittarius	Cultivate. Destroy weeds and pests. Harvest fruits and root crops for food. Trim to retard growth.

Did you know there are only two perennial vegetables? Asparagus and rhubarb. If you are lucky enough to have an established asparagus plant, take note: Snap off stems when they are 7–9 inches tall and before the heads start to spread out to seed. Stop harvesting when most of the spears are extremely thin (less than 3/8 inch).

_____

_____

_____

_____

○
May 25
12:25 am EDT

MAY

S	M	T	W	T	F	S
			1	2	3	4
5	6	7	8	9	10	11
12	13	14	15	16	17	18
19	20	21	22	23	24	25
26	27	28	29	30	31	

June

May 26–June 1

The white chrysanthemum, even when lifted to the eye,
remains immaculate.

~MATSUO BASHO

Date	Qtr.	Sign	Activity
May 25, 12:25 am–May 26, 5:28 pm	3rd	Sagittarius	Cultivate. Destroy weeds and pests. Harvest fruits and root crops for food. Trim to retard growth.
May 26, 5:28 pm–May 28, 5:48 pm	3rd	Capricorn	Plant potatoes and tubers. Trim to retard growth.
May 28, 5:48 pm–May 30, 8:30 pm	3rd	Aquarius	Cultivate. Destroy weeds and pests. Harvest fruits and root crops for food. Trim to retard growth.
May 30, 8:30 pm–May 31, 2:58 pm	3rd	Pisces	Plant biennials, perennials, bulbs and roots. Prune. Irrigate. Fertilize (organic).
May 31, 2:58 pm–Jun 2, 2:33 am	4th	Pisces	Plant biennials, perennials, bulbs and roots. Prune. Irrigate. Fertilize (organic).

I have a neighbor who uses old wire fencing to make her tomato cages. She created boxes as opposed to circles around the sprouts. The fencing is sturdy and can support the tallest and heaviest of plants, is a great way to recycle, and is easy to work around. —Tracci, Ohio

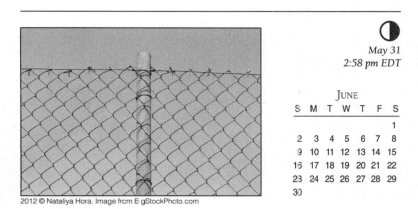

May 31
2:58 pm EDT

JUNE

S	M	T	W	T	F	S
						1
2	3	4	5	6	7	8
9	10	11	12	13	14	15
16	17	18	19	20	21	22
23	24	25	26	27	28	29
30						

2012 © Nataliya Hora. Image from E gStockPhoto.com

♊ June 2–8

Ho! 'Tis the time of salads.   ~Laurence Stone

Date	Qtr.	Sign	Activity
May 31, 2:58 pm– Jun 2, 2:33 am	4th	Pisces	Plant biennials, perennials, bulbs and roots. Prune. Irrigate. Fertilize (organic).
Jun 2, 2:33 am– Jun 4, 11:53 am	4th	Aries	Cultivate. Destroy weeds and pests. Harvest fruits and root crops for food. Trim to retard growth.
Jun 4, 11:53 am– Jun 6, 11:32 pm	4th	Taurus	Plant potatoes and tubers. Trim to retard growth.
Jun 6, 11:32 pm– Jun 8, 11:56 am	4th	Gemini	Cultivate. Destroy weeds and pests. Harvest fruits and root crops for food. Trim to retard growth.

Place a bench under a mature tree or pergola to enjoy summer rains. As long as there is no lightning, there's no reason you can't enjoy rain as much as your plants do. Try sitting on a covered bench to simply listen to the rain. Notice where it soaks in quickly and where it puddles. Savor the cooling breezes and fresh smells.

_____

_____

_____

_____

●
June 8
11:56 am EDT

JUNE

S	M	T	W	T	F	S
						1
2	3	4	5	6	7	8
9	10	11	12	13	14	15
16	17	18	19	20	21	22
23	24	25	26	27	28	29
30						

June 9–15 ♊

The earth is alive. If it was not, it could not produce.
~HEBER C. KIMBALL

Date	Qtr.	Sign	Activity
Jun 9, 12:16 pm– Jun 12, 12:58 am	1st	Cancer	Plant grains, leafy annuals. Fertilize (chemical). Graft or bud plants. Irrigate. Trim to increase growth.

Many plants need lots of sun to flourish, and that means you get lots of sun as you work on them. You probably wear a hat to keep the sun off your face, but what about your arms and legs? Consider using a daily lotion with SPF protection to keep skin looking and feeling its best. Choose a lotion with wide-spectrum protection against UVA and UVB rays and apply it to your arms and legs before heading outside.

2012 © Lisa F. Young. Image from BigStockPhoto.com

JUNE

S	M	T	W	T	F	S
						1
2	3	4	5	6	7	8
9	10	11	12	13	14	15
16	17	18	19	20	21	22
23	24	25	26	27	28	29
30						

♊ June 16–22

*After all, a weed is just a plant in a place you don't want it
to be.*   ~AGATHA CHRISTIE AS MISS MARPLE

Date	Qtr.	Sign	Activity
Jun 16, 9:19 pm– Jun 19, 2:38 am	2nd	Libra	Plant annuals for fragrance and beauty. Trim to increase growth.
Jun 19, 2:38 am– Jun 21, 4:31 am	2nd	Scorpio	Plant grains, leafy annuals. Fertilize (chemical). Graft or bud plants. Irrigate. Trim to increase growth.

I use herbs to brew a fantastic organic fertilizer. Loosely fill a
bucket or larger container with chopped comfrey and stinging
nettle leaves. Fill the container with water. Cover with a lid. Let
container sit in sunlight for a week or so. Be careful when you
take the cover off, as the odor isn't exactly pleasant! You now have
a "sun tea" fertilizer, filled with the nutrients from the herbs. Use
this fertilizer to water your herbs, veggies, fruits, and flowers. —
Betty, New York

◗
*June 16
1:24 pm EDT*

JUNE

S	M	T	W	T	F	S
						1
2	3	4	5	6	7	8
9	10	11	12	13	14	15
16	17	18	19	20	21	22
23	24	25	26	27	28	29
30						

2012 © Selyutina Olga. Image from BigStockPhoto.com

June 23–29 ♋

I sing of brooks, of blossoms, birds, and bowers: Of April,
May, of June, and July flowers.   ~ROBERT HERRICK

Date	Qtr.	Sign	Activity
Jun 23, 4:08 am– Jun 23, 7:32 am	2nd	Capricorn	Graft or bud plants. Trim to increase growth.
Jun 23, 7:32 am– Jun 25, 3:27 am	3rd	Capricorn	Plant potatoes and tubers. Trim to retard growth.
Jun 25, 3:27 am– Jun 27, 4:32 am	3rd	Aquarius	Cultivate. Destroy weeds and pests. Harvest fruits and root crops for food. Trim to retard growth.
Jun 27, 4:32 am– Jun 29, 9:07 am	3rd	Pisces	Plant biennials, perennials, bulbs and roots. Prune. Irrigate. Fertilize (organic).
Jun 29, 9:07 am– Jun 30, 12:54 am	3rd	Aries	Cultivate. Destroy weeds and pests. Harvest fruits and root crops for food. Trim to retard growth.

Pesto and refrigerated dough can be used to make a quick and easy appetizer. Simply unroll a tube of dough. You can use the lines already scored or cut those in half to make mini appetizers. Spread pesto on the dough and roll as usual. Bake as directed and serve warm. Homemade pesto will brown a bit, but the flavor won't suffer.

2012 © David Smith. Image from BigStockPhoto.com

○
June 23
7:32 am EDT

JUNE

S	M	T	W	T	F	S
						1
2	3	4	5	6	7	8
9	10	11	12	13	14	15
16	17	18	19	20	21	22
23	24	25	26	27	28	29
30						

♋ July

June 30–July 6

And young and old came forth to play on a sunshine holiday.

~JOHN MILTON

Date	Qtr.	Sign	Activity
Jun 29, 9:07 am– Jun 30, 12:54 am	3rd	Aries	Cultivate. Destroy weeds and pests. Harvest fruits and root crops for food. Trim to retard growth.
Jun 30, 12:54 am– Jul 1, 5:43 pm	4th	Aries	Cultivate. Destroy weeds and pests. Harvest fruits and root crops for food. Trim to retard growth.
Jul 1, 5:43 pm– Jul 4, 5:21 am	4th	Taurus	Plant potatoes and tubers. Trim to retard growth.
Jul 4, 5:21 am– Jul 6, 6:14 pm	4th	Gemini	Cultivate. Destroy weeds and pests. Harvest fruits and root crops for food. Trim to retard growth.
Jul 6, 6:14 pm– Jul 8, 3:14 am	4th	Cancer	Plant biennials, perennials, bulbs and roots. Prune. Irrigate. Fertilize (organic).

Moles do not like fennel. They will not cross a line of fennel plants, plus the dwarf varieties make an attractive border.
—Jen, Missouri

_____

_____

_____

_____

◑

June 30
12:54 am EDT

JULY

S	M	T	W	T	F	S
	1	2	3	4	5	6
7	8	9	10	11	12	13
14	15	16	17	18	19	20
21	22	23	24	25	26	27
28	29	30	31			

July 7–13 ♋

Sometimes, I can only dream when you are watching me;
waxing and waning as you do.   ~PETER J. HEPBURN

Date	Qtr.	Sign	Activity
Jul 6, 6:14 pm– Jul 8, 3:14 am	4th	Cancer	Plant biennials, perennials, bulbs and roots. Prune. Irrigate. Fertilize (organic).
Jul 8, 3:14 am– Jul 9, 6:48 am	1st	Cancer	Plant grains, leafy annuals. Fertilize (chemical). Graft or bud plants. Irrigate. Trim to increase growth.

Rhubarb is also known as pie plant in some areas, thanks to its most common use: rhubarb pie. But you can also use rhubarb in jams, savory dishes, and even as a pickle. Hit the Internet for creative ideas on using up an excess of rhubarb. More tender stalks can be washed and simply dipped in a personal dish of sugar for a sweet treat. Remember to always discard the toxic leaves of rhubarb before preparing, as only the stalk is edible.

●
July 8
3:14 am EDT

JULY

S	M	T	W	T	F	S
	1	2	3	4	5	6
7	8	9	10	11	12	13
14	15	16	17	18	19	20
21	22	23	24	25	26	27
28	29	30	31			

2012 © Michael Hendricks. Image from BigStockPhoto.com

July 14–20

All that in this delightful garden grows, should happy be, and
have immortal bliss.   ~EDMUND SPENSER

Date	Qtr.	Sign	Activity
Jul 14, 3:41 am– Jul 15, 11:18 pm	1st	Libra	Plant annuals for fragrance and beauty. Trim to increase growth.
Jul 15, 11:18 pm– Jul 16, 10:24 am	2nd	Libra	Plant annuals for fragrance and beauty. Trim to increase growth.
Jul 16, 10:24 am– Jul 18, 1:54 pm	2nd	Scorpio	Plant grains, leafy annuals. Fertilize (chemical). Graft or bud plants. Irrigate. Trim to increase growth.
Jul 20, 2:39 pm– Jul 22, 2:07 pm	2nd	Capricorn	Graft or bud plants. Trim to increase growth.

Your garden can help keep you fit even before you harvest your vegetables! The Centers for Disease Control and Prevention recommends 150 minutes of moderate aerobic activity per week and two or more days of muscle-strengthening activity. Vigorous gardening, such as shoveling, counts as muscle-building work, so dig in!

◖

July 15
11:18 pm EDT

JULY

S	M	T	W	T	F	S
	1	2	3	4	5	6
7	8	9	10	11	12	13
14	15	16	17	18	19	20
21	22	23	24	25	26	27
28	29	30	31			

July 21–27 ♌

*When you get to the end of your rope, tie a knot in it and
hang on.* ～ELEANOR ROOSEVELT

Date	Qtr.	Sign	Activity
Jul 20, 2:39 pm– Jul 22, 2:07 pm	2nd	Capricorn	Graft or bud plants. Trim to increase growth.
Jul 22, 2:16 pm– Jul 24, 2:22 pm	3rd	Aquarius	Cultivate. Destroy weeds and pests. Harvest fruits and root crops for food. Trim to retard growth.
Jul 24, 2:22 pm– Jul 26, 5:29 pm	3rd	Pisces	Plant biennials, perennials, bulbs and roots. Prune. Irrigate. Fertilize (organic).
Jul 26, 5:29 pm– Jul 29, 12:43 am	3rd	Aries	Cultivate. Destroy weeds and pests. Harvest fruits and root crops for food. Trim to retard growth.

Some foods are actually harmed by refrigeration, including members of the family Solanaceae, or Nightshade, including potatoes, tomatoes, eggplants, and tobacco. Refrigerating these plants can cause spots and unpleasant flavor changes as the starch converts to sugars. Keep these goods in a dry, cool place out of sunlight for optimum shelf life.

_____

_____

_____

○
July 22
2:16 pm EDT

JULY

S	M	T	W	T	F	S
	1	2	3	4	5	6
7	8	9	10	11	12	13
14	15	16	17	18	19	20
21	22	23	24	25	26	27
28	29	30	31			

2012 © Kaulin Boris Georgievich. Image from BigStockPhoto.com

♍ August

July 28–August 3

Certain things would make anybody ugly. Some of these we consume; others consume us. ∼VICTORIA MORAN

Date	Qtr.	Sign	Activity
Jul 26, 5:29 pm– Jul 29, 12:43 am	3rd	Aries	Cultivate. Destroy weeds and pests. Harvest fruits and root crops for food. Trim to retard growth.
Jul 29, 12:43 am– Jul 29, 1:43 pm	3rd	Taurus	Plant potatoes and tubers. Trim to retard growth.
Jul 29, 1:43 pm– Jul 31, 11:42 am	4th	Taurus	Plant potatoes and tubers. Trim to retard growth.
Jul 31, 11:42 am– Aug 3, 12:29 am	4th	Gemini	Cultivate. Destroy weeds and pests. Harvest fruits and root crops for food. Trim to retard growth.
Aug 3, 12:29 am– Aug 5, 12:58 pm	4th	Cancer	Plant biennials, perennials, bulbs and roots. Prune. Irrigate. Fertilize (organic).

Calcium isn't the only bone-protecting vitamin out there; vitamin D is crucial in maintaining strong bones. The Recommended Dietary Allowance (RDA) of Vitamin D is 600 IU for ages 1 to 70. Sources include fatty fish (salmon, tuna), fish liver oils, egg yolks, and UV-treated mushrooms. In the US, all milk is fortified with 100 IU of Vitamin D per cup.

◑

July 29
1:43 pm EDT

AUGUST

S	M	T	W	T	F	S
				1	2	3
4	5	6	7	8	9	10
11	12	13	14	15	16	17
18	19	20	21	22	23	24
25	26	27	28	29	30	31

2012 © Auremar. Image from BigStockPhoto.com

August 4–10 ♌

Beauty in things exists in the mood which contemplates them.

~David Hume

Date	Qtr.	Sign	Activity
Aug 3, 12:29 am– Aug 5, 12:58 pm	4th	Cancer	Plant biennials, perennials, bulbs and roots. Prune. Irrigate. Fertilize (organic).
Aug 5, 12:58 pm– Aug 6, 5:51 pm	4th	Leo	Cultivate. Destroy weeds and pests. Harvest fruits and root crops for food. Trim to retard growth.
Aug 10, 9:08 am– Aug 12, 4:18 pm	1st	Libra	Plant annuals for fragrance and beauty. Trim to increase growth.

Taxonomy is the science of classifying plants and animals. Living things are grouped by seven levels of category: kingdom, phylum, class, order, family, genus, and species. Most plants are identified just by their genus and species; common basil, for instance, is *Ocimum basilicum*. Today most taxonomic work is done using DNA profiling to determine similarities among organisms and classify them into groups.

●

August 6
5:51 pm EDT

AUGUST

S	M	T	W	T	F	S
				1	2	3
4	5	6	7	8	9	10
11	12	13	14	15	16	17
18	19	20	21	22	23	24
25	26	27	28	29	30	31

℥ August 11–17

You will find something more in woods than in books. Trees
and stones will teach you that which you can never learn
from masters.   ~St. Bernard

Date	Qtr.	Sign	Activity
Aug 10, 9:08 am– Aug 12, 4:18 pm	1st	Libra	Plant annuals for fragrance and beauty. Trim to increase growth.
Aug 12, 4:18 pm– Aug 14, 6:56 am	1st	Scorpio	Plant grains, leafy annuals. Fertilize (chemical). Graft or bud plants. Irrigate. Trim to increase growth.
Aug 14, 6:56 am– Aug 14, 9:04 pm	2nd	Scorpio	Plant grains, leafy annuals. Fertilize (chemical). Graft or bud plants. Irrigate. Trim to increase growth.
Aug 16, 11:25 pm– Aug 19, 12:07 am	2nd	Capricorn	Graft or bud plants. Trim to increase growth.

I live in a hot and dry summer area (southern Oregon) and found out by trial and error that raised beds are not good when summers are too hot and you get a lot of direct sun. The key is root temperature. On raised beds, roots don't have a chance to cool down during a hot day when the sun is hitting the plant. If you use a drip line, the water actually heats up and "cooks" the roots!
—Dario, Oregon

August 14
6:56 am EDT

August

S	M	T	W	T	F	S
				1	2	3
4	5	6	7	8	9	10
11	12	13	14	15	16	17
18	19	20	21	22	23	24
25	26	27	28	29	30	31

August 18–24

A good night's sleep, or a ten-minute brawl, or a pint of chocolate ice cream, or all three together, is good medicine.

~RAY BRADBURY

Date	Qtr.	Sign	Activity
Aug 16, 11:25 pm– Aug 19, 12:07 am	2nd	Capricorn	Graft or bud plants. Trim to increase growth.
Aug 20, 9:45 pm– Aug 21, 12:43 am	3rd	Aquarius	Cultivate. Destroy weeds and pests. Harvest fruits and root crops for food. Trim to retard growth.
Aug 21, 12:43 am– Aug 23, 3:13 am	3rd	Pisces	Plant biennials, perennials, bulbs and roots. Prune. Irrigate. Fertilize (organic).
Aug 23, 3:13 am– Aug 25, 9:13 am	3rd	Aries	Cultivate. Destroy weeds and pests. Harvest fruits and root crops for food. Trim to retard growth.

Nursery plant tags often indicate the level of sunlight a plant should receive. These terms include:

- Full sun, 6 or more hours daily
- Partial sun, 5–6 hours daily
- Partial shade, 3–4 hours daily
- Full shade, fewer than 3 hours daily

2012 © Barbara Helgason. Image from BigStockPhoto.com

○
August 20
9:45 pm EDT

AUGUST

S	M	T	W	T	F	S
				1	2	3
4	5	6	7	8	9	10
11	12	13	14	15	16	17
18	19	20	21	22	23	24
25	26	27	28	29	30	31

♍ August 25–31

I have often regretted my speech, never my silence.

~PUBLILIUS SYRUS

Date	Qtr.	Sign	Activity
Aug 23, 3:13 am– Aug 25, 9:13 am	3rd	Aries	Cultivate. Destroy weeds and pests. Harvest fruits and root crops for food. Trim to retard growth.
Aug 25, 9:13 am– Aug 27, 7:08 pm	3rd	Taurus	Plant potatoes and tubers. Trim to retard growth.
Aug 27, 7:08 pm– Aug 28, 5:35 am	3rd	Gemini	Cultivate. Destroy weeds and pests. Harvest fruits and root crops for food. Trim to retard growth.
Aug 28, 5:35 am– Aug 30, 7:33 am	4th	Gemini	Cultivate. Destroy weeds and pests. Harvest fruits and root crops for food. Trim to retard growth.
Aug 30, 7:33 am– Sep 1, 8:01 pm	4th	Cancer	Plant biennials, perennials, bulbs and roots. Prune. Irrigate. Fertilize (organic).

You can take energy conservation to the next level by using your landscaping to create a more stable microclimate around your house through shading. Plant leafy trees to shade south-facing walls and roof areas to keep them cool in summer but allow for sunlight in the winter. You can also try growing climbing plants on trellises against sunny east and west walls. If your home is made of masonry, ivy can grow directly on the walls.

◑

August 28
5:35 am EDT

AUGUST

S	M	T	W	T	F	S
				1	2	3
4	5	6	7	8	9	10
11	12	13	14	15	16	17
18	19	20	21	22	23	24
25	26	27	28	29	30	31

September ♍

September 1–7

What delights us in visible beauty is the invisible.

~MARIE VON EBNER-ESCHENBACH

Date	Qtr.	Sign	Activity
Aug 30, 7:33 am– Sep 1, 8:01 pm	4th	Cancer	Plant biennials, perennials, bulbs and roots. Prune. Irrigate. Fertilize (organic).
Sep 1, 8:01 pm– Sep 4, 6:43 am	4th	Leo	Cultivate. Destroy weeds and pests. Harvest fruits and root crops for food. Trim to retard growth.
Sep 4, 6:43 am– Sep 5, 7:36 am	4th	Virgo	Cultivate, especially medicinal plants. Destroy weeds and pests. Trim to retard growth.
Sep 6, 3:12 pm– Sep 8, 9:44 pm	1st	Libra	Plant annuals for fragrance and beauty. Trim to increase growth.

When choosing deciduous trees for shade, take into consideration the mature height and spread of the tree. You will need to plant the trees quite close to your home in order to shade the roof from the hot midday summer sun, so choose a slower-growing species that is not inclined to breakage, and be sure to clean your gutters each fall.

2012 © Greg McGill. Image from BigStockPhoto.com

●

September 5
7:36 am EDT

SEPTEMBER

S	M	T	W	T	F	S
1	2	3	4	5	6	7
8	9	10	11	12	13	14
15	16	17	18	19	20	21
22	23	24	25	26	27	28
29	30					

♍ September 8–14

It's time to start living the life you've imagined.

~Henry James

Date	Qtr.	Sign	Activity
Sep 6, 3:12 pm– Sep 8, 9:44 pm	1st	Libra	Plant annuals for fragrance and beauty. Trim to increase growth.
Sep 8, 9:44 pm– Sep 11, 2:36 am	1st	Scorpio	Plant grains, leafy annuals. Fertilize (chemical). Graft or bud plants. Irrigate. Trim to increase growth.
Sep 13, 5:56 am– Sep 15, 8:05 am	2nd	Capricorn	Graft or bud plants. Trim to increase growth.

I love an early morning cup of coffee while watering the garden. But I'd often discover our vegetable box topped off with fresh scat, courtesy of the neighborhood felines. How happy I was to discover that coffee grounds not only acidify the soil, helping plants grow beautifully, but the scent also keeps cats away! Now I bring the grounds with me for an eco-friendly compost that also protects my veggies from unwanted "fertilizer." —Andrea, California

_____

_____

_____

◐
September 12
1:08 pm EDT

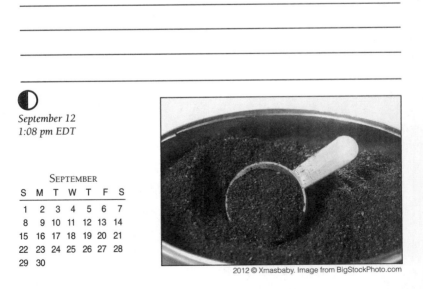

2012 © Xmasbaby. Image from BigStockPhoto.com

SEPTEMBER

S	M	T	W	T	F	S
1	2	3	4	5	6	7
8	9	10	11	12	13	14
15	16	17	18	19	20	21
22	23	24	25	26	27	28
29	30					

September 15–21 ♍

The sun set in the sea; the same odd sun rose from the sea,
and there was one of it and one of me.

~ELIZABETH BISHOP

Date	Qtr.	Sign	Activity
Sep 13, 5:56 am– Sep 15, 8:05 am	2nd	Capricorn	Graft or bud plants. Trim to increase growth.
Sep 17, 9:58 am– Sep 19, 7:13 am	2nd	Pisces	Plant grains, leafy annuals. Fertilize (chemical). Graft or bud plants. Irrigate. Trim to increase growth.
Sep 19, 7:13 am– Sep 19, 12:58 pm	3rd	Pisces	Plant biennials, perennials, bulbs and roots. Prune. Irrigate. Fertilize (organic).
Sep 19, 12:58 pm– Sep 21, 6:33 pm	3rd	Aries	Cultivate. Destroy weeds and pests. Harvest fruits and root crops for food. Trim to retard growth.
Sep 21, 6:33 pm– Sep 24, 3:34 am	3rd	Taurus	Plant potatoes and tubers. Trim to retard growth.

For a quick boost of gardening self-esteem, plant mint. There are myriad species of mint, almost all of which grow easily. They will even overrun other plants if given a chance, so mint is best grown in containers. Try spearmint (*Mentha spicata*) and use the quick-growing leaves to make mint tea.

2012 © Melinda Fawver. Image from BigStockPhoto.com

○
September 19
7:13 am EDT

SEPTEMBER

S	M	T	W	T	F	S
1	2	3	4	5	6	7
8	9	10	11	12	13	14
15	16	17	18	19	20	21
22	23	24	25	26	27	28
29	30					

♎ September 22–28

Leaves and stems weave in hymns of light in the last glow of
September sunset and dusk.   ~H. ARNETT, "WEEDS"

Date	Qtr.	Sign	Activity
Sep 21, 6:33 pm– Sep 24, 3:34 am	3rd	Taurus	Plant potatoes and tubers. Trim to retard growth.
Sep 24, 3:34 am– Sep 26, 3:24 pm	3rd	Gemini	Cultivate. Destroy weeds and pests. Harvest fruits and root crops for food. Trim to retard growth.
Sep 26, 3:24 pm– Sep 26, 11:55 pm	3rd	Cancer	Plant biennials, perennials, bulbs and roots. Prune. Irrigate. Fertilize (organic).
Sep 26, 11:55 pm– Sep 29, 3:57 am	4th	Cancer	Plant biennials, perennials, bulbs and roots. Prune. Irrigate. Fertilize (organic).

While kale is great as a cooked green, you should also try kale chips. Wash and remove the tough stems. Tear leaves into bite-sized pieces and toss in olive oil, using your fingers to make sure each piece is evenly coated, then lay out in a single layer and sprinkle with salt or seasoned salt. Bake at 350° F for 10–15 minutes, removing before the leaves begin to char.

◑
September 26
11:55 pm EDT

SEPTEMBER

S	M	T	W	T	F	S
1	2	3	4	5	6	7
8	9	10	11	12	13	14
15	16	17	18	19	20	21
22	23	24	25	26	27	28
29	30					

October ⚎

September 29–October 5

*No spring, nor summer beauty hath such grace, as I have
seen in one autumnal face.*   ~JOHN DONNE

Date	Qtr.	Sign	Activity
Sep 26, 11:55 pm– Sep 29, 3:57 am	4th	Cancer	Plant biennials, perennials, bulbs and roots. Prune. Irrigate. Fertilize (organic).
Sep 29, 3:57 am– Oct 1, 2:52 pm	4th	Leo	Cultivate. Destroy weeds and pests. Harvest fruits and root crops for food. Trim to retard growth.
Oct 1, 2:52 pm– Oct 3, 10:59 pm	4th	Virgo	Cultivate, especially medicinal plants. Destroy weeds and pests. Trim to retard growth.
Oct 4, 8:35 pm– Oct 6, 4:33 am	1st	Libra	Plant annuals for fragrance and beauty. Trim to increase growth.

The language of flowers was a popular means of communication in the repressed world of Victorian England. This went beyond just red roses for true love: lavender indicated devotion, iris meant good news, white lilies signaled purity, mint spelled suspicion, oak leaves signified strength, arborvitae was for lasting friendship, aloe for grief, rosemary for remembrance, and daisies for innocence.

2012 © Kristof Degreef. Image from BigStockPhoto.com

● October 4
8:35 pm EDT

OCTOBER

S	M	T	W	T	F	S
		1	2	3	4	5
6	7	8	9	10	11	12
13	14	15	16	17	18	19
20	21	22	23	24	25	26
27	28	29	30	31		

October 6–12

If we couldn't laugh, we would all go insane.

~Jimmy Buffet

Date	Qtr.	Sign	Activity
Oct 4, 8:35 pm– Oct 6, 4:33 am	1st	Libra	Plant annuals for fragrance and beauty. Trim to increase growth.
Oct 6, 4:33 am– Oct 8, 8:21 am	1st	Scorpio	Plant grains, leafy annuals. Fertilize (chemical). Graft or bud plants. Irrigate. Trim to increase growth.
Oct 10, 11:17 am– Oct 11, 7:02 pm	1st	Capricorn	Graft or bud plants. Trim to increase growth.
Oct 11, 7:02 pm– Oct 12, 2:00 pm	2nd	Capricorn	Graft or bud plants. Trim to increase growth.

Gardening can present the perfect opportunity for conversation and companionship. Start a gardening group with a few friends and set a time each week to get together. You can rotate meeting location and work together to tackle larger outdoor projects: hauling compost, digging up old plants, or doing landscaping work. The extra hands will allow each person to improve their space while fostering friendship.

◑
October 11
7:02 pm EDT

OCTOBER

S	M	T	W	T	F	S
		1	2	3	4	5
6	7	8	9	10	11	12
13	14	15	16	17	18	19
20	21	22	23	24	25	26
27	28	29	30	31		

2012 © Barbara Helgason. Image from BigStockPhoto.com

October 13–19 ♎

Always a rainbow after the rain, always a solace following
pain; Spring follows winter, warmth after cold, always a
balance, green turning gold.

~ANITA MCLEAN WASHINGTON

Date	Qtr.	Sign	Activity
Oct 14, 5:06 pm– Oct 16, 9:18 pm	2nd	Pisces	Plant grains, leafy annuals. Fertilize (chemical). Graft or bud plants. Irrigate. Trim to increase growth.
Oct 18, 7:38 pm– Oct 19, 3:27 am	3rd	Aries	Cultivate. Destroy weeds and pests. Harvest fruits and root crops for food. Trim to retard growth.
Oct 19, 3:27 am– Oct 21, 12:14 pm	3rd	Taurus	Plant potatoes and tubers. Trim to retard growth.

I have an old blender in my kitchen where I place my fruit and vegetable scraps, egg shells, etc. (anything compostable) while preparing meals. I add water, blend it all together, and then work the mixture into the garden soil or pour into my compost bin. Blending the scraps helps to speed up the breakdown (composting) process. —Teri, New Hampshire

2012 © Ben Andrews. Image from BigStockPhoto.com

○
October 18
7:38 pm EDT

OCTOBER

S	M	T	W	T	F	S
		1	2	3	4	5
6	7	8	9	10	11	12
13	14	15	16	17	18	19
20	21	22	23	24	25	26
27	28	29	30	31		

October 20–26

A bad neighbor is a misfortune, as much as a good one is a
great blessing.   ~Hesiod

Date	Qtr.	Sign	Activity
Oct 19, 3:27 am– Oct 21, 12:14 pm	3rd	Taurus	Plant potatoes and tubers. Trim to retard growth.
Oct 21, 12:14 pm– Oct 23, 11:36 pm	3rd	Gemini	Cultivate. Destroy weeds and pests. Harvest fruits and root crops for food. Trim to retard growth.
Oct 23, 11:36 pm– Oct 26, 12:12 pm	3rd	Cancer	Plant biennials, perennials, bulbs and roots. Prune. Irrigate. Fertilize (organic).
Oct 26, 12:12 pm– Oct 26, 7:40 pm	3rd	Leo	Cultivate. Destroy weeds and pests. Harvest fruits and root crops for food. Trim to retard growth.
Oct 26, 7:40 pm– Oct 28, 11:45 pm	4th	Leo	Cultivate. Destroy weeds and pests. Harvest fruits and root crops for food. Trim to retard growth.

I'm growing spinach and lettuce indoors using three hydroponic systems I built. My tip to hydroponic growers of non-fruiting plants like spinach and lettuce is to feed one-third of the level recommended on the nutrient solution's bottle. Feed less until your plants ask for more, otherwise you risk burning and killing them. The bottles often provide recommended feeding levels that reflect the needs of fruiting plants, like tomatoes. Giving non-fruit plants that much food will kill them. —Kenny, Minnesota

◑
October 26
7:40 pm EDT

OCTOBER

S	M	T	W	T	F	S
		1	2	3	4	5
6	7	8	9	10	11	12
13	14	15	16	17	18	19
20	21	22	23	24	25	26
27	28	29	30	31		

2012 © Noppadon Chanruangdecha. Image from BigStockPhoto.com

November ♏

October 27–November 2

*They who dream by day are cognizant of many things which
escape those who dream only by night.*

~EDGAR ALLEN POE

Date	Qtr.	Sign	Activity
Oct 26, 7:40 pm– Oct 28, 11:45 pm	4th	Leo	Cultivate. Destroy weeds and pests. Harvest fruits and root crops for food. Trim to retard growth.
Oct 28, 11:45 pm– Oct 31, 8:22 am	4th	Virgo	Cultivate, especially medicinal plants. Destroy weeds and pests. Trim to retard growth.
Nov 2, 1:35 pm– Nov 3, 7:50 am	4th	Scorpio	Plant biennials, perennials, bulbs and roots. Prune. Irrigate. Fertilize (organic).

We all know plants need chlorophyll, but it turns out humans need it as well. Studies are still being done on delivery systems and diseases, but there's no arguing that eating lots of green vegetables can lead to better health. All green vegetables contain chlorophyll, but spinach is king of the hill with 300–600 mg per ounce.

2012 © Jason Stitt. Image from BigStockPhoto.com

NOVEMBER

S	M	T	W	T	F	S
					1	2
3	4	5	6	7	8	9
10	11	12	13	14	15	16
17	18	19	20	21	22	23
24	25	26	27	28	29	30

♏ November 3–9

Peace is our true nature like the vast sky above the clouds and rain.

~DEBRA MOFFITT

Date	Qtr.	Sign	Activity
Nov 2, 1:35 pm– Nov 3, 7:50 am	4th	Scorpio	Plant biennials, perennials, bulbs and roots. Prune. Irrigate. Fertilize (organic).
Nov 3, 7:50 am– Nov 4, 3:14 pm	1st	Scorpio	Plant grains, leafy annuals. Fertilize (chemical). Graft or bud plants. Irrigate. Trim to increase growth.
Nov 6, 4:44 pm– Nov 8, 6:30 pm	1st	Capricorn	Graft or bud plants. Trim to increase growth.

Most pumpkin pie recipes start with canned pumpkin, but you can also make your own unseasoned filling. Start with a pie pumpkin, meant for baking; these are usually smaller than jack o'lanterns, which are grown for size rather than flavor. Wash and seed the pumpkin. Cut into quarters if you prefer, or roast whole. Bake at 400° F for about 40 minutes, until a paring knife easily pierces all the pieces.

November 3
7:50 am EST
Daylight Saving Time ends
  November 3, 2:00 am

NOVEMBER

S	M	T	W	T	F	S
					1	2
3	4	5	6	7	8	9
10	11	12	13	14	15	16
17	18	19	20	21	22	23
24	25	26	27	28	29	30

2012 © Viktar Malyshchyts. Image from BigStockPhoto.com

November 10–16 ♏

The dusky night rides down the sky, and ushers in the morn.

~HENRY FIELDING

Date	Qtr.	Sign	Activity
Nov 10, 9:36 pm– Nov 13, 2:39 am	2nd	Pisces	Plant grains, leafy annuals. Fertilize (chemical). Graft or bud plants. Irrigate. Trim to increase growth.
Nov 15, 9:49 am– Nov 17, 10:16 am	2nd	Taurus	Plant annuals for hardiness. Trim to increase growth.

L et your roasted pumpkin cool and then scrape the skin away from the flesh. Puree the flesh until smooth, adding a touch of water if needed. You'll need about 16 ounces of puree for a regular 9-inch pie, so plan to roast 4–6 pounds of pumpkin. You may need to buy two smaller pumpkins for this purpose.

◑

November 10
12:57 am EST

NOVEMBER

S	M	T	W	T	F	S
					1	2
3	4	5	6	7	8	9
10	11	12	13	14	15	16
17	18	19	20	21	22	23
24	25	26	27	28	29	30

2012 © Lisa F. Young. Image from BigStockPhoto.com

♏ November 17–23

You can keep going on much less attention than you crave.

~IDRIES SHAH

Date	Qtr.	Sign	Activity
Nov 15, 9:49 am– Nov 17, 10:16 am	2nd	Taurus	Plant annuals for hardiness. Trim to increase growth.
Nov 17, 10:16 am– Nov 17, 7:07 pm	3rd	Taurus	Plant potatoes and tubers. Trim to retard growth.
Nov 17, 7:07 pm– Nov 20, 6:23 am	3rd	Gemini	Cultivate. Destroy weeds and pests. Harvest fruits and root crops for food. Trim to retard growth.
Nov 20, 6:23 am– Nov 22, 6:56 pm	3rd	Cancer	Plant biennials, perennials, bulbs and roots. Prune. Irrigate. Fertilize (organic).
Nov 22, 6:56 pm– Nov 25, 7:11 am	3rd	Leo	Cultivate. Destroy weeds and pests. Harvest fruits and root crops for food. Trim to retard growth.

A worm is a worm is a worm, right? Wrong! Vermes is an old taxon (classification of species) that is no longer in use. Today we use the word *worm* to describe species from thirteen different phyla. Gardeners are most familiar with earthworms, members of the Annelida phylum. It is the earthworms' movements that benefit gardeners by mixing and aerating the soil.

○
November 17
10:16 am EST

NOVEMBER

S	M	T	W	T	F	S
					1	2
3	4	5	6	7	8	9
10	11	12	13	14	15	16
17	18	19	20	21	22	23
24	25	26	27	28	29	30

2012 © Enoxh the Digital Art Director. Image from BigStockPhoto.com

November 24–30

When everything seems to be going against you, remember that the airplane takes off against the wind, not with it.

~HENRY FORD

Date	Qtr.	Sign	Activity
Nov 22, 6:56 pm– Nov 25, 7:11 am	3rd	Leo	Cultivate. Destroy weeds and pests. Harvest fruits and root crops for food. Trim to retard growth.
Nov 25, 7:11 am– Nov 25, 2:28 pm	3rd	Virgo	Cultivate, especially medicinal plants. Destroy weeds and pests. Trim to retard growth.
Nov 25, 2:28 pm– Nov 27, 5:00 pm	4th	Virgo	Cultivate, especially medicinal plants. Destroy weeds and pests. Trim to retard growth.
Nov 29, 11:03 pm– Dec 2, 1:31 am	4th	Scorpio	Plant biennials, perennials, bulbs and roots. Prune. Irrigate. Fertilize (organic).

Sweet potato wedges are a great option for those who don't care for the sometimes-mushy marshmallow-covered dish. Wash sweet potatoes, peel if desired, and cut into wedges or thick fries. Toss with olive oil, spread on a baking sheet, and sprinkle with seasoned salt and paprika. Bake at 450° F until soft. Serve with ketchup or an aioli mayonnaise.

November 25
2:28 pm EST

NOVEMBER

S	M	T	W	T	F	S
					1	2
3	4	5	6	7	8	9
10	11	12	13	14	15	16
17	18	19	20	21	22	23
24	25	26	27	28	29	30

⌁ December

December 1–7

*A crust eaten in peace is better than a banquet partaken
in anxiety.*   ~Aesop

Date	Qtr.	Sign	Activity
Nov 29, 11:03 pm– Dec 2, 1:31 am	4th	Scorpio	Plant biennials, perennials, bulbs and roots. Prune. Irrigate. Fertilize (organic).
Dec 2, 1:31 am– Dec 2, 7:22 pm	4th	Sagittarius	Cultivate. Destroy weeds and pests. Harvest fruits and root crops for food. Trim to retard growth.
Dec 4, 1:49 am– Dec 6, 1:53 am	1st	Capricorn	Graft or bud plants. Trim to increase growth.

L oose leaf teas can be brewed in a number of ways. Paper filters can be purchased for a single cup or for a pot; these are generally only good for one use. Tea balls are filled, closed, and submerged in hot water. The same idea applies to open-topped baskets, though these usually sit at or above water level. For tea lovers, there are many specialty pots and mugs on the market that incorporate an infuser right in their design.

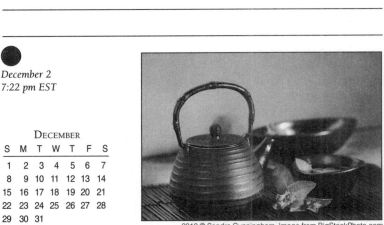

●

December 2
7:22 pm EST

DECEMBER

S	M	T	W	T	F	S
1	2	3	4	5	6	7
8	9	10	11	12	13	14
15	16	17	18	19	20	21
22	23	24	25	26	27	28
29	30	31				

2012 © Sandra Cunningham. Image from BigStockPhoto.com

December 8–14

The earth seems to rest in silent meditation; and the waters and mountains and the sky and the heavens seem all to be in meditation.   ~CHANDOGYA UPANISHAD

Date	Qtr.	Sign	Activity
Dec 8, 3:34 am–Dec 9, 10:12 am	1st	Pisces	Plant grains, leafy annuals. Fertilize (chemical). Graft or bud plants. Irrigate. Trim to increase growth.
Dec 9, 10:12 am–Dec 10, 8:06 am	2nd	Pisces	Plant grains, leafy annuals. Fertilize (chemical). Graft or bud plants. Irrigate. Trim to increase growth.
Dec 12, 3:40 pm–Dec 15, 1:40 am	2nd	Taurus	Plant annuals for hardiness. Trim to increase growth.

Tea brewing is a high art form in some countries, and tea experts all seem to have a few common tips. Start with good quality water and never use boiling water, which will cook the tea leaves instead of steeping them. Preheat your pot or mug so that it won't cool the brew water. It is better to understeep your tea than to oversteep. Finally, purchase high-quality loose tea from a reputable tea source.

December 9
10:12 am EST

DECEMBER

S	M	T	W	T	F	S
1	2	3	4	5	6	7
8	9	10	11	12	13	14
15	16	17	18	19	20	21
22	23	24	25	26	27	28
29	30	31				

December 15–21

Happiness is letting go of your ideas about happiness.

~GUY FINLEY

Date	Qtr.	Sign	Activity
Dec 12, 3:40 pm– Dec 15, 1:40 am	2nd	Taurus	Plant annuals for hardiness. Trim to increase growth.
Dec 17, 4:28 am– Dec 17, 1:17 pm	3rd	Gemini	Cultivate. Destroy weeds and pests. Harvest fruits and root crops for food. Trim to retard growth.
Dec 17, 1:17 pm– Dec 20, 1:48 am	3rd	Cancer	Plant biennials, perennials, bulbs and roots. Prune. Irrigate. Fertilize (organic).
Dec 20, 1:48 am– Dec 22, 2:19 pm	3rd	Leo	Cultivate. Destroy weeds and pests. Harvest fruits and root crops for food. Trim to retard growth.

Skip the holiday cookie tray this year in favor of a bowl of in-shell almonds, cashews, Brazil nuts, and chestnuts. Put out a nutcracker and have fun breaking the shells to reveal the delicious and nutritious nut meat. You'll cut down on sugar intake, and having to crack each shell will eliminate mindless snacking. Put out a second bowl for all those shells!

O

December 17
4:28 am EST

DECEMBER

S	M	T	W	T	F	S
1	2	3	4	5	6	7
8	9	10	11	12	13	14
15	16	17	18	19	20	21
22	23	24	25	26	27	28
29	30	31				

2012 © Adrian Hughes. Image from BigStockPhoto.com

December 22–28 ♑

All truths are easy to understand once they are discovered;
the point is to discover them.   ~GALILEO GALILEI

Date	Qtr.	Sign	Activity
Dec 20, 1:48 am– Dec 22, 2:19 pm	3rd	Leo	Cultivate. Destroy weeds and pests. Harvest fruits and root crops for food. Trim to retard growth.
Dec 22, 2:19 pm– Dec 25, 1:17 am	3rd	Virgo	Cultivate, especially medicinal plants. Destroy weeds and pests. Trim to retard growth.
Dec 27, 8:58 am– Dec 29, 12:37 pm	4th	Scorpio	Plant biennials, perennials, bulbs and roots. Prune. Irrigate. Fertilize (organic).

Add some color to your holiday greenery with cranberries. String them together to decorate trees or garlands, fill clear vases with piles of the red berries, or use them in a dish to hold a candle upright. You can also freeze washed cranberries in an individual layer to act as ice cubes in those cool holiday cocktails; they won't water down your beverage like regular ice cubes.

_____

_____

_____

2012 © Dale Woodall. Image from BigStockPhoto.com

◑

December 25
8:48 am EST

DECEMBER

S	M	T	W	T	F	S
1	2	3	4	5	6	7
8	9	10	11	12	13	14
15	16	17	18	19	20	21
22	23	24	25	26	27	28
29	30	31				

♑ December 29–January 4, 2014

If we had no winter, the spring would not be so pleasant.

~ANNE BRADSTREET

Date	Qtr.	Sign	Activity
Dec 27, 8:58 am– Dec 29, 12:37 pm	4th	Scorpio	Plant biennials, perennials, bulbs and roots. Prune. Irrigate. Fertilize (organic).
Dec 29, 12:37 pm– Dec 31, 1:01 pm	4th	Sagittarius	Cultivate. Destroy weeds and pests. Harvest fruits and root crops for food. Trim to retard growth.

The familiar candy cane is made of corn syrup, sugar, and flavoring—peppermint is the most popular flavor. This brown mixture is pulled like taffy, and the exposure to the air turns it white. Red stripes are then added to form a log, which is rolled thin, twisted, and wrapped while it's still warm. It is only then that the famous bend is made so you can hang your treats as holiday decorations.

_____

_____

_____

_____

DECEMBER

S	M	T	W	T	F	S
	1	2	3	4	5	6	7
8	9	10	11	12	13	14
15	16	17	18	19	20	21
22	23	24	25	26	27	28
29	30	31

2012 © Thomas Perkins. Image from BigStockPhoto.com

Gardening by the Moon

Today, people often reject the notion of gardening according to the Moon's phase and sign. The usual nonbeliever is not a scientist but the city dweller who has never had any real contact with nature and little experience of natural rhythms.

Camille Flammarion, the French astronomer, testifies to the success of Moon planting, though:

"Cucumbers increase at Full Moon, as well as radishes, turnips, leeks, lilies, horseradish, and saffron; onions, on the contrary, are much larger and better nourished during the decline and old age of the Moon than at its increase, during its youth and fullness, which is the reason the Egyptians abstained from onions, on account of their antipathy to the Moon. Herbs gathered while the Moon increases are of great efficiency. If the vines are trimmed at night when the Moon is in the sign of the Lion, Sagittarius, the Scorpion, or the Bull, it will save them from field rats, moles, snails, flies, and other animals."

Dr. Clark Timmins is one of the few modern scientists to have conducted tests in Moon planting. Following is a summary of his experiments:

Beets: When sown with the Moon in Scorpio, the germination rate was 71 percent; when sown in Sagittarius, the germination rate was 58 percent.

Scotch marigold: When sown with the Moon in Cancer, the germination rate was 90 percent; when sown in Leo, the rate was 32 percent.

Carrots: When sown with the Moon in Scorpio, the germination rate was 64 percent; when sown in Sagittarius, the germination rate was 47 percent.

Tomatoes: When sown with the Moon in Cancer, the germination rate was 90 percent; but when sown with the Moon in Leo, the germination rate was 58 percent.

Two things should be emphasized. First, remember that this is only a summary of the results of the experiments; the experiments themselves were conducted in a scientific manner to eliminate any variation in soil, temperature, moisture, and so on, so that only the Moon sign is varied. Second, note that these astonishing results were obtained without regard to the phase of the Moon—the other factor we use in Moon planting, and which presumably would have increased the differential in germination rates.

Dr. Timmins also tried transplanting Cancer- and Leo-planted tomato seedlings while the Cancer Moon was waxing. The result was 100 percent survival. When transplanting was done with the waning Sagittarius Moon, there was 0 percent survival. Dr. Timmins' tests show that the Cancer-planted tomatoes had blossoms twelve days earlier than those planted under Leo; the Cancer-planted tomatoes had an average height of twenty inches at that time compared to fifteen inches for the Leo-planted; the first ripe tomatoes were gathered from the Cancer plantings eleven days ahead of the Leo plantings; and a count of the hanging fruit and its size and weight shows an advantage to the Cancer plants over the Leo plants of 45 percent.

Dr. Timmins also observed that there have been similar tests that did not indicate results favorable to the Moon planting theory. As a scientist, he asked why one set of experiments indicated a positive verification of Moon planting, and others did not. He checked these other tests and found that the experimenters had not followed the geocentric system for determining the Moon sign positions, but the heliocentric. When the times used in these other tests were converted to the geocentric system, the dates chosen often were found to be in barren, rather than fertile, signs. Without going into a technical explanation, it is sufficient to point out that geocentric and heliocentric positions often vary by as much as four days. This is a large enough differential to place the Moon in Cancer, for example, in the heliocentric system, and at the same time in Leo by the geocentric system.

Most almanacs and calendars show the Moon's signs heliocentrically—and thus incorrectly for Moon planting—while the *Moon Sign Book* is calculated correctly for planting purposes, using the geocentric system. Some readers are confused because the *Moon Sign Book* talks about first, second, third, and fourth quarters, while other almanacs refer to these same divisions as New Moon, first quarter, Full Moon, and fourth quarter. Thus the almanacs say first quarter when the *Moon Sign Book* says second quarter.

There is nothing complicated about using astrology in agriculture and horticulture in order to increase both pleasure and profit, but there is one very important rule that is often neglected—use common sense! Of course this is one rule that should be remembered in every activity we undertake, but in the case of gardening and farming by the Moon, if it is not possible to use the best dates for planting or harvesting, we must select the next best and just try to do the best we can.

This brings up the matter of the other factors to consider in your gardening work. The dates we give as best for a certain activity apply to the entire country (with slight time correction), but in your section of the country you may be buried under three feet of snow on a date we say is good to plant your flowers. So we have factors of weather, season, temperature, and moisture variations, soil conditions, your own available time and opportunity, and so forth. Some astrologers like to think it is all a matter of science, but gardening is also an art. In art, you develop an instinctive identification with your work and influence it with your feelings and wishes.

The *Moon Sign Book* gives you the place of the Moon for every day of the year so that you can select the best times once you have become familiar with the rules and practices of lunar agriculture. We give you specific, easy-to-follow directions so that you can get right down to work.

We give you the best dates for planting, and also for various related activities, including cultivation, fertilizing, harvesting, irrigation, and getting rid of weeds and pests. But we cannot tell you exactly when it's good to plant. Many of these rules were learned by observation and experience; as the body of experience grew, we could see various patterns emerging that allowed us to make judgments about new things. That's what you should do, too. After you have worked with lunar agriculture for a while and have gained a working knowledge, you will probably begin to try new things—and we hope you will share your experiments and findings with us. That's how the science grows.

Here's an example of what we mean. Years ago Llewellyn George suggested that we try to combine our bits of knowledge about what to expect in planting under each of the Moon signs in order to benefit from several lunar factors in one plant. From this came our rule for developing "thoroughbred seed." To develop thoroughbred seed, save the seed for three successive years from plants grown by the correct Moon sign and phase. You can plant in the first quarter phase and in the sign of Cancer for fruitfulness; the second year, plant seeds from the first year plants in Libra for beauty; and in the third year, plant the seeds from the second year plants in Taurus to produce hardiness. In a similar manner you can combine the fruitfulness of Cancer, the good root growth of Pisces, and the sturdiness and good vine growth of Scorpio. And don't forget the characteristics of Capricorn: hardy like Taurus, but drier and perhaps more resistant to drought and disease.

Unlike common almanacs, we consider both the Moon's phase and the Moon's sign in making our calculations for the proper timing of our work. It is perhaps a little easier to understand this if we remind you that we are all living in the center of a vast electromagnetic field that is the Earth and its environment in space. Everything that occurs within this electromagnetic field has an effect on everything else within the field. The Moon and the Sun are the most important of the factors affecting the life of the Earth, and it is their relative positions to the Earth that we project for each day of the year.

Many people claim that not only do they achieve larger crops gardening by the Moon, but that their fruits and vegetables are much tastier. A number of organic gardeners have also become lunar gardeners using the natural rhythm of life forces that we experience through the relative movements of the Sun and Moon. We provide a few basic rules and then give you day-by-day guidance for your gardening work. You will be able to choose the best dates to meet your own needs and opportunities.

Planting by the Moon's Phases

During the increasing or waxing light—from New Moon to Full Moon—plant annuals that produce their yield above the ground. An annual is a plant that completes its entire life cycle within one growing season and has to be seeded each year. During the decreasing or waning light—from Full Moon to New Moon—plant biennials, perennials, and bulb and root plants. Biennials include crops that are planted one season to winter over and produce crops the next, such as winter wheat. Perennials and bulb and root plants include all plants that grow from the same root each year.

A simpler, less-accurate rule is to plant crops that produce above the ground during the waxing Moon, and to plant crops that produce below the ground during the waning Moon. Thus the old adage, "Plant potatoes during the dark of the Moon." Llewellyn George's system divided the lunar month into quarters. The first two from New Moon to Full Moon are the first and second quarters, and the last two from Full Moon to New Moon the third and fourth quarters. Using these divisions, we can increase our accuracy in timing our efforts to coincide with natural forces.

First Quarter

Plant annuals producing their yield above the ground, which are generally of the leafy kind that produce their seed outside the fruit. Some examples are asparagus, broccoli, brussels sprouts, cabbage, cauliflower, celery, cress, endive, kohlrabi, lettuce, parsley, and spinach. Cucumbers are an exception, as they do best in the first quarter rather than the second, even though the seeds are inside the fruit. Also plant cereals and grains.

Second Quarter

Plant annuals producing their yield above the ground, which are generally of the viney kind that produce their seed inside the fruit. Some examples include beans, eggplant, melons, peas, peppers, pumpkins, squash, tomatoes, etc. These are not hard-and-fast divisions. If you can't plant during the first quarter, plant during the second, and vice versa. There are many plants that seem to do equally well planted in either quarter. such as water-melon, hay, and cereals and grains.

Third Quarter

Plant biennials, perennials, bulbs, root plants, trees, shrubs, berries, grapes, strawberries, beets, carrots, onions, parsnips, rutabagas, potatoes, radishes, peanuts, rhubarb, turnips, winter wheat, etc.

Fourth Quarter

This is the best time to cultivate, turn sod, pull weeds, and destroy pests of all kinds, especially when the Moon is in Aries, Leo, Virgo, Gemini, Aquarius, and Sagittarius.

The Moon in the Signs

Moon in Aries

Barren, dry, fiery, and masculine. Use for destroying noxious weeds.

Moon in Taurus

Productive, moist, earthy, and feminine. Use for planting many crops when hardiness is important, particularly root crops. Also used for lettuce, cabbage, and similar leafy vegetables.

Moon in Gemini

Barren and dry, airy and masculine. Use for destroying noxious growths, weeds, and pests, and for cultivation.

Moon in Cancer

Fruitful, moist, feminine. Use for planting and irrigation.

Moon in Leo

Barren, dry, fiery, masculine. Use for killing weeds or cultivation.

Moon in Virgo

Barren, dry, earthy, and feminine. Use for cultivation and destroying weeds and pests.

Moon in Libra

Semi-fruitful, moist, and airy. Use for planting crops that need good pulp growth. A very good sign for flowers and vines. Also used for seeding hay, corn fodder, and the like.

Moon in Scorpio

Very fruitful and moist, watery and feminine. Nearly as productive as Cancer; use for the same purposes. Especially good for vine growth and sturdiness.

Moon in Sagittarius

Barren and dry, fiery and masculine. Use for planting onions, seeding hay, and for cultivation.

Moon in Capricorn

Productive and dry, earthy and feminine. Use for planting potatoes and other tubers.

Moon in Aquarius

Barren, dry, airy, and masculine. Use for cultivation and destroying noxious growths and pests.

Moon in Pisces

Very fruitful, moist, watery, and feminine. Especially good for root growth.

A Guide to Planting

Plant	Quarter	Sign
Annuals	1st or 2nd	
Apple tree	2nd or 3rd	Cancer, Pisces, Virgo
Artichoke	1st	Cancer, Pisces
Asparagus	1st	Cancer, Scorpio, Pisces
Aster	1st or 2nd	Virgo, Libra
Barley	1st or 2nd	Cancer, Pisces, Libra, Capricorn, Virgo
Beans (bush & pole)	2nd	Cancer, Taurus, Pisces, Libra
Beans (kidney, white, & navy)	1st or 2nd	Cancer, Pisces
Beech tree	2nd or 3rd	Virgo, Taurus
Beets	3rd	Cancer, Capricorn, Pisces, Libra
Biennials	3rd or 4th	
Broccoli	1st	Cancer, Scorpio, Pisces, Libra
Brussels sprouts	1st	Cancer, Scorpio, Pisces, Libra
Buckwheat	1st or 2nd	Capricorn
Bulbs	3rd	Cancer, Scorpio, Pisces
Bulbs for seed	2nd or 3rd	
Cabbage	1st	Cancer, Scorpio, Pisces, Taurus, Libra
Canes (raspberry, blackberry, & gooseberry)	2nd	Cancer, Scorpio, Pisces
Cantaloupe	1st or 2nd	Cancer, Scorpio, Pisces, Taurus, Libra
Carrots	3rd	Cancer, Scorpio, Pisces, Taurus, Libra
Cauliflower	1st	Cancer, Scorpio, Pisces, Libra
Celeriac	3rd	Cancer, Scorpio, Pisces
Celery	1st	Cancer, Scorpio, Pisces
Cereals	1st or 2nd	Cancer, Scorpio, Pisces, Libra
Chard	1st or 2nd	Cancer, Scorpio, Pisces
Chicory	2nd or 3rd	Cancer, Scorpio, Pisces
Chrysanthemum	1st or 2nd	Virgo
Clover	1st or 2nd	Cancer, Scorpio, Pisces

Plant	Quarter	Sign
Coreopsis	2nd or 3rd	Libra
Corn	1st	Cancer, Scorpio, Pisces
Corn for fodder	1st or 2nd	Libra
Cosmo	2nd or 3rd	Libra
Cress	1st	Cancer, Scorpio, Pisces
Crocus	1st or 2nd	Virgo
Cucumber	1st	Cancer, Scorpio, Pisces
Daffodil	1st or 2nd	Libra, Virgo
Dahlia	1st or 2nd	Libra, Virgo
Deciduous trees	2nd or 3rd	Cancer, Scorpio, Pisces, Virgo, Libra
Eggplant	2nd	Cancer, Scorpio, Pisces, Libra
Endive	1st	Cancer, Scorpio, Pisces, Libra
Flowers	1st	Cancer, Scorpio, Pisces, Libra, Taurus, Virgo
Garlic	3rd	Libra, Taurus, Pisces
Gladiola	1st or 2nd	Libra, Virgo
Gourds	1st or 2nd	Cancer, Scorpio, Pisces, Libra
Grapes	2nd or 3rd	Cancer, Scorpio, Pisces, Virgo
Hay	1st or 2nd	Cancer, Scorpio, Pisces, Libra, Taurus
Herbs	1st or 2nd	Cancer, Scorpio, Pisces
Honeysuckle	1st or 2nd	Scorpio, Virgo
Hops	1st or 2nd	Scorpio, Libra
Horseradish	1st or 2nd	Cancer, Scorpio, Pisces
Houseplants	1st	Cancer, Scorpio, Pisces, Libra
Hyacinth	3rd	Cancer, Scorpio, Pisces
Iris	1st or 2nd	Cancer, Virgo
Kohlrabi	1st or 2nd	Cancer, Scorpio, Pisces, Libra
Leek	2nd or 3rd	Sagittarius
Lettuce	1st	Cancer, Scorpio, Pisces, Libra, Taurus
Lily	1st or 2nd	Cancer, Scorpio, Pisces
Maple tree	2nd or 3rd	Taurus, Virgo, Cancer, Pisces
Melon	2nd	Cancer, Scorpio, Pisces
Moon vine	1st or 2nd	Virgo

Plant	Quarter	Sign
Morning glory	1st or 2nd	Cancer, Scorpio, Pisces, Virgo
Oak tree	2nd or 3rd	Taurus, Virgo, Cancer, Pisces
Oats	1st or 2nd	Cancer, Scorpio, Pisces, Libra
Okra	1st or 2nd	Cancer, Scorpio, Pisces, Libra
Onion seed	2nd	Cancer, Scorpio, Sagittarius
Onion set	3rd or 4th	Cancer, Pisces, Taurus, Libra
Pansies	1st or 2nd	Cancer, Scorpio, Pisces
Parsley	1st	Cancer, Scorpio, Pisces, Libra
Parsnip	3rd	Cancer, Scorpio, Taurus, Capricorn
Peach tree	2nd or 3rd	Cancer, Taurus, Virgo, Libra
Peanuts	3rd	Cancer, Scorpio, Pisces
Pear tree	2nd or 3rd	Cancer, Scorpio, Pisces, Libra
Peas	2nd	Cancer, Scorpio, Pisces, Libra
Peony	1st or 2nd	Virgo
Peppers	2nd	Cancer, Scorpio, Pisces
Perennials	3rd	
Petunia	1st or 2nd	Libra, Virgo
Plum tree	2nd or 3rd	Cancer, Pisces, Taurus, Virgo
Poppies	1st or 2nd	Virgo
Portulaca	1st or 2nd	Virgo
Potatoes	3rd	Cancer, Scorpio, Libra, Taurus, Capricorn
Privet	1st or 2nd	Taurus, Libra
Pumpkin	2nd	Cancer, Scorpio, Pisces, Libra
Quince	1st or 2nd	Capricorn
Radishes	3rd	Cancer, Scorpio, Pisces, Libra, Capricorn
Rhubarb	3rd	Cancer, Pisces
Rice	1st or 2nd	Scorpio
Roses	1st or 2nd	Cancer, Virgo
Rutabaga	3rd	Cancer, Scorpio, Pisces, Taurus
Saffron	1st or 2nd	Cancer, Scorpio, Pisces
Sage	3rd	Cancer, Scorpio, Pisces

Plant	Quarter	Sign
Salsify	1st	Cancer, Scorpio, Pisces
Shallot	2nd	Scorpio
Spinach	1st	Cancer, Scorpio, Pisces
Squash	2nd	Cancer, Scorpio, Pisces, Libra
Strawberries	3rd	Cancer, Scorpio, Pisces
String beans	1st or 2nd	Taurus
Sunflowers	1st or 2nd	Libra, Cancer
Sweet peas	1st or 2nd	Any
Tomatoes	2nd	Cancer, Scorpio, Pisces, Capricorn
Trees, shade	3rd	Taurus, Capricorn
Trees, ornamental	2nd	Libra, Taurus
Trumpet vine	1st or 2nd	Cancer, Scorpio, Pisces
Tubers for seed	3rd	Cancer, Scorpio, Pisces, Libra
Tulips	1st or 2nd	Libra, Virgo
Turnips	3rd	Cancer, Scorpio, Pisces, Taurus, Capricorn, Libra
Valerian	1st or 2nd	Virgo, Gemini
Watermelon	1st or 2nd	Cancer, Scorpio, Pisces, Libra
Wheat	1st or 2nd	Cancer, Scorpio, Pisces, Libra

Companion Planting Guide

Plant	Companions	Hindered by
Asparagus	Tomatoes, parsley, basil	None known
Beans	Tomatoes, carrots, cucumbers, garlic, cabbage, beets, corn	Onions, gladiolas
Beets	Onions, cabbage, lettuce, mint, catnip	Pole beans
Brocccli	Beans, celery, potatoes, onions	Tomatoes
Cabbage	Peppermint, sage, thyme, tomatoes	Strawberries, grapes
Carrots	Peas, lettuce, chives, radishes, leeks, onions, sage	Dill, anise
Citrus trees	Guava, live oak, rubber trees, peppers	None known
Corn	Potatoes, beans, peas, melon, squash, pumpkin, sunflowers, soybeans	Quack grass, wheat, straw, mulch
Cucumbers	Beans, cabbage, radishes, sunflowers, lettuce, broccoli, squash	Aromatic herbs
Eggplant	Green beans, lettuce, kale	None known
Grapes	Peas, beans, blackberries	Cabbage, radishes
Melons	Corn, peas	Potatoes, gourds
Onions, leeks	Beets, chamomile, carrots, lettuce	Peas, beans, sage
Parsnip	Peas	None known
Peas	Radishes, carrots, corn, cucumbers, beans, tomatoes, spinach, turnips	Onion, garlic
Potatoes	Beans, corn, peas, cabbage, hemp, cucumbers, eggplant, catnip	Raspberries, pumpkins, tomatoes, sunflowers
Radishes	Peas, lettuce, nasturtiums, cucumbers	Hyssop
Spinach	Strawberries	None known
Squash/Pumpkin	Nasturtiums, corn, mint, catnip	Potatoes
Tomatoes	Asparagus, parsley, chives, onions, carrots, marigolds, nasturtiums, dill	Black walnut roots, fennel, potatoes
Turnips	Peas, beans, brussels sprouts	Potatoes

73

Plant	Companions	Uses
Anise	Coriander	Flavor candy, pastry, cheeses, cookies
Basil	Tomatoes	Dislikes rue; repels flies and mosquitoes
Borage	Tomatoes, squash	Use in teas
Buttercup	Clover	Hinders delphinium, peonies, monkshood, columbine
Catnip		Repels flea beetles
Chamomile	Peppermint, wheat, onions, cabbage	Roman chamomile may control damping-off disease; use in herbal sprays
Chervil	Radishes	Good in soups and other dishes
Chives	Carrots	Use in spray to deter black spot on roses
Coriander	Plant anywhere	Hinders seed formation in fennel
Cosmos		Repels corn earworms
Dill	Cabbage	Hinders carrots and tomatoes
Fennel	Plant in borders	Disliked by all garden plants
Horseradish		Repels potato bugs
Horsetail		Makes fungicide spray
Hyssop		Attracts cabbage flies; harmful to radishes
Lavender	Plant anywhere	Use in spray to control insects on cotton, repels clothes moths
Lovage		Lures horn worms away from tomatoes
Marigolds		Pest repellent; use against Mexican bean beetles and nematodes
Mint	Cabbage, tomatoes	Repels ants, flea beetles, cabbage worm butterflies
Morning glory	Corn	Helps melon germination
Nasturtium	Cabbage, cucumbers	Deters aphids, squash bugs, pumpkin beetles
Okra	Eggplant	Attracts leafhopper (lure insects from other plants)
Parsley	Tomatoes, asparagus	Freeze chopped up leaves to flavor foods
Purslane		Good ground cover
Rosemary		Repels cabbage moths, bean beetles, carrot flies
Savory		Plant with onions for added sweetness
Tansy		Deters Japanese beetles, striped cucumber beetles, squash bugs
Thyme		Repels cabbage worms
Yarrow		Increases essential oils of neighbors

Moon Void-of-Course

By Kim Rogers-Gallagher

The Moon circles the Earth in about twenty-eight days, moving through each zodiac sign in two-and-a-half days. As she passes through the thirty degrees of each sign, she "visits" with the planets in numerical order, forming aspects with them. Because she moves one degree in just two to two-and-a-half hours, her influence on each planet lasts only a few hours. She eventually reaches the planet that's in the highest degree of any sign and forms what will be her final aspect before leaving the sign. From this point until she enters the next sign, she is referred to as void-of-course.

Think of it this way: the Moon is the emotional "tone" of the day, carrying feelings with her particular to the sign she's "wearing" at the moment. After she has contacted each of the planets, she symbolically "rests" before changing her costume, so her instinct is temporarily on hold. It's during this time that many people feel "fuzzy" or "vague." Plans or decisions made now often do not pan out. Without the instinctual "knowing" the Moon provides as she touches each planet, we tend to be unrealistic or exercise poor judgment. The traditional definition of the void Moon is that "nothing will come of this." Actions initiated under a void Moon are often wasted, irrelevant, or incorrect—usually because information is hidden, missing, or has been overlooked.

Although it's not a good time to initiate plans, routine tasks seem to go along just fine. This period is ideal for reflection. On the lighter side, remember there are good uses for the void Moon. It is the period when the universe seems to be most open to loopholes. It's a great time to make plans you don't want to fulfill or schedule things you don't want to do. See the table on pages 76–81 for a schedule of the Moon's void-of-course times.

Last Aspect **Moon Enters New Sign**

		January		
3	7:15 am	3	Libra	8:11 pm
5	6:13 pm	6	Scorpio	1:09 am
7	6:31 am	8	Sagittarius	3:28 am
8	9:28 pm	10	Capricorn	3:54 am
11	2:44 pm	12	Aquarius	4:01 am
13	3:37 am	14	Pisces	5:49 am
16	4:32 am	16	Aries	11:07 am
18	7:40 pm	18	Taurus	8:36 pm
20	1:16 pm	21	Gemini	9:04 am
23	6:42 am	23	Cancer	10:00 pm
25	3:35 pm	26	Leo	9:20 am
28	11:59 am	28	Virgo	6:27 pm
30	8:59 pm	31	Libra	1:36 am
		February		
1	8:03 pm	2	Scorpio	7:02 am
4	7:31 am	4	Sagittarius	10:45 am
5	3:42 pm	6	Capricorn	12:55 pm
7	7:44 am	8	Aquarius	2:16 pm
10	2:20 am	10	Pisces	4:20 pm
11	12:03 pm	12	Aries	8:51 pm
14	10:35 pm	15	Taurus	5:08 am
17	3:31 pm	17	Gemini	4:50 pm
19	1:48 pm	20	Cancer	5:45 am
21	9:08 pm	22	Leo	5:12 pm
24	11:50 pm	25	Virgo	1:52 am
26	1:13 pm	27	Libra	8:02 am
28	3:37 am	3/1	Scorpio	12:33 pm

Last Aspect   **Moon Enters New Sign**

		March		
3	4:19 am	3	Sagittarius	4:11 pm
5	10:28 am	5	Capricorn	7:14 pm
7	4:14 pm	7	Aquarius	10:01 pm
8	5:08 pm	10	Pisces	1:19 am
11	3:51 pm	12	Aries	7:17 am
13	4:02 am	14	Taurus	3:08 pm
16	7:11 pm	17	Gemini	2:09 am
19	1:27 pm	19	Cancer	2:55 pm
20	2:02 pm	22	Leo	2:50 am
22	11:28 pm	24	Virgo	11:49 am
25	8:46 am	26	Libra	5:32 pm
27	2:14 pm	28	Scorpio	8:53 pm
29	4:25 pm	30	Sagittarius	11:13 pm
		April		
1	1:00 am	2	Capricorn	1:35 am
3	6:35 am	4	Aquarius	4:41 am
5	1:22 pm	6	Pisces	9:00 am
8	12:10 am	8	Aries	3:02 pm
10	12:25 pm	10	Taurus	11:22 pm
13	8:30 am	13	Gemini	10:13 am
15	3:41 pm	15	Cancer	10:49 pm
18	8:31 am	18	Leo	11:13 am
19	5:06 pm	20	Virgo	9:08 pm
22	2:02 am	23	Libra	3:25 am
24	8:12 am	25	Scorpio	6:25 am
26	4:56 am	27	Sagittarius	7:32 am
29	12:37 am	29	Capricorn	8:21 am

Last Aspect   **Moon Enters New Sign**

			May	
1	10:07 am	1	Aquarius	10:20 am
3	12:24 am	3	Pisces	2:25 pm
5	12:00 pm	5	Aries	9:03 pm
7	8:40 am	8	Taurus	6:09 am
9	8:28 pm	10	Gemini	5:21 pm
12	9:32 am	13	Cancer	5:57 am
15	8:14 am	15	Leo	6:38 pm
18	12:35 am	18	Virgo	5:33 am
20	12:48 pm	20	Libra	1:07 pm
22	3:35 am	22	Scorpio	4:55 pm
24	9:55 am	24	Sagittarius	5:49 pm
26	6:22 am	26	Capricorn	5:28 pm
28	2:40 pm	28	Aquarius	5:48 pm
30	7:57 pm	30	Pisces	8:30 pm
			June	
2	12:30 am	2	Aries	2:33 am
4	2:09 am	4	Taurus	11:53 am
5	9:25 am	6	Gemini	11:32 pm
9	4:29 am	9	Cancer	12:16 pm
10	5:15 pm	12	Leo	12:58 am
14	7:14 am	14	Virgo	12:26 pm
16	5:26 pm	16	Libra	9:19 pm
18	11:55 pm	19	Scorpio	2:38 am
20	3:16 pm	21	Sagittarius	4:31 am
23	3:08 am	23	Capricorn	4:08 am
24	10:24 pm	25	Aquarius	3:27 am
26	9:08 am	27	Pisces	4:32 am
28	8:16 pm	29	Aries	9:07 am

Last Aspect		Moon Enters New Sign		
		July		
1	2:48 am	1	Taurus	5:43 pm
3	11:51 am	4	Gemini	5:21 am
6	8:30 am	6	Cancer	6:14 pm
8	7:44 am	9	Leo	6:48 am
11	3:54 pm	11	Virgo	6:12 pm
13	11:26 am	14	Libra	3:41 am
15	11:18 pm	16	Scorpio	10:24 am
18	7:12 am	18	Sagittarius	1:54 pm
20	11:00 am	20	Capricorn	2:39 pm
21	11:53 am	22	Aquarius	2:07 pm
23	10:01 am	24	Pisces	2:22 pm
25	2:43 pm	26	Aries	5:29 pm
27	10:19 pm	29	Taurus	12:43 am
30	11:58 am	31	Gemini	11:42 am
		August		
1	12:48 pm	3	Cancer	12:29 am
5	2:49 am	5	Leo	12:58 pm
6	5:51 pm	7	Virgo	11:57 pm
9	6:05 pm	10	Libra	9:08 am
11	9:29 pm	12	Scorpio	4:18 pm
14	5:30 pm	14	Sagittarius	9:04 pm
16	1:32 pm	16	Capricorn	11:25 pm
18	2:26 pm	19	Aquarius	12:07 am
20	9:45 pm	21	Pisces	12:43 am
22	9:38 pm	23	Aries	3:13 am
25	6:02 am	25	Taurus	9:13 am
27	6:58 pm	27	Gemini	7:08 pm
29	12:44 am	30	Cancer	7:33 am
31	8:06 pm	9/1	Leo	8:01 pm

Last Aspect   Moon Enters New Sign

		September		
3	1:52 pm	4	Virgo	6:43 am
6	6:10 am	6	Libra	3:12 pm
8	4:46 pm	8	Scorpio	9:44 pm
10	5:21 am	11	Sagittarius	2:36 am
12	1:08 pm	13	Capricorn	5:56 am
14	7:17 pm	15	Aquarius	8:05 am
16	4:19 am	17	Pisces	9:58 am
19	7:13 am	19	Aries	12:58 pm
20	9:25 pm	21	Taurus	6:33 pm
23	3:13 am	24	Gemini	3:34 am
26	7:21 am	26	Cancer	3:24 pm
29	3:30 am	29	Leo	3:57 am
		October		
1	12:48 am	1	Virgo	2:52 pm
3	2:57 pm	3	Libra	10:59 pm
5	6:28 pm	6	Scorpio	4:33 am
8	12:54 am	8	Sagittarius	8:21 am
10	6:10 am	10	Capricorn	11:17 am
11	8:04 pm	12	Aquarius	2:00 pm
14	4:28 pm	14	Pisces	5:06 pm
16	3:15 am	16	Aries	9:18 pm
18	7:38 pm	19	Taurus	3:27 am
20	5:02 pm	21	Gemini	12:14 pm
22	8:35 pm	23	Cancer	11:36 pm
25	4:31 pm	26	Leo	12:12 pm
28	8:26 am	28	Virgo	11:45 pm
30	10:48 pm	31	Libra	8:22 am

Last Aspect   Moon Enters New Sign

November				
2	8:47 am	2	Scorpio	1:35 pm
3	11:23 pm	4	Sagittarius	3:14 pm
5	11:48 am	6	Capricorn	4:44 pm
8	2:39 am	8	Aquarius	6:30 pm
10	12:57 am	10	Pisces	9:36 pm
12	9:34 am	13	Aries	2:39 am
14	3:57 pm	15	Taurus	9:49 am
17	10:16 am	17	Gemini	7:07 pm
19	10:59 am	20	Cancer	6:23 am
22	2:11 am	22	Leo	6:56 pm
24	3:59 am	25	Virgo	7:11 am
27	6:44 am	27	Libra	5:00 pm
29	6:13 am	29	Scorpio	11:03 pm
December				
1	8:34 pm	2	Sagittarius	1:31 am
3	10:45 pm	4	Capricorn	1:49 am
6	12:31 am	6	Aquarius	1:53 am
7	7:11 am	8	Pisces	3:34 am
10	1:41 am	10	Aries	8:06 am
12	10:37 am	12	Taurus	3:40 pm
14	9:54 pm	15	Gemini	1:40 am
17	4:28 am	17	Cancer	1:17 pm
19	11:37 pm	20	Leo	1:48 am
22	8:25 am	22	Virgo	2:19 pm
24	10:55 pm	25	Libra	1:17 am
27	6:00 am	27	Scorpio	8:58 am
29	8:54 am	29	Sagittarius	12:37 pm
30	6:36 am	31	Capricorn	1:01 pm

The Moon's Rhythm

The Moon journeys around Earth in an elliptical orbit that takes about 27.33 days, which is known as a sidereal month (period of revolution of one body about another). She can move up to 15 degrees or as few as 11 degrees in a day, with the fastest motion occurring when the Moon is at perigee (closest approach to Earth). The Moon is never retrograde, but when her motion is slow, the effect is similar to a retrograde period.

Astrologers have observed that people born on a day when the Moon is fast will process information differently from those who are born when the Moon is slow in motion. People born when the Moon is fast process information quickly and tend to react quickly, while those born during a slow Moon will be more deliberate.

The time from New Moon to New Moon is called the synodic month (involving a conjunction), and the average time span between this Sun-Moon alignment is 29.53 days. Since 29.53

won't divide into 365 evenly, we can have a month with two Full
Moons or two New Moons.

Moon Aspects

The aspects the Moon will make during the times you are considering are also important. A trine or sextile, and sometimes a
conjunction, are considered favorable aspects. A trine or sextile
between the Sun and Moon is an excellent foundation for success. Whether or not a conjunction is considered favorable depends upon the planet the Moon is making a conjunction to. If
it's joining the Sun, Venus, Mercury, Jupiter, or even Saturn, the
aspect is favorable. If the Moon joins Pluto or Mars, however,
that would not be considered favorable. There may be excep-
tions, but it would depend on what you are electing to do. For
example, a trine to Pluto might hasten the end of a relationship
you want to be free of.

It is important to avoid times when the Moon makes an aspect to or is conjoining any retrograde planet, unless, of course,
you want the thing started to end in failure.

After the Moon has completed an aspect to a planet, that
planetary energy has passed. For example, if the Moon squares
Saturn at 10:00 am, you can disregard Saturn's influence on your
activity if it will occur after that time. You should always look
ahead at aspects the Moon will make on the day in question,
though, because if the Moon opposes Mars at 11:30 pm on that
day, you can expect events that stretch into the evening to be affected by the Moon-Mars aspect. A testy conversation might lead
to an argument, or more.

Moon Signs

Much agricultural work is ruled by earth signs—Virgo, Capricorn, and Taurus; and the air signs—Gemini, Aquarius, and
Libra—rule flying and intellectual pursuits.

Each planet has one or two signs in which its characteristics are enhanced or "dignified," and the planet is said to "rule" that sign. The Sun rules Leo and the Moon rules Cancer, for example. The ruling planet for each sign is listed below. These should not be considered complete lists. We recommend that you purchase a book of planetary rulerships for more complete information.

Aries Moon

The energy of an Aries Moon is masculine, dry, barren, and fiery. Aries provides great start-up energy, but things started at this time may be the result of impulsive action that lacks research or necessary support. Aries lacks staying power.

Use this assertive, outgoing Moon sign to initiate change, but have a plan in place for someone to pick up the reins when you're impatient to move on to the next thing. Work that requires skillful, but not necessarily patient, use of tools—hammering, cutting down trees, etc.—is appropriate in Aries. Expect things to occur rapidly but to also quickly pass. If you are prone to injury or accidents, exercise caution and good judgment in Aries-related activities.

RULER: Mars

IMPULSE: Action

RULES: Head and face

Taurus Moon

A Taurus Moon's energy is feminine, semi-fruitful, and earthy. The Moon is exalted—very strong—in Taurus. Taurus is known as the farmer's sign because of its associations with farmland and precipitation that is the typical day-long "soaker" variety. Taurus energy is good to incorporate into your plans when patience, practicality, and perseverance are needed. Be aware, though, that you may also experience stubbornness in this sign.

Things started in Taurus tend to be long lasting and to increase in value. This can be very supportive energy in a marriage election. On the downside, the fixed energy of this sign resists change or the letting go of even the most difficult situations. A divorce following a marriage that occurred during a Taurus Moon may be difficult and costly to end. Things begun now tend to become habitual and hard to alter. If you want to make changes in something you started, it would be better to wait for Gemini. This is a good time to get a loan, but expect the people in charge of money to be cautious and slow to make decisions.

RULER: Venus

IMPULSE: Stability

RULES: Neck, throat, and voice

Gemini Moon

A Gemini Moon's energy is masculine, dry, barren, and airy. People are more changeable than usual and may prefer to follow intellectual pursuits and play mental games rather than apply themselves to practical concerns.

This sign is not favored for agricultural matters, but it is an excellent time to prepare for activities, to run errands, and write letters. Plan to use a Gemini Moon to exchange ideas, meet people, go on vacations that include walking or biking, or be in situations that require versatility and quick thinking on your feet.

RULER: Mercury

IMPULSE: Versatility

RULES: Shoulders, hands, arms, lungs, and nervous system

Cancer Moon

A Cancer Moon's energy is feminine, fruitful, moist, and very strong. Use this sign when you want to grow things—flowers, fruits, vegetables, commodities, stocks, or collections—for example. This sensitive sign stimulates rapport between people. Considered the most fertile of the signs, it is often associated with mothering. You can use this moontime to build personal friendships that support mutual growth.

Cancer is associated with emotions and feelings. Prominent Cancer energy promotes growth, but it can also turn people pouty and prone to withdrawing into their shells.

RULER: The Moon

IMPULSE: Tenacity

RULES: Chest area, breasts, and stomach

Leo Moon

A Leo Moon's energy is masculine, hot, dry, fiery, and barren. Use it whenever you need to put on a show, make a presentation, or entertain colleagues or guests. This is a proud yet playful energy that exudes self-confidence and is often associated with romance.

This is an excellent time for fund-raisers and ceremonies or to be straightforward, frank, and honest about something. It is advisable not to put yourself in a position of needing public approval or where you might have to cope with underhandedness, as trouble in these areas can bring out the worst Leo traits. There is a tendency in this sign to become arrogant or self-centered.

RULER: The Sun

IMPULSE: I am

RULES: Heart and upper back

Virgo Moon

A Virgo Moon is feminine, dry, barren, earthy energy. It is favorable for anything that needs painstaking attention—especially those things where exactness rather than innovation is preferred.

Use this sign for activities when you must analyze information or when you must determine the value of something. Virgo is the sign of bargain hunting. It's friendly toward agricultural matters with an emphasis on animals and harvesting vegetables. It is an excellent time to care for animals, especially training them and veterinary work.

This sign is most beneficial when decisions have already been made and now need to be carried out. The inclination here is to see details rather than the bigger picture.

There is a tendency in this sign to overdo. Precautions should be taken to avoid becoming too dull from all work and no play. Build a little relaxation and pleasure into your routine from the beginning.

RULER: Mercury

IMPULSE: Discriminating

RULES: Abdomen and intestines

Libra Moon

A Libra Moon's energy is masculine, semi-fruitful, and airy. This energy will benefit any attempt to bring beauty to a place or thing. Libra is considered good energy for starting things of an intellectual nature. Libra is the sign of partnership and unions, which make it an excellent time to form partnerships of any kind, to make agreements, and to negotiate. Even though this sign is good for initiating things, it is crucial to work with a partner who will provide incentive and encouragement, however. A Libra Moon accentuates teamwork (particularly teams of two) and artistic work (especially work that involves color). Make use of this sign when you are decorating your home or shopping for better-quality clothing.

RULER: Venus

IMPULSE: Balance

RULES: Lower back, kidneys, and buttocks

Scorpio Moon

The Scorpio Moon is feminine, fruitful, cold, and moist. It is useful when intensity (that sometimes borders on obsession) is needed. Scorpio is considered a very psychic sign. Use this Moon sign when you must back up something you strongly believe in, such as union or employer relations. There is strong group loyalty here, but a Scorpio Moon is also a good time to end connections thoroughly. This is also a good time to conduct research.

The desire nature is so strong here that there is a tendency to manipulate situations to get what one wants or to not see one's responsibility in an act.

RULER: Pluto, Mars (traditional)

IMPULSE: Transformation

RULES: Reproductive organs, genitals, groin, and pelvis

Sagittarius Moon

The Moon's energy is masculine, dry, barren, and fiery in Sagittarius, encouraging flights of imagination and confidence in the flow of life. Sagittarius is the most philosophical sign. Candor and honesty are enhanced when the Moon is here. This is an excellent time to "get things off your chest" and to deal with institutions of higher learning, publishing companies, and the law. It's also a good time for sport and adventure.

Sagittarians are the crusaders of this world. This is a good time to tackle things that need improvement, but don't try to be the diplomat while influenced by this energy. Opinions can run strong, and the tendency to proselytize is increased.

RULER: Jupiter

IMPULSE: Expansion

RULES: Thighs and hips

Capricorn Moon

In Capricorn the Moon's energy is feminine, semi-fruitful, and earthy. Because Cancer and Capricorn are polar opposites, the Moon's energy is thought to be weakened here. This energy encourages the need for structure, discipline, and organization. This is a good time to set goals and plan for the future, tend to family business, and to take care of details requiring patience or a businesslike manner. Institutional activities are favored. This sign should be avoided if you're seeking favors, as those in authority can be insensitive under this influence.

RULER: Saturn

IMPULSE: Ambitious

RULES: Bones, skin, and knees

Aquarius Moon

An Aquarius Moon's energy is masculine, barren, dry, and airy. Activities that are unique, individualistic, concerned with humanitarian issues, society as a whole, and making improvements are favored under this Moon. It is this quality of making improvements that has caused this sign to be associated with inventors and new inventions.

An Aquarius Moon promotes the gathering of social groups for friendly exchanges. People tend to react and speak from an intellectual rather than emotional viewpoint when the Moon is in this sign.

RULER: Uranus and Saturn

IMPULSE: Reformer

RULES: Calves and ankles

Pisces Moon

A Pisces Moon is feminine, fruitful, cool, and moist. This is an excellent time to retreat, meditate, sleep, pray, or make that dreamed-of escape into a fantasy vacation. However, things are not always what they seem to be with the Moon in Pisces. Personal boundaries tend to be fuzzy, and you may not be seeing things clearly. People tend to be idealistic under this sign, which can prevent them from seeing reality.

There is a live-and-let-live philosophy attached to this sign, which in the idealistic world may work well enough, but chaos is frequently the result. That's why this sign is also associated with alcohol and drug abuse, drug trafficking, and counterfeiting. On the lighter side, many musicians and artists are ruled by Pisces. It's only when they move too far away from reality that the dark side of substance abuse, suicide, or crime takes away life.

RULER: Jupiter and Neptune
IMPULSE: Empathetic
RULES: Feet

More About Zodiac Signs

Element (Triplicity)

Each of the zodiac signs is classified as belonging to an element; these are the four basic elements:

Fire Signs

Aries, Sagittarius, and Leo are action-oriented, outgoing, energetic, and spontaneous.

Earth Signs

Taurus, Capricorn, and Virgo are stable, conservative, practical, and oriented to the physical and material realm.

Air Signs

Gemini, Aquarius, and Libra are sociable and critical, and they tend to represent intellectual responses rather than feelings.

Water Signs

Cancer, Scorpio, and Pisces are emotional, receptive, intuitive, and can be very sensitive.

Quality (Quadruplicity)

Each zodiac sign is further classified as being cardinal, mutable, or fixed. There are four signs in each quadruplicity, one sign from each element.

Cardinal Signs

Aries, Cancer, Libra, and Capricorn represent beginnings and newly initiated action. They initiate each new season in the cycle of the year.

Fixed Signs

Taurus, Leo, Scorpio, and Aquarius want to maintain the status quo through stubbornness and persistence; they represent that "between" time. For example, Leo is the month when summer really feels like summer.

Mutable Signs

Pisces, Gemini, Virgo, and Sagittarius adapt to change and tolerate situations. They represent the last month of each season, when things are changing in preparation for the coming season.

Nature and Fertility

In addition to a sign's element and quality, each sign is further classified as either fruitful, semi-fruitful, or barren. This classification is the most important for readers who use the gardening information in the *Moon Sign Book* because the timing of most events depends on the fertility of the sign occupied by the Moon. The water signs of Cancer, Scorpio, and Pisces are the most fruitful. The semi-fruitful signs are the earth signs Taurus and Capricorn, and the air sign Libra. The barren signs correspond to fire-signs Aries, Leo, and Sagittarius; air-signs Gemini and Aquarius; and earth-sign Virgo.

Good Timing

By Sharon Leah

Electional astrology is the art of electing times to begin any un-dertaking. Say, for example, you want to start a business. That business will experience ups and downs, as well as reach its poten-tial, according to the promise held in the universe at the time the business was started—its birth time. The horoscope (birth chart) set for the date, time, and place that a business starts would indicate the outcome—its potential to succeed.

So, you might ask yourself the question: If the horoscope for a business start can show success or failure, why not begin at a time that is more favorable to the venture? Well, you can.

While no time is perfect, there are better times and better days to undertake specific activities. There are thousands of examples that prove electional astrology is not only practical, but that it can make a difference in our lives. There are rules for electing times to begin various activities—even shopping. You'll find detailed instructions about how to make elections beginning on page 107.

Personalizing Elections

The election rules in this almanac are based upon the planetary positions at the time for which the election is made. They do not depend on any type of birth chart. However, a birth chart based upon the time, date, and birthplace of an event has advantages. No election is effective for every person. For example, you may leave home to begin a trip at the same time as a friend, but each of you will have a different experience according to whether or not your birth chart favors the trip.

Not all elections require a birth chart, but the timing of very important events—business starts, marriages, etc.—would benefit from the additional accuracy a birth chart provides. To order a birth chart for yourself or a planned event, visit our Web site at www. llewellyn.com.

Some Things to Consider

You've probably experienced good timing in your life. Maybe you were at the right place at the right time to meet a friend whom you hadn't seen in years. Frequently, when something like that happens, it is the result of following an intuitive impulse—that "gut instinct." Consider for a moment that you were actually responding to planetary energies. Electional astrology is a tool that can help you to align with energies, present and future, that are available to us through planetary placements.

Significators

Decide upon the important significators (planet, sign, and house ruling the matter) for which the election is being made. The Moon is the most important significator in any election, so the Moon should always be fortified (strong by sign and making favorable aspects to other planets). The Moon's aspects to other planets are more important than the sign the Moon is in.

Other important considerations are the significators of the Ascendant and Midheaven—the house ruling the election matter and the ruler of the sign on that house cusp. Finally, any planet or sign that has a general rulership over the matter in question should be taken into consideration.

Nature and Fertility

Determine the general nature of the sign that is appropriate for your election. For example, much agricultural work is ruled by the earth signs of Virgo, Capricorn, and Taurus; while the air signs—Gemini, Aquarius, and Libra—rule intellectual pursuits.

One Final Comment

Use common sense. If you must do something, like plant your garden or take an airplane trip on a day that doesn't have the best aspects, proceed anyway, but try to minimize problems. For example, leave early for the airport to avoid being left behind due to delays in the security lanes. When you have no other choice, do the best that you can under the circumstances at the time.

If you want to personalize your elections, please turn to page 107 for more information. If you want a quick and easy answer, you can refer to Llewellyn's Astro Almanac.

Llewellyn's Astro Almanac

The Astro Almanac tables, beginning on the next page, can help you find the dates best suited to particular activities. The dates provided are determined from the Moon's sign, phase, and aspects to other planets. Please note that the Astro Almanac does not take personal factors, such as your Sun and Moon sign, into account. The dates are general, and they will apply for everyone. Some activities will not have ideal dates during a particular month.

Activity	January
Animals (Neuter or spay)	8, 9, 10
Animals (Sell or buy)	12, 14, 16, 26
Automobile (Buy)	1, 2, 10, 11, 21, 29
Brewing	6, 7
Build (Start foundation)	12, 13
Business (Conducting for self and others)	2, 7, 16, 21
Business (Start new)	no ideal dates
Can Fruits and Vegetables	6, 7
Can Preserves	6, 7
Concrete (Pour)	27, 28
Construction (Begin new)	2, 4, 12, 16, 21, 26, 31
Consultants (Begin work with)	1, 4, 6, 11, 12, 16, 21, 26, 31
Contracts (Bid on)	12, 16, 21, 22, 26
Cultivate	no ideal dates
Decorating	12, 13, 21, 22, 23
Demolition	8, 9, 26, 27
Electronics (Buy)	12, 21
Entertain Guests	5, 20
Floor Covering (Laying new)	1, 2, 3, 4, 5, 27, 28, 29, 30, 31
Habits (Break)	10
Hair (Cut to increase growth)	11, 15, 18, 19, 20, 21, 22, 26
Hair (Cut to decrease growth)	8, 9, 10
Harvest (Grain for storage)	1, 27, 28
Harvest (Root crops)	1, 8, 9, 27, 28
Investments (New)	2, 21
Loan (Ask for)	18, 19, 20
Massage (Relaxing)	5, 20
Mow Lawn (Decrease growth)	1, 2, 3, 4, 5, 6, 7, 8, 9, 10, 27, 28, 29, 30, 31
Mow Lawn (Increase growth)	12, 13, 14, 15, 16, 17, 18, 19, 20, 21, 22, 23, 24, 25
Mushrooms (Pick)	25, 26, 27
Negotiate (Business for the elderly)	10, 24, 29
Prune for Better Fruit	6, 7, 8, 9
Prune to Promote Healing	10, 11
Wean Children	8, 9, 10, 11, 12, 13
Wood Floors (Installing)	10, 11
Write Letters or Contracts	8, 11, 21, 26

Activity	February
Animals (Neuter or spay)	5, 6, 7, 8
Animals (Sell or buy)	13, 14, 19, 23
Automobile (Buy)	6, 7, 18, 25
Brewing	3
Build (Start foundation)	16, 17
Business (Conducting for self and others)	1, 5, 14, 20
Business (Start new)	no ideal dates
Can Fruits and Vegetables	3
Can Preserves	3
Concrete (Pour)	no ideal dates
Construction (Begin new)	1, 5, 9, 13, 14, 20, 23, 27
Consultants (Begin work with)	1, 6, 9, 11, 13, 16, 18, 21, 23, 27
Contracts (Bid on)	11, 13, 16, 18, 21, 23
Cultivate	9
Decorating	10, 17, 18, 19
Demolition	4, 5
Electronics (Buy)	1, 9, 18
Entertain Guests	19
Floor Covering (Laying new)	1, 8, 9, 26, 27, 28
Habits (Break)	6, 7, 8
Hair (Cut to increase growth)	11, 15, 16, 17, 18, 19, 22
Hair (Cut to decrease growth)	4, 5, 6, 7
Harvest (Grain for storage)	no ideal dates
Harvest (Root crops)	4, 5, 8
Investments (New)	1, 20
Loan (Ask for)	15, 16, 17, 22, 23, 24
Massage (Relaxing)	9
Mow Lawn (Decrease growth)	1, 2, 3, 4, 5, 6, 7, 8, 26, 27, 28
Mow Lawn (Increase growth)	11, 12, 13, 14, 15, 16, 17, 18, 19, 20, 21, 22, 23, 24
Mushrooms (Pick)	24, 25, 26
Negotiate (Business for the elderly)	11, 25
Prune for Better Fruit	2, 3, 4, 5
Prune to Promote Healing	6, 7, 8
Wean Children	5, 6, 7, 8, 9, 10
Wood Floors (Installing)	6, 7, 8
Write Letters or Contracts	4, 9, 11, 18, 23

Activity	March
Animals (Neuter or spay)	4, 6, 7, 10, 11, 31
Animals (Sell or buy)	16, 22
Automobile (Buy)	6, 17, 25
Brewing	2, 3, 10, 29, 30
Build (Start foundation)	15, 16
Business (Conducting for self and others)	2, 6, 16, 22, 31
Business (Start new)	25
Can Fruits and Vegetables	2, 3, 10, 11, 29, 30
Can Preserves	2, 3, 29, 30
Concrete (Pour)	8
Construction (Begin new)	6, 8, 12, 16, 22, 27, 31
Consultants (Begin work with)	2, 6, 8, 10, 12, 15, 17, 20, 22, 27, 29
Contracts (Bid on)	12, 15, 17, 20, 22
Cultivate	4, 8, 9, 31
Decorating	17, 18, 19, 27
Demolition	3, 4, 31
Electronics (Buy)	8, 17
Entertain Guests	16
Floor Covering (Laying new)	1, 8, 9, 28
Habits (Break)	6, 7, 8, 9
Hair (Cut to increase growth)	14, 15, 16, 17, 18
Hair (Cut to decrease growth)	3, 4, 5, 6, 10, 11, 31
Harvest (Grain for storage)	3, 4, 30, 31
Harvest (Root crops)	3, 4, 5, 8, 9, 31
Investments (New)	2, 22, 31
Loan (Ask for)	14, 15, 16, 22, 23, 24
Massage (Relaxing)	16, 22
Mow Lawn (Decrease growth)	1, 2, 3, 4, 5, 6, 7, 8, 9, 10, 28, 29, 30, 31
Mow Lawn (Increase growth)	12, 13, 14, 15, 16, 17, 18, 19, 20, 21, 22, 23, 24, 25, 26
Mushrooms (Pick)	26, 27, 28
Negotiate (Business for the elderly)	6, 10, 20
Prune for Better Fruit	1, 2, 3, 4, 29, 30, 31
Prune to Promote Healing	6, 7
Wean Children	4, 5, 6, 7, 8, 9, 31
Wood Floors (Installing)	6, 7
Write Letters or Contracts	4, 8, 10, 17, 22, 31

Activity	April
Animals (Neuter or spay)	1, 2, 4, 6, 7, 8, 27, 28, 29, 30
Animals (Sell or buy)	16, 19, 21, 24
Automobile (Buy)	2, 3, 14, 21, 29
Brewing	7, 8, 26
Build (Start foundation)	11, 12
Business (Conducting for self and others)	5, 15, 20, 30
Business (Start new)	21, 22
Can Fruits and Vegetables	7, 8, 26
Can Preserves	26
Concrete (Pour)	5
Construction (Begin new)	5, 9, 15, 19, 20, 24, 30
Consultants (Begin work with)	3, 5, 8, 9, 13, 14, 19, 24, 29
Contracts (Bid on)	13, 14, 19, 23, 24
Cultivate	1, 2, 4, 5, 9, 28, 29
Decorating	13, 14, 15, 23, 24, 25
Demolition	1, 2, 8, 9, 27, 28
Electronics (Buy)	4, 14
Entertain Guests	16
Floor Covering (Laying new)	4, 5
Habits (Break)	4, 5, 8, 9
Hair (Cut to increase growth)	10, 11, 13, 14, 18
Hair (Cut to decrease growth)	1, 2, 3, 7, 27, 28, 29, 30
Harvest (Grain for storage)	1, 2, 27, 28, 29
Harvest (Root crops)	1, 4, 5, 8, 9, 27, 28
Investments (New)	20, 30
Loan (Ask for)	10, 11, 13, 18, 19, 20
Massage (Relaxing)	5, 16
Mow Lawn (Decrease growth)	1, 2, 3, 4, 5, 6, 7, 8, 9, 26, 27, 28, 29, 30
Mow Lawn (Increase growth)	11, 13, 14, 15, 16, 17, 18, 19, 20, 21, 22, 23, 24
Mushrooms (Pick)	24, 25, 26
Negotiate (Business for the elderly)	2, 16, 21, 29
Prune for Better Fruit	25, 26, 27, 28
Prune to Promote Healing	2, 3, 4, 29, 30
Wean Children	1, 2, 3, 4, 5, 28, 29, 30
Wood Floors (Installing)	2, 3, 4, 29, 30
Write Letters or Contracts	4, 8, 14, 19, 28

Activity	May
Animals (Neuter or spay)	3, 4, 5, 25, 26, 27, 28, 31
Animals (Sell or buy)	16, 21, 22
Automobile (Buy)	11, 18, 27
Brewing	4, 5, 31
Build (Start foundation)	10, 16, 17, 18
Business (Conducting for self and others)	4, 15, 20, 29
Business (Start new)	18, 19
Can Fruits and Vegetables	4, 5, 31
Can Preserves	9
Concrete (Pour)	2, 29, 30
Construction (Begin new)	2, 7, 15, 17, 20, 22, 29, 30
Consultants (Begin work with)	2, 3, 7, 9, 12, 15, 17, 21, 22, 30
Contracts (Bid on)	12, 15, 17, 21, 22
Cultivate	2, 3, 6, 7, 25, 26
Decorating	10, 11, 12, 20, 21, 22
Demolition	6, 7, 25
Electronics (Buy)	2, 11, 21, 29, 30
Entertain Guests	10, 21
Floor Covering (Laying new)	1, 2, 8, 9, 29, 30
Habits (Break)	3, 6, 7
Hair (Cut to increase growth)	11, 11, 12, 15
Hair (Cut to decrease growth)	4, 8, 9, 26, 27
Harvest (Grain for storage)	1, 26, 28, 29, 30
Harvest (Root crops)	1, 2, 3, 6, 7, 25, 26, 29, 30
Investments (New)	20, 29
Loan (Ask for)	10, 15, 16, 17, 18
Massage (Relaxing)	16, 21, 30
Mow Lawn (Decrease growth)	1, 2, 3, 4, 5, 6, 7, 8, 26, 27, 28, 29, 30, 31
Mow Lawn (Increase growth)	10, 11, 12, 13, 14, 15, 16, 17, 18, 19, 20, 21, 22, 23
Mushrooms (Pick)	24, 25, 26
Negotiate (Business for the elderly)	13, 18
Prune for Better Fruit	25
Prune to Promote Healing	1, 27, 28
Wean Children	1, 2, 3, 25, 26, 27, 28, 29, 30
Wood Floors (Installing)	1, 27, 28
Write Letters or Contracts	2, 9, 11, 16, 25, 29

Activity	June
Animals (Neuter or spay)	23, 24, 27, 29
Animals (Sell or buy)	14, 18, 20
Automobile (Buy)	7, 14, 16, 23
Brewing	28
Build (Start foundation)	12, 13, 14
Business (Conducting for self and others)	3, 13, 18, 27
Business (Start new)	14, 16
Can Fruits and Vegetables	28
Can Preserves	5, 6
Concrete (Pour)	5, 6, 25, 26
Construction (Begin new)	3, 4, 13, 14, 18
Consultants (Begin work with)	4, 5, 9, 10, 14, 16, 18, 20, 24, 28
Contracts (Bid on)	9, 10, 14, 16, 18, 20
Cultivate	2, 3, 4, 7, 8, 30
Decorating	8, 9, 17, 18, 19
Demolition	2, 3, 29, 30
Electronics (Buy)	7, 25
Entertain Guests	10
Floor Covering (Laying new)	4, 5, 6, 7, 8, 25 26
Habits (Break)	2, 3, 4, 7, 30
Hair (Cut to increase growth)	8, 21, 22
Hair (Cut to decrease growth)	1, 2, 4, 5, 6, 7, 24, 28
Harvest (Grain for storage)	25, 26, 29
Harvest (Root crops)	2, 3, 7, 25, 26, 29, 30
Investments (New)	18, 27
Loan (Ask for)	12, 13, 14
Massage (Relaxing)	4, 10
Mow Lawn (Decrease growth)	1, 2, 3, 4, 5, 6, 7, 24, 25, 26, 27, 28, 29, 30
Mow Lawn (Increase growth)	9, 10, 11, 12, 13, 14, 15, 16, 17, 18, 19, 20, 21, 22
Mushrooms (Pick)	22, 23, 24
Negotiate (Business for the elderly)	9, 14, 23, 27
Prune for Better Fruit	no ideal dates
Prune to Promote Healing	23, 24, 25
Wean Children	21, 22, 23, 24. 25, 26, 27
Wood Floors (Installing)	23, 24, 25
Write Letters or Contracts	7, 13, 22, 25

Activity	July
Animals (Neuter or spay)	25, 26
Animals (Sell or buy)	12, 16
Automobile (Buy)	5, 12, 13, 20
Brewing	7, 25, 26
Build (Start foundation)	9, 10, 11
Business (Conducting for self and others)	2, 13, 18, 27
Business (Start new)	12, 20
Can Fruits and Vegetables	7, 25, 26
Can Preserves	2, 3, 7, 29, 30
Concrete (Pour)	2, 3, 23, 29, 30
Construction (Begin new)	1, 2, 12, 13, 27, 29
Consultants (Begin work with)	1, 3, 6, 8, 12, 13, 16, 17, 25, 29, 30
Contracts (Bid on)	12, 13, 16, 17
Cultivate	1, 4, 5, 6
Decorating	14, 15, 16
Demolition	26, 27, 28
Electronics (Buy)	5, 23
Entertain Guests	4, 10, 15, 29
Floor Covering (Laying new)	1, 2, 3, 4, 5, 23, 29, 30, 31
Habits (Break)	1, 4, 5, 6, 31
Hair (Cut to increase growth)	9, 18, 19, 20, 21
Hair (Cut to decrease growth)	1, 2, 3, 4, 5, 25, 29, 30, 31
Harvest (Grain for storage)	23, 26, 27
Harvest (Root crops)	1, 4, 5, 6, 22, 23, 24, 26, 27, 28, 31
Investments (New)	18, 27
Loan (Ask for)	9, 10, 11
Massage (Relaxing)	10, 15, 29
Mow Lawn (Decrease growth)	1, 2, 3, 4, 5, 6, 7, 23, 24, 25, 26, 27, 28, 29, 30, 31
Mow Lawn (Increase growth)	9, 10, 11, 12, 13, 14, 15, 16, 17, 18, 19, 20, 21
Mushrooms (Pick)	21, 22, 23
Negotiate (Business for the elderly)	20, 24
Prune for Better Fruit	no ideal dates
Prune to Promote Healing	no ideal dates
Wean Children	19, 20, 21, 22, 23, 24
Wood Floors (Installing)	no ideal dates
Write Letters or Contracts	5, 8, 10, 19, 23

Activity	August
Animals (Neuter or spay)	21, 22, 23
Animals (Sell or buy)	8, 13, 19
Automobile (Buy)	1, 8, 17, 28
Brewing	3, 4, 5, 21, 22, 31
Build (Start foundation)	13
Business (Conducting for self and others)	1, 11, 16, 25, 30
Business (Start new)	8, 17
Can Fruits and Vegetables	3, 4, 21, 22, 31
Can Preserves	3, 4, 26, 27, 31
Concrete (Pour)	26, 27
Construction (Begin new)	1, 8, 11, 16, 25, 26, 30
Consultants (Begin work with)	3, 5, 8, 10, 13, 15, 21, 25, 26, 31
Contracts (Bid on)	8, 10, 13, 15
Cultivate	1, 2, 6, 28, 29
Decorating	10, 11, 12, 19, 20
Demolition	5, 6, 23, 24
Electronics (Buy)	1, 10, 19, 28
Entertain Guests	8, 29
Floor Covering (Laying new)	1, 2, 5, 6, 25, 26, 27, 28, 29
Habits (Break)	1, 2, 5, 29
Hair (Cut to increase growth)	15, 16, 17, 18, 21, 22, 25, 26, 27
Hair (Cut to decrease growth)	1, 2, 5, 28, 29
Harvest (Grain for storage)	23, 24, 27
Harvest (Root crops)	1, 2, 5, 23, 24, 28, 29
Investments (New)	16, 25
Loan (Ask for)	7
Massage (Relaxing)	4, 19
Mow Lawn (Decrease growth)	1, 2, 3, 4, 5, 21, 22, 23, 24, 25, 26, 27, 28, 29, 30, 31
Mow Lawn (Increase growth)	7, 8, 9, 10, 11, 12, 13, 14, 15, 16, 17, 18, 19
Mushrooms (Pick)	19, 20, 21
Negotiate (Business for the elderly)	3, 8, 17, 21, 30
Prune for Better Fruit	no ideal dates
Prune to Promote Healing	no ideal dates
Wean Children	15, 16, 17, 18, 19, 20
Wood Floors (Installing)	no ideal dates
Write Letters or Contracts	1, 5, 6, 15, 19

Activity	September
Animals (Neuter or spay)	19
Animals (Sell or buy)	10, 13, 17, 18
Automobile (Buy)	4, 6, 13, 25, 26
Brewing	1, 27, 28
Build (Start foundation)	9, 10
Business (Conducting for self and others)	10, 14, 24, 29
Business (Start new)	5, 13, 14
Can Fruits and Vegetables	1, 27, 28
Can Preserves	1, 22, 23, 27, 28
Concrete (Pour)	2, 3, 22, 23, 29, 30
Construction (Begin new)	5, 14, 23, 24, 29
Consultants (Begin work with)	5, 6, 10, 11, 16, 18, 23, 26, 28
Contracts (Bid on)	6, 10, 11, 16, 18
Cultivate	2, 3, 4, 5, 29, 30
Decorating	6, 7, 8, 15, 16, 17
Demolition	2, 3, 20, 29, 30
Electronics (Buy)	16, 25, 26
Entertain Guests	3, 8, 28
Floor Covering (Laying new)	2, 3, 4, 5, 22, 23, 24, 25, 29, 30
Habits (Break)	2, 3, 4, 29, 30
Hair (Cut to increase growth)	11, 12, 13, 14, 18
Hair (Cut to decrease growth)	1, 21, 22, 23, 24, 25, 29
Harvest (Grain for storage)	20, 21, 24, 25, 26
Harvest (Root crops)	2, 3, 20, 21, 24, 25, 26, 29, 30
Investments (New)	14, 24
Loan (Ask for)	no ideal dates
Massage (Relaxing)	3, 8, 28
Mow Lawn (Decrease growth)	1, 2, 3, 4, 20, 21, 22, 23, 24, 25, 26, 27, 28, 29, 30
Mow Lawn (Increase growth)	6, 7, 8, 9, 10, 11, 12, 13, 14, 15, 16, 17, 18
Mushrooms (Pick)	18, 19, 20
Negotiate (Business for the elderly)	4, 13, 27
Prune for Better Fruit	no ideal dates
Prune to Promote Healing	no ideal dates
Wean Children	11, 12, 13, 14, 15, 16, 17
Wood Floors (Installing)	no ideal dates
Write Letters or Contracts	2, 6, 11, 16, 25, 30

Activity	October
Animals (Neuter or spay)	no ideal dates
Animals (Sell or buy)	13, 16, 17
Automobile (Buy)	1, 2, 11, 22, 30
Brewing	24, 25, 26
Build (Start foundation)	6, 7
Business (Conducting for self and others)	9, 14, 24, 29
Business (Start new)	11
Can Fruits and Vegetables	24, 25
Can Preserves	19, 20, 24, 25
Concrete (Pour)	19, 20, 27, 28
Construction (Begin new)	3, 9, 14, 20, 24, 29, 30
Consultants (Begin work with)	1, 3, 6, 7, 11, 15, 16, 20, 25, 30
Contracts (Bid on)	6, 7, 11, 15, 16
Cultivate	1, 2, 3, 27, 28, 29, 30, 31
Decorating	4, 5, 12, 13, 14
Demolition	18, 26, 27
Electronics (Buy)	13, 22
Entertain Guests	28
Floor Covering (Laying new)	1, 2, 3, 4, 19, 20, 21, 22, 23, 26, 27, 28, 29, 30
Habits (Break)	1, 27, 28
Hair (Cut to increase growth)	8, 9, 10, 11, 15
Hair (Cut to decrease growth)	19, 20, 21, 22, 26
Harvest (Grain for storage)	21, 22, 23, 26
Harvest (Root crops)	1, 21, 22, 23, 26, 27, 28
Investments (New)	14, 24
Loan (Ask for)	no ideal dates
Massage (Relaxing)	13, 28
Mow Lawn (Decrease growth)	1, 2, 3, 19, 20, 21, 22, 23, 24, 25, 26, 27, 28, 29, 30, 31
Mow Lawn (Increase growth)	5, 6, 7, 8, 9, 10, 11, 12, 13, 14, 15, 16, 17
Mushrooms (Pick)	17, 18, 19
Negotiate (Business for the elderly)	2, 15
Prune for Better Fruit	no ideal dates
Prune to Promote Healing	no ideal dates
Wean Children	9, 10, 11, 12, 13, 14
Wood Floors (Installing)	no ideal dates
Write Letters or Contracts	6, 9, 13, 22

Activity	November
Animals (Neuter or spay)	no ideal dates
Animals (Sell or buy)	16
Automobile (Buy)	6, 7, 18, 26
Brewing	21, 22, 30
Build (Start foundation)	3, 4, 9
Business (Conducting for self and others)	7, 12, 22, 28
Business (Start new)	7, 8, 17
Can Fruits and Vegetables	21, 22, 30
Can Preserves	21, 22, 30
Concrete (Pour)	23, 24
Construction (Begin new)	7, 17, 22, 26, 28
Consultants (Begin work with)	3, 6, 11, 12, 17, 21, 26
Contracts (Bid on)	6, 11, 12
Cultivate	25, 26, 27
Decorating	8, 9, 10
Demolition	22, 23, 24
Electronics (Buy)	9, 18
Entertain Guests	2
Floor Covering (Laying new)	1, 2, 18, 19, 22, 23, 24, 25, 26, 27, 28, 29
Habits (Break)	no ideal dates
Hair (Cut to increase growth)	4, 5, 6, 7, 11, 12, 15, 16
Hair (Cut to decrease growth)	18, 19, 22
Harvest (Grain for storage)	18, 19, 22, 23, 24
Harvest (Root crops)	18, 19, 22, 23, 24
Investments (New)	12, 22
Loan (Ask for)	15, 16
Massage (Relaxing)	2, 16
Mow Lawn (Decrease growth)	1, 2, 18, 19, 20, 21, 22, 23, 24, 25, 26, 27, 28, 29, 30
Mow Lawn (Increase growth)	4, 5, 6, 7, 8, 9, 10, 11, 12, 13, 14, 15, 16
Mushrooms (Pick)	16, 17, 18
Negotiate (Business for the elderly)	7, 11, 21, 26
Prune for Better Fruit	2, 30
Prune to Promote Healing	no ideal dates
Wean Children	5, 6, 7, 8, 9, 10
Wood Floors (Installing)	no ideal dates
Write Letters or Contracts	3, 5, 9, 18

Activity	December
Animals (Neuter or spay)	2, 29, 30, 31
Animals (Sell or buy)	14
Automobile (Buy)	5, 15, 24
Brewing	18, 28, 29
Build (Start foundation)	6, 7
Business (Conducting for self and others)	7, 11, 22, 27
Business (Start new)	5, 14
Can Fruits and Vegetables	18, 28
Can Preserves	18, 28
Concrete (Pour)	20, 21
Construction (Begin new)	7, 11, 14, 22, 24
Consultants (Begin work with)	1, 6, 9, 11, 14, 19, 22, 24, 27, 28
Contracts (Bid on)	6, 9, 11, 14
Cultivate	no ideal dates
Decorating	6, 7, 8, 15, 16
Demolition	2, 20, 21, 29, 30
Electronics (Buy)	6, 15
Entertain Guests	14
Floor Covering (Laying new)	20, 21, 22, 23, 24, 25, 26, 27
Habits (Break)	31
Hair (Cut to increase growth)	3, 4, 5, 6, 9, 12, 13, 14, 15, 16
Hair (Cut to decrease growth)	2, 29, 30, 31
Harvest (Grain for storage)	20, 21, 22
Harvest (Root crops)	17, 20, 21, 22, 29, 30
Investments (New)	11, 22
Loan (Ask for)	12, 13, 14
Massage (Relaxing)	14
Mow Lawn (Decrease growth)	1, 18, 19, 20, 21, 22, 23, 24, 25, 26, 27, 28, 29, 30, 31
Mow Lawn (Increase growth)	3, 4, 5, 6, 7, 8, 9, 10, 11, 12, 13, 14, 15, 16
Mushrooms (Pick)	16, 17, 18
Negotiate (Business for the elderly)	9
Prune for Better Fruit	1, 2, 27, 28, 29, 30
Prune to Promote Healing	no ideal dates
Wean Children	2, 3, 4, 5, 6, 7, 8, 30, 31
Wood Floors (Installing)	31
Write Letters or Contracts	1, 2, 6, 15, 20, 30

Choose the Best Time for Your Activities

When rules for elections refer to "favorable" and "unfavorable" aspects to your Sun or other planets, please refer to the Favorable and Unfavorable Days Tables and Lunar Aspectarian for more information. You'll find instructions beginning on page 129 and the tables beginning on page 136.

The material in this section came from several sources including: *The New A to Z Horoscope Maker and Delineator* by Llewellyn George (Llewellyn, 1999), *Moon Sign Book* (Llewellyn, 1945), and *Electional Astrology* by Vivian Robson (Slingshot Publishing, 2000). Robson's book was originally published in 1937.

Advertise (Internet)

The Moon should be conjunct, sextile, or trine Mercury or Uranus and in the sign of Gemini, Capricorn, or Aquarius.

Advertise (Print)

Write ads on a day favorable to your Sun. The Moon should be conjunct, sextile, or trine Mercury or Venus. Avoid hard aspects to Mars and Saturn. Ad campaigns produce the best results when the Moon is well aspected in Gemini (to enhance communication) or Capricorn (to build business).

Animals

Take home new pets when the day is favorable to your Sun, or when the Moon is trine, sextile, or conjunct Mercury, Venus, or Jupiter, or in the sign of Virgo or Pisces. However, avoid days when the Moon is either square or opposing the Sun, Mars, Saturn, Uranus, Neptune, or Pluto. When selecting a pet, have the Moon well aspected by the planet that rules the animal. Cats are ruled by the Sun, dogs by Mercury, birds by Venus, horses by Jupiter, and fish by Neptune. Buy large animals when the Moon is in Sagittarius or Pisces and making favorable aspects to Jupiter or Mercury. Buy animals smaller than sheep when the Moon is in Virgo with favorable aspects to Mercury or Venus.

Animals (Breed)

Animals are easiest to handle when the Moon is in Taurus, Cancer, Libra, or Pisces, but try to avoid the Full Moon. To encourage healthy births, animals should be mated so births occur when the Moon is increasing in Taurus, Cancer, Pisces, or Libra. Those born during a semi-fruitful sign (Taurus and Capricorn) will produce leaner meat. Libra yields beautiful animals for showing and racing.

Animals (Declaw)

Declaw cats for medical purposes in the dark of the Moon. Avoid the week before and after the Full Moon and the sign of Pisces.

Animals (Neuter or spay)

Have livestock and pets neutered or spayed when the Moon is in Sagittarius, Capricorn, or Pisces, after it has passed through Scorpio, the sign that rules reproductive organs. Avoid the week before and after the Full Moon.

Animals (Sell or buy)

In either buying or selling, it is important to keep the Moon and Mercury free from any aspect to Mars. Aspects to Mars will create discord and increase the likelihood of wrangling over price and quality. The Moon should be passing from the first quarter to full and sextile or trine Venus or Jupiter. When buying racehorses, let the Moon be in an air sign. The Moon should be in air signs when you buy birds. If the birds are to be pets, let the Moon be in good aspect to Venus.

Animals (Train)

Train pets when the Moon is in Virgo or trine to Mercury.

Animals (Train dogs to hunt)

Let the Moon be in Aries in conjunction with Mars, which makes them courageous and quick to learn. But let Jupiter also be in aspect to preserve them from danger in hunting.

Automobiles

When buying an automobile, select a time when the Moon is conjunct, sextile, or trine to Mercury, Saturn, or Uranus and in the sign of Gemini or Capricorn. Avoid times when Mercury is in retrograde motion.

Baking Cakes

Your cakes will have a lighter texture if you see that the Moon is in Gemini, Libra, or Aquarius and in good aspect to Venus or

Mercury. If you are decorating a cake or confections are being made, have the Moon placed in Libra.

Beauty Treatments (Massage, etc.)

See that the Moon is in Taurus, Cancer, Leo, Libra, or Aquarius and in favorable aspect to Venus. In the case of plastic surgery, aspects to Mars should be avoided, and the Moon should not be in the sign ruling the part to be operated on.

Borrow (Money or goods)

See that the Moon is not placed between 15 degrees Libra and 15 degrees Scorpio. Let the Moon be waning and in Leo, Scorpio (16 to 30 degrees), Sagittarius, or Pisces. Venus should be in good aspect to the Moon, and the Moon should not be square, opposing, or conjunct either Saturn or Mars.

Brewing

Start brewing during the third or fourth quarter, when the Moon is in Cancer, Scorpio, or Pisces.

Build (Start foundation)

Turning the first sod for the foundation marks the beginning of the building. For best results, excavate the site when the Moon is in the first quarter of a fixed sign and making favorable aspects to Saturn.

Business (Start new)

When starting a business, have the Moon be in Taurus, Virgo, or Capricorn and increasing. The Moon should be sextile or trine Jupiter or Saturn, but avoid oppositions or squares. The planet ruling the business should be well aspected, too.

Buy Goods

Buy during the third quarter, when the Moon is in Taurus for quality or in a mutable sign (Gemini, Sagittarius, Virgo, or Pisces) for savings. Good aspects to Venus or the Sun are desirable. If you are buying for yourself, it is good if the day is favorable for your Sun sign. You may also apply rules for buying specific items.

Canning

Can fruits and vegetables when the Moon is in either the third or fourth quarter and in the water sign Cancer or Pisces. Preserves and jellies use the same quarters and the signs Cancer, Pisces, or Taurus.

Clothing

Buy clothing on a day that is favorable for your Sun sign and when Venus or Mercury is well aspected. Avoid aspects to Mars and Saturn. Buy your clothing when the Moon is in Taurus if you want to remain satisfied. Do not buy clothing or jewelry when the Moon is in Scorpio or Aries. See that the Moon is sextile or trine the Sun during the first or second quarters.

Collections

Try to make collections on days when your Sun is well aspected. Avoid days when the Moon is opposing or square Mars or Saturn. If possible, the Moon should be in a cardinal sign (Aries, Cancer, Libra, or Capricorn). It is more difficult to collect when the Moon is in Taurus or Scorpio.

Concrete

Pour concrete when the Moon is in the third quarter of the fixed sign Taurus, Leo, or Aquarius.

Construction (Begin new)

The Moon should be sextile or trine Jupiter. According to Hermes, no building should be begun when the Moon is in Scorpio or Pisces. The best time to begin building is when the Moon is in Aquarius.

Consultants (Work with)

The Moon should be conjunct, sextile, or trine Mercury or Jupiter.

Contracts (Bid on)

The Moon should be in Gemini or Capricorn and either the Moon or Mercury should be conjunct, sextile, or trine Jupiter.

Copyrights/Patents

The Moon should be conjunct, trine, or sextile either Mercury or Jupiter.

Coronations and Installations

Let the Moon be in Leo and in favorable aspect to Venus, Jupiter, or Mercury. The Moon should be applying to these planets.

Cultivate

Cultivate when the Moon is in a barren sign and waning, ideally the fourth quarter in Aries, Gemini, Leo, Virgo, or Aquarius. The third quarter in the sign of Sagittarius will also work.

Cut Timber

Timber cut during the waning Moon does not become worm-eaten; it will season well and not warp, decay, or snap during burning. Cut when the Moon is in Taurus, Gemini, Virgo, or Capricorn—especially in August. Avoid the water signs. Look for favorable aspects to Mars.

Decorating or Home Repairs

Have the Moon waxing and in the sign of Libra, Gemini, or Aquarius. Avoid squares or oppositions to either Mars or Saturn. Venus in good aspect to Mars or Saturn is beneficial.

Demolition

Let the waning Moon be in Leo, Sagittarius, or Aries.

Dental and Dentists

Visit the dentist when the Moon is in Virgo, or pick a day marked favorable for your Sun sign. Mars should be marked sextile, conjunct, or trine; avoid squares or oppositions to Saturn, Uranus, or Jupiter.

Teeth are best removed when the Moon is in Gemini, Virgo, Sagittarius, or Pisces and during the first or second quarter. Avoid the Full Moon! The day should be favorable for your lunar cycle, and Mars and Saturn should be marked conjunct, trine, or sextile. Fillings should be done in the third or fourth quarters in the sign of Taurus, Leo, Scorpio, or Pisces. The same applies for dentures.

Dressmaking

William Lilly wrote in 1676: "Make no new clothes, or first put them on when the Moon is in Scorpio or afflicted by Mars, for they will be apt to be torn and quickly worn out." Design, repair, and sew clothes in the first and second quarters of Taurus, Leo, or Libra on a day marked favorable for your Sun sign. Venus, Jupiter, and Mercury should be favorably aspected, but avoid hard aspects to Mars or Saturn.

Egg-setting (see p. 161)

Eggs should be set so chicks will hatch during fruitful signs. To set eggs, subtract the number of days given for incubation or gestation from the fruitful dates. Chickens incubate in twenty-one days, turkeys and geese in twenty-eight days.

A freshly laid egg loses quality rapidly if it is not handled properly. Use plenty of clean litter in the nests to reduce the number of dirty or cracked eggs. Gather eggs daily in mild weather and at least two times daily in hot or cold weather. The eggs should be placed in a cooler immediately after gathering and stored at 50 to

55° F. Do not store eggs with foods or products that give off pungent odors since eggs may absorb the odors.

Eggs saved for hatching purposes should not be washed. Only clean and slightly soiled eggs should be saved for hatching. Dirty eggs should not be incubated. Eggs should be stored in a cool place with the large ends up. It is not advisable to store the eggs longer than one week before setting them in an incubator.

Electricity and Gas (Install)

The Moon should be in a fire sign, and there should be no squares, oppositions, or conjunctions with Uranus (ruler of electricity), Neptune (ruler of gas), Saturn, or Mars. Hard aspects to Mars can cause fires.

Electronics (Buying)

Choose a day when the Moon is in an air sign (Gemini, Libra, Aquarius) and well aspected by Mercury and/or Uranus when buying electronics.

Electronics (Repair)

The Moon should be sextile or trine Mars or Uranus and in a fixed sign (Taurus, Leo, Scorpio, Aquarius).

Entertain Friends

Let the Moon be in Leo or Libra and making good aspects to Venus. Avoid squares or oppositions to either Mars or Saturn by the Moon or Venus.

Eyes and Eyeglasses

Have your eyes tested and glasses fitted on a day marked favorable for your Sun sign, and on a day that falls during your favorable lunar cycle. Mars should not be in aspect with the Moon. The same applies for any treatment of the eyes, which should also be started during the Moon's first or second quarter.

2012 © Steve Mcsweeny. Image from BigStockPhoto.com

Fence Posts

Set posts when the Moon is in the third or fourth quarter of the fixed sign Taurus or Leo.

Fertilize and Compost

Fertilize when the Moon is in a fruitful sign (Cancer, Scorpio, Pisces). Organic fertilizers are best when the Moon is waning. Use chemical fertilizers when the Moon is waxing. Start compost when the Moon is in the fourth quarter in a water sign.

Find Hidden Treasure

Let the Moon be in good aspect to Jupiter or Venus. If you erect a horoscope for this election, place the Moon in the Fourth House.

Find Lost Articles

Search for lost articles during the first quarter and when your Sun sign is marked favorable. Also check to see that the planet ruling the lost item is trine, sextile, or conjunct the Moon. The Moon rules household utensils; Mercury rules letters and books; and Venus rules clothing, jewelry, and money.

Fishing

During the summer months, the best time of the day to fish is from sunrise to three hours after and from two hours before sunset until one hour after. Fish do not bite in cooler months until the air is warm, from noon to 3 pm. Warm, cloudy days are good. The most favorable winds are from the south and southwest. Easterly winds are unfavorable. The best days of the month for fishing are when the Moon changes quarters, especially if the change occurs on a day when the Moon is in a water sign (Cancer, Scorpio, Pisces). The best period in any month is the day after the Full Moon.

Friendship

The need for friendship is greater when the Moon is in Aquarius or when Uranus aspects the Moon. Friendship prospers when Venus or Uranus is trine, sextile, or conjunct the Moon. The Moon in Gemini facilitates the chance meeting of acquaintances and friends.

Grafting or Budding

Grafting is the process of introducing new varieties of fruit on less desirable trees. For this process you should use the increasing phase of the Moon in fruitful signs such as Cancer, Scorpio, or Pisces. Capricorn may be used, too. Cut your grafts while trees are dormant, from December to March. Keep them in a cool, dark place, not too dry or too damp. Do the grafting before the sap starts to flow and while the Moon is waxing, preferably while it is in Cancer, Scorpio, or Pisces. The type of plant should determine both cutting and planting times.

Habit (Breaking)

To end an undesirable habit, and this applies to ending everything from a bad relationship to smoking, start on a day when the Moon is in the fourth quarter and in the barren sign of Gemini, Leo, or

Aquarius. Aries, Virgo, and Capricorn may be suitable as well, depending on the habit you want to be rid of. Make sure that your lunar cycle is favorable. Avoid lunar aspects to Mars or Jupiter. However, favorable aspects to Pluto are helpful.

Haircuts

Cut hair when the Moon is in Gemini, Sagittarius, Pisces, Taurus, or Capricorn, but not in Virgo. Look for favorable aspects to Venus. For faster growth, cut hair when the Moon is increasing in Cancer or Pisces. To make hair grow thicker, cut when the Moon is full in the signs of Taurus, Cancer, or Leo. If you want your hair to grow more slowly, have the Moon be decreasing in Aries, Gemini, or Virgo, and have the Moon square or opposing Saturn.

Permanents, straightening, and hair coloring will take well if the Moon is in Taurus or Leo and trine or sextile Venus. Avoid hair treatments if Mars is marked as square or in opposition, especially if heat is to be used. For permanents, a trine to Jupiter is helpful. The Moon also should be in the first quarter. Check the lunar cycle for a favorable day in relation to your Sun sign.

Harvest Crops

Harvest root crops when the Moon is in a dry sign (Aries, Leo, Sagittarius, Gemini, Aquarius) and waning. Harvest grain for storage just after the Full Moon, avoiding Cancer, Scorpio, or Pisces. Harvest in the third and fourth quarters in dry signs. Dry crops in the third quarter in fire signs.

Health

A diagnosis is more likely to be successful when the Moon is in Aries, Cancer, Libra, or Capricorn and less so when in Gemini, Sagittarius, Pisces, or Virgo. Begin a recuperation program or enter a hospital when the Moon is in a cardinal or fixed sign and the day is favorable to your Sun sign. For surgery, see "Surgical Procedures." Buy medicines when the Moon is in Virgo or Scorpio.

Home (Buy new)

If you desire a permanent home, buy when the New Moon is in a fixed sign—Taurus or Leo—for example. Each sign will affect your decision in a different way. A house bought when the Moon is in Taurus is likely to be more practical and have a country look—right down to the split-rail fence. A house purchased when the Moon is in Leo will more likely be a real showplace.

If you're buying for speculation and a quick turnover, be certain that the Moon is in a cardinal sign (Aries, Cancer, Libra, Capricorn). Avoid buying when the Moon is in a fixed sign (Leo, Scorpio, Aquarius, Taurus).

Home (Make repairs)

In all repairs, avoid squares, oppositions, or conjunctions to the planet ruling the place or thing to be repaired. For example, bathrooms are ruled by Scorpio and Cancer. You would not want to start a project in those rooms when the Moon or Pluto is receiving hard aspects. The front entrance, hall, dining room, and porch are ruled by the Sun. So you would want to avoid times when Saturn or Mars are square, opposing, or conjunct the Sun. Also, let the Moon be waxing.

Home (Sell)

Make a strong effort to list your property for sale when the Sun is marked favorable in your sign and in good aspect to Jupiter. Avoid adverse aspects to as many planets as possible.

Home Furnishings (Buy new)

Saturn days (Saturday) are good for buying, and Jupiter days (Thursday) are good for selling. Items bought on days when Saturn is well aspected tend to wear longer and purchases tend to be more conservative.

Job (Start new)

Jupiter and Venus should be sextile, trine, or conjunct the Moon. A day when your Sun is receiving favorable aspects is preferred.

Legal Matters

Good Moon-Jupiter aspects improve the outcome in legal decisions. To gain damages through a lawsuit, begin the process during the increasing Moon. To avoid paying damages, a court date during the decreasing Moon is desirable. Good Moon-Sun aspects strengthen your chance of success. A well-aspected Moon in Cancer or Leo, making good aspects to the Sun, brings the best results in custody cases. In divorce cases, a favorable Moon-Venus aspect is best.

Loan (Ask for)

A first and second quarter phase favors the lender, the third and fourth quarters favor the borrower. Good aspects of Jupiter and Venus to the Moon are favorable to both, as is having the Moon in Leo or Taurus.

Machinery, Appliances, or Tools (Buy)

Tools, machinery, and other implements should be bought on days when your lunar cycle is favorable and when Mars and Uranus are trine, sextile, or conjunct the Moon. Any quarter of the Moon is suitable. When buying gas or electrical appliances, the Moon should be in Aquarius.

Make a Will

Let the Moon be in a fixed sign (Taurus, Leo, Scorpio, or Aquarius) to ensure permanence. If the Moon is in a cardinal sign (Aries, Cancer, Libra, or Capricorn), the will could be altered. Let the Moon be waxing—increasing in light—and in good aspect to Saturn, Venus, or Mercury. In case the will is made in an emergency during illness and the Moon is slow in motion, void-of-course, combust, or under the Sun's beams, the testator will die and the will remain unaltered. There is some danger that it will be lost or stolen, however.

Marriage

The best time for marriage to take place is when the Moon is increasing, but not yet full. Good signs for the Moon to be in are Taurus, Cancer, Leo, or Libra.

The Moon in Taurus produces the most steadfast marriages, but if the partners later want to separate, they may have a difficult time. Make sure that the Moon is well aspected, especially to Venus or Jupiter. Avoid aspects to Mars, Uranus, or Pluto and the signs Aries, Gemini, Virgo, Scorpio, or Aquarius.

The values of the signs are as follows:

- Aries is not favored for marriage
- Taurus from 0 to 19 degrees is good, the remaining degrees are less favorable
- Cancer is unfavorable unless you are marrying a widow
- Leo is favored, but it may cause one party to deceive the other as to his or her money or possessions
- Virgo is not favored except when marrying a widow
- Libra is good for engagements but not for marriage
- Scorpio from 0 to 15 degrees is good, but the last 15 degrees are entirely unfortunate. The woman may be fickle, envious, and quarrelsome
- Sagittarius is neutral
- Capricorn, from 0 to 10 degrees, is difficult for marriage; however, the remaining degrees are favorable, especially when marrying a widow
- Aquarius is not favored
- Pisces is favored, although marriage under this sign can incline a woman to chatter a lot

These effects are strongest when the Moon is in the sign. If the Moon and Venus are in a cardinal sign, happiness between the couple may not continue long.

On no account should the Moon apply to Saturn or Mars, even by good aspect.

Medical Treatment for the Eyes

Let the Moon be increasing in light and motion and making favorable aspects to Venus or Jupiter and be unaspected by Mars. Keep the Moon out of Taurus, Capricorn, or Virgo. If an aspect between the Moon and Mars is unavoidable, let it be separating.

Medical Treatment for the Head

If possible, have Mars and Saturn free of hard aspects. Let the Moon be in Aries or Taurus, decreasing in light, in conjunction or aspect with Venus or Jupiter and free of hard aspects. The Sun should not be in any aspect to the Moon.

Medical Treatment for the Nose

Let the Moon be in Cancer, Leo, or Virgo and not aspecting Mars or Saturn and also not in conjunction with a retrograde or weak planet.

Mining

Saturn rules mining. Begin work when Saturn is marked conjunct, trine, or sextile. Mine for gold when the Sun is marked conjunct, trine, or sextile. Mercury rules quicksilver, Venus rules copper, Jupiter rules tin, Saturn rules lead and coal, Uranus rules radioactive elements, Neptune rules oil, the Moon rules water. Mine for these items when the ruling planet is marked conjunct, trine, or sextile.

Move to New Home

If you have a choice, and sometimes you don't, make sure that Mars is not aspecting the Moon. Move on a day favorable to your Sun sign or when the Moon is conjunct, sextile, or trine the Sun.

Mow Lawn

Mow in the first and second quarters (waxing phase) to increase growth and lushness, and in the third and fourth quarters (waning phase) to decrease growth.

Negotiate

When you are choosing a time to negotiate, consider what the meeting is about and what you want to have happen. If it is agreement or compromise between two parties that you desire, have the Moon be in the sign of Libra. When you are making contracts, it is best to have the Moon in the same element. For example, if your concern is communication, then elect a time when the Moon is in an air sign. If, on the other hand, your concern is about possessions, an earth sign would be more appropriate. Fixed signs are unfavorable, with the exception of Leo; so are cardinal signs, except for Capricorn. If you are negotiating the end of something, use the rules that apply to ending habits.

Occupational Training

When you begin training, see that your lunar cycle is favorable that day and that the planet ruling your occupation is marked conjunct or trine.

Paint

Paint buildings during the waning Libra or Aquarius Moon. If the weather is hot, paint when the Moon is in Taurus. If the weather is cold, paint when the Moon is in Leo. Schedule the painting to start in the fourth quarter as the wood is drier and paint will penetrate wood better. Avoid painting around the New Moon, though, as the wood is likely to be damp, making the paint subject to scalding when hot weather hits it. If the temperature is below 70° F, it is not advisable to paint while the Moon is in Cancer, Scorpio, or Pisces as the paint is apt to creep, check, or run.

Party (Host or attend)

A party timed so the Moon is in Gemini, Leo, Libra, or Sagittarius, with good aspects to Venus and Jupiter, will be fun and well attended. There should be no aspects between the Moon and Mars or Saturn.

Pawn

Do not pawn any article when Jupiter is receiving a square or opposition from Saturn or Mars or when Jupiter is within 17 degrees of the Sun, for you will have little chance to redeem the items.

Pick Mushrooms

Mushrooms, one of the most promising traditional medicines in the world, should be gathered at the Full Moon.

Plant

Root crops, like carrots and potatoes, are best if planted in the sign Taurus or Capricorn. Beans, peas, tomatoes, peppers, and other fruit-bearing plants are best if planted in a sign that supports seed growth. Leaf plants, like lettuce, broccoli, or cauliflower, are best planted when the Moon is in a water sign.

It is recommended that you transplant during a decreasing Moon, when forces are streaming into the lower part of the plant. This helps root growth.

Promotion (Ask for)

Choose a day favorable to your Sun sign. Mercury should be marked conjunct, trine, or sextile. Avoid days when Mars or Saturn is aspected.

Prune

Prune during the third and fourth quarter of a Scorpio Moon to retard growth and to promote better fruit. Prune when the Moon is in cardinal Capricorn to promote healing.

Reconcile with People

If the reconciliation is with a woman, let Venus be strong and well aspected. If elders or superiors are involved, see that Saturn is receiving good aspects; if the reconciliation is between young people or between an older and younger person, see that Mercury is well aspected.

Romance

There is less control of when a romance starts, but romances begun under an increasing Moon are more likely to be permanent or satisfying, while those begun during the decreasing Moon tend to transform the participants. The tone of the relationship can be guessed from the sign the Moon is in. Romances begun with the Moon in Aries may be impulsive. Those begun in Capricorn will take greater effort to bring to a desirable conclusion, but they may be very rewarding. Good aspects between the Moon and Venus will have a positive influence on the relationship. Avoid unfavorable aspects to Mars, Uranus, and Pluto. A decreasing Moon, particularly the fourth quarter, facilitates ending a relationship and causes the least pain.

Roof a Building

Begin roofing a building during the third or fourth quarter, when the Moon is in Aries or Aquarius. Shingles laid during the New Moon have a tendency to curl at the edges.

Sauerkraut

The best-tasting sauerkraut is made just after the Full Moon in the fruitful signs of Cancer, Scorpio, or Pisces.

Select a Child's Sex

Count from the last day of menstruation to the first day of the next cycle and divide the interval between the two dates in half. Pregnancy in the first half produces females, but copulation should take place with the Moon in a feminine sign. Pregnancy in the latter half, up to three days before the beginning of menstruation, produces males, but copulation should take place with the Moon in a masculine sign. The three-day period before the next period again produces females.

Sell or Canvass

Begin these activities during a day favorable to your Sun sign. Otherwise, sell on days when Jupiter, Mercury, or Mars is trine, sextile, or conjunct the Moon. Avoid days when Saturn is square or opposing the Moon, for that always hinders business and causes discord. If the Moon is passing from the first quarter to full, it is best to have the Moon swift in motion and in good aspect with Venus and/or Jupiter.

Sign Papers

Sign contracts or agreements when the Moon is increasing in a fruitful sign and on a day when the Moon is making favorable aspects to Mercury. Avoid days when Mars, Saturn, or Neptune are square or opposite the Moon.

Spray and Weed

Spray pests and weeds during the fourth quarter when the Moon is in the barren sign Leo or Aquarius and making favorable aspects to Pluto. Weed during a waning Moon in a barren sign.

Staff (Fire)

Have the Moon in the third or fourth quarter, but not full. The Moon should not be square any planets.

Staff (Hire)

The Moon should be in the first or second quarter, and preferably in the sign of Gemini or Virgo. The Moon should be conjunct, trine, or sextile Mercury or Jupiter.

Stocks (Buy)

The Moon should be in Taurus or Capricorn, and there should be a sextile or trine to Jupiter or Saturn.

Surgical Procedures

Blood flow, like ocean tides, appears to be related to Moon phases. To reduce hemorrhage after a surgery, schedule it within one week before or after a New Moon. Schedule surgery to occur during the increase of the Moon if possible, as wounds heal better and vitality is greater than during the decrease of the Moon. Avoid surgery within one week before or after the Full Moon. Select a date when the Moon is past the sign governing the part of the body involved in the operation. For example, abdominal operations should be done when the Moon is in Sagittarius,

Capricorn, or Aquarius. The further removed the Moon sign is from the sign ruling the afflicted part of the body, the better.

For successful operations, avoid times when the Moon is applying to any aspect of Mars. (This tends to promote inflammation and complications.) See the Lunar Aspectarian on odd pages 137–159 to find days with negative Mars aspects and positive Venus and Jupiter aspects. Never operate with the Moon in the same sign as a person's Sun sign or Ascendant. Let the Moon be in a fixed sign and avoid square or opposing aspects. The Moon should not be void-of-course. Cosmetic surgery should be done in the increase of the Moon, when the Moon is not square or in opposition to Mars. Avoid days when the Moon is square or opposing Saturn or the Sun.

Travel (Air)

Start long trips when the Moon is making favorable aspects to the Sun. For enjoyment, aspects to Jupiter are preferable; for visiting, look for favorable aspects to Mercury. To prevent accidents, avoid squares or oppositions to Mars, Saturn, Uranus, or Pluto. Choose a day when the Moon is in Sagittarius or Gemini and well aspected to Mercury, Jupiter, or Uranus. Avoid adverse aspects of Mars, Saturn, or Uranus.

Visit

On setting out to visit a person, let the Moon be in aspect with any retrograde planet, for this ensures that the person you're visiting will be at home. If you desire to stay a long time in a place, let the Moon be in good aspect to Saturn. If you desire to leave the place quickly, let the Moon be in a cardinal sign.

Wean Children

To wean a child successfully, do so when the Moon is in Sagittarius, Capricorn, Aquarius, or Pisces—signs that do not rule vital

human organs. By observing this astrological rule, much trouble for parents and child may be avoided.

Weight (Reduce)

If you want to lose weight, the best time to get started is when the Moon is in the third or fourth quarter and in the barren sign of Virgo. Review the section on How to Use the Moon Tables and Lunar Aspectarian beginning on page 136 to help you select a date that is favorable to begin your weight-loss program.

Wine and Drink Other Than Beer

Start brewing when the Moon is in Pisces or Taurus. Sextiles or trines to Venus are favorable, but avoid aspects to Mars or Saturn.

Write

Write for pleasure or publication when the Moon is in Gemini. Mercury should be making favorable aspects to Uranus and Neptune.

How to Use the Moon Tables and Lunar Aspectarian

Timing activities is one of the most important things you can do to ensure success. In many Eastern countries, timing by the planets is so important that practically no event takes place without first setting up a chart for it. Weddings have occurred in the middle of the night because the influences were best then. You may not want to take it that far, but you can still make use of the influences of the Moon whenever possible. It's easy and it works!

Llewellyn's Moon Sign Book has information to help you plan just about any activity: weddings, fishing, making purchases, cutting your hair, traveling, and more. We provide the guidelines you need to pick the best day out of the several from which you have to choose. The Moon Tables are the *Moon Sign Book's* primary method for choosing dates. Following are instructions, examples, and directions on how to read the Moon Tables. More advanced information on using the tables containing the Lunar Aspectarian and favorable and unfavorable days (found on odd-numbered pages opposite the Moon Tables), Moon void-of-course and retrograde information to choose the dates best for you is also included.

The Five Basic Steps

Step 1: Directions for Choosing Dates
Look up the directions for choosing dates for the activity that you wish to begin, then go to step 2.

Step 2: Check the Moon Tables
You'll find two tables for each month of the year beginning on page 136. The Moon Tables (on the left-hand pages) include the day, date, and sign the Moon is in; the element and nature of the sign; the Moon's phase; and when it changes sign or phase. If there is a time listed after a date, that time is the time when the Moon moves into that zodiac sign. Until then, the Moon is considered to be in the sign for the previous day.

The abbreviation Full signifies Full Moon and New signifies New Moon. The times listed with dates indicate when the Moon changes sign. The times listed after the phase indicate when the Moon changes phase.

Turn to the month you would like to begin your activity. You will be using the Moon's sign and phase information most often when you begin choosing your own dates. Use the Time Zone Map on page 164 and the Time Zone Conversions table on page 165 to convert time to your own time zone.

When you find dates that meet the criteria for the correct Moon phase and sign for your activity, you may have completed the process. For certain simple activities, such as getting a haircut, the phase and sign information is all that is needed. If the directions for your activity include information on certain lunar aspects, however, you should consult the Lunar Aspectarian. An example of this would be if the directions told you not to perform a certain activity when the Moon is square (Q) Jupiter.

Step 3: Check the Lunar Aspectarian

On the pages opposite the Moon Tables you will find tables containing the Lunar Aspectarian and Favorable and Unfavorable Days. The Lunar Aspectarian gives the aspects (or angles) of the Moon to other planets. Some aspects are favorable, while others are not. To use the Lunar Aspectarian, find the planet that the directions list as favorable for your activity, and run down the column to the date desired. For example, you should avoid aspects to Mars if you are planning surgery. So you would look for Mars across the top and then run down that column looking for days where there are no aspects to Mars (as signified by empty boxes). If you want to find a favorable aspect (sextile (X) or trine (T)) to Mercury, run your finger down the column under Mercury until you find an X or T. Adverse aspects to planets are squares (Q) or oppositions (O). A conjunction (C) is sometimes beneficial, sometimes not, depending on the activity or planets involved.

Step 4: Favorable and Unfavorable Days

The tables listing favorable and unfavorable days are helpful when you want to choose your personal best dates because your Sun sign is taken into consideration. The twelve Sun signs are listed on the right side of the tables. Once you have determined which days meet your criteria for phase, sign, and aspects, you can determine whether or not those days are positive for you by checking the favorable and unfavorable days for your Sun sign.

To find out if a day is positive for you, find your Sun sign and then look down the column. If it is marked F, it is very favorable. The Moon is in the same sign as your Sun on a favorable day. If it is marked f, it is slightly favorable; U is very unfavorable; and u means slightly unfavorable. A day marked very unfavorable (U) indicates that the Moon is in the sign opposing your Sun.

Once you have selected good dates for the activity you are about to begin, you can go straight to "Using What You've Learned," beginning on the next page. To learn how to fine-tune your selections even further, read on.

Step 5: Void-of-Course Moon and Retrogrades

This last step is perhaps the most advanced portion of the procedure. It is generally considered poor timing to make decisions, sign important papers, or start special activities during a Moon void-of-course period or during a Mercury retrograde. Once you have chosen the best date for your activity based on steps one through four, you can check the Void-of-Course tables, beginning on page 76, to find out if any of the dates you have chosen have void periods.

The Moon is said to be void-of-course after it has made its last aspect to a planet within a particular sign, but before it has moved into the next sign. Put simply, the Moon is "resting" during the void-of-course period, so activities initiated at this time generally don't come to fruition. You will notice that there are many void periods during the year, and it is nearly impossible to avoid all of them. Some people choose to ignore these altogether and do not take them into consideration when planning activities.

Next, you can check the Retrograde Planets tables on page 160 to see what planets are retrograde during your chosen date(s).

A planet is said to be retrograde when it appears to move backward in the sky as viewed from the Earth. Generally, the farther a planet is away from the Sun, the longer it can stay retrograde. Some planets will retrograde for several months at a time. Avoiding retrogrades is not as important in lunar planning as avoiding the Moon void-of-course, with the exception of the planet Mercury.

Mercury rules thought and communication, so it is advisable not to sign important papers, initiate important business or legal work, or make crucial decisions during these times. As with the Moon void-of-course, it is difficult to avoid all planetary retrogrades when beginning events, and you may choose to ignore this step of the process. Following are some examples using some or all of the steps outlined above.

Using What You've Learned

Let's say it's a new year and you want to have your hair cut. It's thin and you would like it to look fuller, so you find the directions for hair care and you see that for thicker hair you should cut hair while the Moon is Full and in the sign of Taurus, Cancer, or Leo. You should avoid the Moon in Aries, Gemini, or Virgo. Look at the January Moon Table on page 136. You see that the Full Moon is on January 26 at 11:38 pm. The Moon moves into the sign of Leo at 9:20 am that day and remains in Leo until January 28 at 6:27 pm, so January 27–28 meets both the phase and sign criteria.

Let's move on to a more difficult example using the sign and phase of the Moon. You want to buy a permanent home. After checking the instructions for purchasing a house: "Home (Buy new)" on page 118, you see that you should buy a home when the Moon is in Taurus, Cancer, or Leo. You need to get a loan, so you should also look under "Loan (Ask for)" on page 119. Here it says that the third and fourth quarters favor the borrower (you). You are going to buy the house in October so go to page 154. The Moon is in the third quarter October 18–26. The Moon is in Cancer from 11:36 pm on October 23 until October 26 at 12:12 pm. The best days for obtaining a loan would be October 23–26, while the Moon is in Cancer.

Just match up the best sign and phase (quarter) to come up with the best date. With all activities, be sure to check the favorable and unfavorable days for your Sun sign in the table adjoining the Lunar Aspectarian. If there is a choice between several dates, pick the one most favorable for you. Because buying a home is an important business decision, you may also wish to see if the Moon is void or if Mercury is retrograde during these dates.

Now let's look at an example that uses signs, phases, and aspects. Our example is starting new home construction. We will use the month of April. Look under "Build (Start foundation)" on page 110 and you'll see that the Moon should be in the first quarter of Taurus or Leo. You should select a time when the Moon is not making unfavorable aspects to Saturn. (Conjunctions are usually considered good if they are not to Mars, Saturn, or Neptune.) Look in the April Moon Table. You will see that the Moon is in the first quarter April 10–18. The Moon is in Taurus from 11:22 pm on April 10 until April 13 at 10:13 am. Now, look to the April Lunar Aspectarian. We see that there are no squares or oppositions to Saturn on April 10, 12, or 13, but there is an opposition on April 11. Therefore, April 12 would be the best date to start a foundation.

A Note About Time and Time Zones

All tables in the Moon Sign Book use Eastern Time. You must calculate the difference between your time zone and the Eastern Time Zone. Please refer to the Time Zone Conversions chart on 165 for help with time conversions. The sign the Moon is in at midnight is the sign shown in the Aspectarian and Favorable and Unfavorable Days tables.

How Does the Time Matter?

Due to the three-hour time difference between the East and West Coasts of the United States, those of you living on the East Coast may be, for example, under the influence of a Virgo Moon, while those of you living on the West Coast will still have a Leo Moon influence.

We follow a commonly held belief among astrologers: whatever sign the Moon is in at the start of a day—12 00 am Eastern Time—is considered the dominant influence of the day. That sign is indicated in the Moon Tables. If the date you select for an activity shows the Moon changing signs, you can decide how important the sign change may be for your specific election and adjust your election date and time accordingly.

Use Common Sense

Some activities depend on outside factors. Obviously, you can't go out and plant when there is a foot of snow on the ground. You should adjust to the conditions at hand. If the weather was bad during the first quarter, when it was best to plant crops, do it during the second quarter while the Moon is in a fruitful sign. If the Moon is not in a fruitful sign during the first or second quarter, choose a day when it is in a semi-fruitful sign. The best advice is to choose either the sign or phase that is most favorable, when the two don't coincide.

To Summarize

First, look up the activity under the proper heading, then look for the information given in the tables. Choose the best date considering the number of positive factors in effect. If most of the dates are favorable, there is no problem choosing the one that will fit your schedule. However, if there aren't any really good dates, pick the ones with the least number of negative influences. Please keep in mind that the information found here applies in the broadest sense to the events you want to plan or are considering. To be the most effective, when you use electional astrology, you should also consider your own birth chart in relation to a chart drawn for the time or times you have under consideration. The best advice we can offer you is: read the entire introduction to each section.

January Moon Table

Date	Sign	Element	Nature	Phase
1 Tue 12:35 pm	Virgo	Earth	Barren	3rd
2 Wed	Virgo	Earth	Barren	3rd
3 Thu 8:11 pm	Libra	Air	Semi-fruitful	3rd
4 Fri	Libra	Air	Semi-fruitful	4th 10:58 pm
5 Sat	Libra	Air	Semi-fruitful	4th
6 Sun 1:09 am	Scorpio	Water	Fruitful	4th
7 Mon	Scorpio	Water	Fruitful	4th
8 Tue 3:28 am	Sagittarius	Fire	Barren	4th
9 Wed	Sagittarius	Fire	Barren	4th
10 Thu 3:54 am	Capricorn	Earth	Semi-fruitful	4th
11 Fri	Capricorn	Earth	Semi-fruitful	New 2:44 pm
12 Sat 4:01 am	Aquarius	Air	Barren	1st
13 Sun	Aquarius	Air	Barren	1st
14 Mon 5:49 am	Pisces	Water	Fruitful	1st
15 Tue	Pisces	Water	Fruitful	1st
16 Wed 11:07 am	Aries	Fire	Barren	1st
17 Thu	Aries	Fire	Barren	1st
18 Fri 8:36 pm	Taurus	Earth	Semi-fruitful	2nd 6:45 pm
19 Sat	Taurus	Earth	Semi-fruitful	2nd
20 Sun	Taurus	Earth	Semi-fruitful	2nd
21 Mon 9:04 am	Gemini	Air	Barren	2nd
22 Tue	Gemini	Air	Barren	2nd
23 Wed 10:00 pm	Cancer	Water	Fruitful	2nd
24 Thu	Cancer	Water	Fruitful	2nd
25 Fri	Cancer	Water	Fruitful	2nd
26 Sat 9:20 am	Leo	Fire	Barren	Full 11:38 pm
27 Sun	Leo	Fire	Barren	3rd
28 Mon 6:27 pm	Virgo	Earth	Barren	3rd
29 Tue	Virgo	Earth	Barren	3rd
30 Wed	Virgo	Earth	Barren	3rd
31 Thu 1:36 am	Libra	Air	Semi-fruitful	3rd

January Aspectarian/Favorable & Unfavorable Days

Date	Sun	Mercury	Venus	Mars	Jupiter	Saturn	Uranus	Neptune	Pluto
1	T								O
2	T				Q	X			T
3			Q						
4	Q	Q			T	T		O	Q
5				X					
6		X		Q		C		T	X
7	X								
8					X	O		T	Q
9									
10			C		X	Q	X		C
11	C	C							
12					T	Q	X		
13			C						
14		X		Q				C	X
15						T			
16	X	X			X		C		
17			Q	X					Q
18	Q	Q						X	
19						O			T
20		T	Q						
21	T	T			C		X	Q	
22									
23			T						
24					T	Q	T		O
25		O							
26	O				X	T			
27		O				Q			
28			O					O	
29					Q	X			T
30		T							
31						T		O	Q

Date	Aries	Taurus	Gemini	Cancer	Leo	Virgo	Libra	Scorpio	Sagittarus	Capricorn	Aquarius	Pisces
1	f	u	f		F		f	u	f		U	
2		f	u	f		F		f	u	f		U
3		f	u	f		F		f	u	f		U
4	U		f	u	f		F		f	u	f	
5	U		f	u	f		F		f	u	f	
6		U		f	u	f	F		f	u	f	
7		U		f	u	f	F		f	u	f	
8	f		U		f	u	f	F		f	u	
9	f		U		f	u	f	F		f	u	
10	u	f		U		f	u	f		F		f
11	u	f		U		f	u	f		F		f
12	f	u	f		U		f	u	f		F	
13	f	u	f		U		f	u	f		F	
14		f	u	f		U		f	u	f		F
15		f	u	f		U		f	u	f		F
16	F		f	u	f		U		f	u	f	
17	F		f	u	f		U		f	u	f	
18	F		f	u	f		U		f	u	f	
19		F		f	u	f		U		f	u	f
20		F		f	u	f		U		f	u	f
21	f		F		f	u	f		U		f	u
22	f		F		f	u	f		U		f	u
23	f		F		f	u	f		U		f	u
24	u	f		F		f	u	f		U		f
25	u	f		F		f	u	f		U		f
26	f	u	f		F		f	u	f		U	
27	f	u	f		F		f	u	f		U	
28	f	u	f		F		f	u	f		U	
29		f	u	f		F		f	u	f		U
30		f	u	f		F		f	u	f		U
31	U		f	u	f		F		f	u	f	

February Moon Table

Date	Sign	Element	Nature	Phase
1 Fri	Libra	Air	Semi-fruitful	3rd
2 Sat 7:02 am	Scorpio	Water	Fruitful	3rd
3 Sun	Scorpio	Water	Fruitful	4th 8:56 am
4 Mon 10:45 am	Sagittarius	Fire	Barren	4th
5 Tue	Sagittarius	Fire	Barren	4th
6 Wed 12:55 pm	Capricorn	Earth	Semi-fruitful	4th
7 Thu	Capricorn	Earth	Semi-fruitful	4th
8 Fri 2:16 pm	Aquarius	Air	Barren	4th
9 Sat	Aquarius	Air	Barren	4th
10 Sun 4:20 pm	Pisces	Water	Fruitful	New 2:20 am
11 Mon	Pisces	Water	Fruitful	1st
12 Tue 8:51 pm	Aries	Fire	Barren	1st
13 Wed	Aries	Fire	Barren	1st
14 Thu	Aries	Fire	Barren	1st
15 Fri 5:08 am	Taurus	Earth	Semi-fruitful	1st
16 Sat	Taurus	Earth	Semi-fruitful	1st
17 Sun 4:50 pm	Gemini	Air	Barren	2nd 3:31 pm
18 Mon	Gemini	Air	Barren	2nd
19 Tue	Gemini	Air	Barren	2nd
20 Wed 5:45 am	Cancer	Water	Fruitful	2nd
21 Thu	Cancer	Water	Fruitful	2nd
22 Fri 5:12 pm	Leo	Fire	Barren	2nd
23 Sat	Leo	Fire	Barren	2nd
24 Sun	Leo	Fire	Barren	2nd
25 Mon 1:52 am	Virgo	Earth	Barren	Full 3:26 pm
26 Tue	Virgo	Earth	Barren	3rd
27 Wed 8:02 am	Libra	Air	Semi-fruitful	3rd
28 Thu	Libra	Air	Semi-fruitful	3rd

February Aspectarian/Favorable & Unfavorable Days

Date	Sun	Mercury	Venus	Mars	Jupiter	Saturn	Uranus	Neptune	Pluto
1	T	T							
2			Q	T				T	
3	Q					C			X
4		Q	X	Q	O		T	Q	
5	X								
6		X		X			Q	X	
7						X			C
8									
9			C		T	Q	X		
10	C							C	
11		C		C	Q	T			X
12									
13					X		C		Q
14	X		X						
15								X	
16		X	Q	X		O			T
17	Q							Q	
18				Q	C		X		
19		Q	T						
20	T						Q	T	
21		T		T		T			O
22									
23					X	Q	T		
24			O						
25	O				Q	X		O	T
26		O		O					
27					T		O		
28									Q

Date	Aries	Taurus	Gemini	Cancer	Leo	Virgo	Libra	Scorpio	Sagittarus	Capricorn	Aquarius	Pisces
1	U		f	u	f		F		f	u	f	
2		U		f	u	f		F		f	u	f
3		U		f	u	f		F		f	u	f
4	f		U		f	u	f		F		f	u
5	f		U		f	u	f		F		f	u
6	f		U		f	u	f		F		f	u
7	u	f		U		f	u	f		F		f
8	u	f		U		f	u	f		F		f
9	f	u	f		U		f	u	f		F	
10	f	u	f		U		f	u	f		F	
11		f	u	f		U		f	u	f		F
12		f	u	f		U		f	u	f		F
13	F		f	u	f		U		f	u	f	
14	F		f	u	f		U		f	u	f	
15		F		f	u	f		U		f	u	f
16		F		f	u	f		U		f	u	f
17		F		f	u	f		U		f	u	f
18	f		F		f	u	f		U		f	u
19	f		F		f	u	f		U		f	u
20	u	f		F		f	u	f		U		f
21	u	f		F		f	u	f		U		f
22	u	f		F		f	u	f		U		f
23	f	u	f		F		f	u	f		U	
24	f	u	f		F		f	u	f		U	
25		f	u	f		F		f	u	f		U
26		f	u	f		F		f	u	f		U
27	U		f	u	f		F		f	u	f	
28	U		f	u	f		F		f	u	f	

March Moon Table

Date	Sign	Element	Nature	Phase
1 Fri 12:33 pm	Scorpio	Water	Fruitful	3rd
2 Sat	Scorpio	Water	Fruitful	3rd
3 Sun 4:11 pm	Sagittarius	Fire	Barren	3rd
4 Mon	Sagittarius	Fire	Barren	4th 4:53 pm
5 Tue 7:14 pm	Capricorn	Earth	Semi-fruitful	4th
6 Wed	Capricorn	Earth	Semi-fruitful	4th
7 Thu 10:01 pm	Aquarius	Air	Barren	4th
8 Fri	Aquarius	Air	Barren	4th
9 Sat	Aquarius	Air	Barren	4th
10 Sun 1:19 am	Pisces	Water	Fruitful	4th
11 Mon	Pisces	Water	Fruitful	New 3:51 pm
12 Tue 7:17 am	Aries	Fire	Barren	1st
13 Wed	Aries	Fire	Barren	1st
14 Thu 3:08 pm	Taurus	Earth	Semi-fruitful	1st
15 Fri	Taurus	Earth	Semi-fruitful	1st
16 Sat	Taurus	Earth	Semi-fruitful	1st
17 Sun 2:09 am	Gemini	Air	Barren	1st
18 Mon	Gemini	Air	Barren	1st
19 Tue 2:55 pm	Cancer	Water	Fruitful	2nd 1:27 pm
20 Wed	Cancer	Water	Fruitful	2nd
21 Thu	Cancer	Water	Fruitful	2nd
22 Fri 2:50 am	Leo	Fire	Barren	2nd
23 Sat	Leo	Fire	Barren	2nd
24 Sun 11:49 am	Virgo	Earth	Barren	2nd
25 Mon	Virgo	Earth	Barren	2nd
26 Tue 5:32 pm	Libra	Air	Semi-fruitful	2nd
27 Wed	Libra	Air	Semi-fruitful	Full 5:27 am
28 Thu 8:53 pm	Scorpio	Water	Fruitful	3rd
29 Fri	Scorpio	Water	Fruitful	3rd
30 Sat 11:13 pm	Sagittarius	Fire	Barren	3rd
31 Sun	Sagittarius	Fire	Barren	3rd

March Aspectarian/Favorable & Unfavorable Days

Date	Sun	Mercury	Venus	Mars	Jupiter	Saturn	Uranus	Neptune	Pluto
1		T						T	
2	T	T				C			X
3			T					Q	
4	Q	Q	Q		O	T			
5				Q					
6	X	X	X			X	Q	X	C
7				X					
8					T	Q	X		
9									
10		C			Q	T		C	X
11	C		C						
12			C	X		C			
13									Q
14								X	
15		X			O				T
16	X		X						
17		Q		X	C		X	Q	
18									
19	Q		Q					T	
20		T		Q	T	Q			O
21									
22	T		T	T	X	Q	T		
23									
24								O	
25		O			Q	X			T
26									
27	O		O	O	T		O		Q
28									
29		T				C		T	X
30									
31	T	Q	T		O			T	Q

Date	Aries	Taurus	Gemini	Cancer	Leo	Virgo	Libra	Scorpio	Sagittarius	Capricorn	Aquarius	Pisces
1	U		f	u	f		F		f	u	f	
2		U		f	u	f		F		f	u	f
3		U		f	u	f		F		f	u	f
4	f		U		f	u	f		F		f	u
5	f		U		f	u	f		F		f	u
6	u	f		U		f	u	f		F		f
7	u	f		U		f	u	f		F		f
8	f	u	f		U		f	u	f		F	
9	f	u	f		U		f	u	f		F	
10		f	u	f		U		f	u	f		F
11		f	u	f		U		f	u	f		F
12	F		f	u	f		U		f	u	f	
13	F		f	u	f		U		f	u	f	
14	F		f	u	f		U		f	u	f	
15		F		f	u	f		U		f	u	f
16		F		f	u	f		U		f	u	f
17	f		F		f	u	f		U		f	u
18	f		F		f	u	f		U		f	u
19	f		F		f	u	f		U		f	u
20	u	f		F		f	u	f		U		f
21	u	f		F		f	u	f		U		f
22	f	u	f		F		f	u	f		U	
23	f	u	f		F		f	u	f		U	
24	f	u	f		F		f	u	f		U	
25		f	u	f		F		f	u	f		U
26		f	u	f		F		f	u	f		U
27	U		f	u	f		F		f	u	f	
28	U		f	u	f		F		f	u	f	
29		U		f	u	f		F		f	u	f
30		U		f	u	f		F		f	u	f
31	f		U		f	u	f		F		f	u

April Moon Table

Date	Sign	Element	Nature	Phase
1 Mon	Sagittarius	Fire	Barren	3rd
2 Tue 1:35 am	Capricorn	Earth	Semi-fruitful	3rd
3 Wed	Capricorn	Earth	Semi-fruitful	4th 12:37 am
4 Thu 4:41 am	Aquarius	Air	Barren	4th
5 Fri	Aquarius	Air	Barren	4th
6 Sat 9:00 am	Pisces	Water	Fruitful	4th
7 Sun	Pisces	Water	Fruitful	4th
8 Mon 3:02 pm	Aries	Fire	Barren	4th
9 Tue	Aries	Fire	Barren	4th
10 Wed 11:22 pm	Taurus	Earth	Semi-fruitful	New 5:35 am
11 Thu	Taurus	Earth	Semi-fruitful	1st
12 Fri	Taurus	Earth	Semi-fruitful	1st
13 Sat 10:13 am	Gemini	Air	Barren	1st
14 Sun	Gemini	Air	Barren	1st
15 Mon 10:49 pm	Cancer	Water	Fruitful	1st
16 Tue	Cancer	Water	Fruitful	1st
17 Wed	Cancer	Water	Fruitful	1st
18 Thu 11:13 am	Leo	Fire	Barren	2nd 8:31 am
19 Fri	Leo	Fire	Barren	2nd
20 Sat 9:08 pm	Virgo	Earth	Barren	2nd
21 Sun	Virgo	Earth	Barren	2nd
22 Mon	Virgo	Earth	Barren	2nd
23 Tue 3:25 am	Libra	Air	Semi-fruitful	2nd
24 Wed	Libra	Air	Semi-fruitful	2nd
25 Thu 6:25 am	Scorpio	Water	Fruitful	Full 3:57 pm
26 Fri	Scorpio	Water	Fruitful	3rd
27 Sat 7:32 am	Sagittarius	Fire	Barren	3rd
28 Sun	Sagittarius	Fire	Barren	3rd
29 Mon 8:21 am	Capricorn	Earth	Semi-fruitful	3rd
30 Tue	Capricorn	Earth	Semi-fruitful	3rd

April Aspectarian/Favorable & Unfavorable Days

Date	Sun	Mercury	Venus	Mars	Jupiter	Saturn	Uranus	Neptune	Pluto
1				T					
2						X	Q	X	C
3	Q	X	Q	Q					
4						Q	X		
5	X		X	X	T				
6								C	
7						Q	T		X
8		C							
9						X		C	Q
10	C		C	C					
11						O		X	T
12									
13		X							Q
14					C		X		
15	X			X					
16		Q	X			T	Q	T	O
17									
18	Q		Q	Q					
19		T			X	Q	T		
20	T			T					
21		T				X		O	T
22						Q			
23								O	Q
24		O			T				
25	O		O			C		T	
26		O							X
27								Q	
28						O	T		
29		T		T		X		X	
30	T			T			Q		C

Date	Aries	Taurus	Gemini	Cancer	Leo	Virgo	Libra	Scorpio	Sagittarus	Capricorn	Aquarius	Pisces
1	f		U		f	u	f		F		f	u
2	u	f		U		f	u	f		F		f
3	u	f		U		f	u	f		F		f
4	f	u	f		U		f	u	f		F	
5	f	u	f		U		f	u	f		F	
6		f	u	f		U		f	u	f		F
7		f	u	f		U		f	u	f		F
8		f	u	f		U		f	u	f		F
9	F		f	u	f		U		f	u	f	
10	F		f	u	f		U		f	u	f	
11		F		f	u	f		U		f	u	f
12		F		f	u	f		U		f	u	f
13	f		F		f	u	f		U		f	u
14	f		F		f	u	f		U		f	u
15	f		F		f	u	f		U		f	u
16	u	f		F		f	u	f		U		f
17	u	f		F		f	u	f		U		f
18	f	u	f		F		f	u	f		U	
19	f	u	f		F		f	u	f		U	
20	f	u	f		F		f	u	f		U	
21		f	u	f		F		f	u	f		U
22		f	u	f		F		f	u	f		U
23	U		f	u	f		F		f	u	f	
24	U		f	u	f		F		f	u	f	
25		U		f	u	f		F		f	u	f
26		U		f	u	f		F		f	u	f
27	f		U		f	u	f		F		f	u
28	f		U		f	u	f		F		f	u
29	u	f		U		f	u	f		F		f
30	u	f		U		f	u	f		F		f

May Moon Table

Date	Sign	Element	Nature	Phase
1 Wed 10:20 am	Aquarius	Air	Barren	3rd
2 Thu	Aquarius	Air	Barren	4th 7:14 am
3 Fri 2:25 pm	Pisces	Water	Fruitful	4th
4 Sat	Pisces	Water	Fruitful	4th
5 Sun 9:03 pm	Aries	Fire	Barren	4th
6 Mon	Aries	Fire	Barren	4th
7 Tue	Aries	Fire	Barren	4th
8 Wed 6:09 am	Taurus	Earth	Semi-fruitful	4th
9 Thu	Taurus	Earth	Semi-fruitful	New 8:28 pm
10 Fri 5:21 pm	Gemini	Air	Barren	1st
11 Sat	Gemini	Air	Barren	1st
12 Sun	Gemini	Air	Barren	1st
13 Mon 5:57 am	Cancer	Water	Fruitful	1st
14 Tue	Cancer	Water	Fruitful	1st
15 Wed 6:38 pm	Leo	Fire	Barren	1st
16 Thu	Leo	Fire	Barren	1st
17 Fri	Leo	Fire	Barren	1st
18 Sat 5:33 am	Virgo	Earth	Barren	2nd 12:35 am
19 Sun	Virgo	Earth	Barren	2nd
20 Mon 1:07 pm	Libra	Air	Semi-fruitful	2nd
21 Tue	Libra	Air	Semi-fruitful	2nd
22 Wed 4:55 pm	Scorpio	Water	Fruitful	2nd
23 Thu	Scorpio	Water	Fruitful	2nd
24 Fri 5:49 pm	Sagittarius	Fire	Barren	2nd
25 Sat	Sagittarius	Fire	Barren	Full 12:25 am
26 Sun 5:28 pm	Capricorn	Earth	Semi-fruitful	3rd
27 Mon	Capricorn	Earth	Semi-fruitful	3rd
28 Tue 5:48 pm	Aquarius	Air	Barren	3rd
29 Wed	Aquarius	Air	Barren	3rd
30 Thu 8:30 pm	Pisces	Water	Fruitful	3rd
31 Fri	Pisces	Water	Fruitful	4th 2:58 pm

May Aspectarian/Favorable & Unfavorable Days

Date	Sun	Mercury	Venus	Mars	Jupiter	Saturn	Uranus	Neptune	Pluto
1		Q				Q			
2	Q			Q	T		X		
3		X	Q					C	
4	X			X	Q	T			X
5			X						
6							C		Q
7					X				
8						O		X	
9	C	C		C					T
10			C						
11							X	Q	
12					C				
13						T		T	
14				X				Q	O
15	X	X							
16			X			Q	T		
17				Q	X				
18	Q	Q					X	O	
19			Q	T	Q				T
20	T								
21		T	T					O	Q
22					T				
23						C		T	X
24				O					
25	O					T	Q		
26		O	O		O				
27						X	Q	X	C
28				T					
29	T					Q	X		
30		T	T	Q	T				
31	Q					T		C	X

Date	Aries	Taurus	Gemini	Cancer	Leo	Virgo	Libra	Scorpio	Sagittarus	Capricorn	Aquarius	Pisces
1	f	u	f		U		f	u	f		F	
2	f	u	f		U		f	u	f		F	
3	f	u	f		U		f	u	f		F	
4		f	u	f		U		f	u	f		F
5		f	u	f		U		f	u	f		F
6	F		f	u	f		U		f	u	f	
7	F		f	u	f		U		f	u	f	
8		F		f	u	f		U		f	u	f
9		F		f	u	f		U		f	u	f
10		F		f	u	f		U		f	u	f
11	f		F		f	u	f		U		f	u
12	f		F		f	u	f		U		f	u
13	u	f		F		f	u	f		U		f
14	u	f		F		f	u	f		U		f
15	u	f		F		f	u	f		U		f
16	f	u	f		F		f	u	f		U	
17	f	u	f		F		f	u	f		U	
18		f	u	f		F		f	u	f		U
19		f	u	f		F		f	u	f		U
20		f	u	f		F		f	u	f		U
21	U		f	u	f		F		f	u	f	
22	U		f	u	f		F		f	u	f	
23		U		f	u	f		F		f	u	f
24		U		f	u	f		F		f	u	f
25	f		U		f	u	f		F		f	u
26	f		U		f	u	f		F		f	u
27	u	f		U		f	u	f		F		f
28	u	f		U		f	u	f		F		f
29	f	u	f		U		f	u	f		F	
30	f	u	f		U		f	u	f		F	
31		f	u	f		U		f	u	f		F

145

June Moon Table

Date	Sign	Element	Nature	Phase
1 Sat	Pisces	Water	Fruitful	4th
2 Sun 2:33 am	Aries	Fire	Barren	4th
3 Mon	Aries	Fire	Barren	4th
4 Tue 11:53 am	Taurus	Earth	Semi-fruitful	4th
5 Wed	Taurus	Earth	Semi-fruitful	4th
6 Thu 11:32 pm	Gemini	Air	Barren	4th
7 Fri	Gemini	Air	Barren	4th
8 Sat	Gemini	Air	Barren	New 11:56 am
9 Sun 12:16 pm	Cancer	Water	Fruitful	1st
10 Mon	Cancer	Water	Fruitful	1st
11 Tue	Cancer	Water	Fruitful	1st
12 Wed 12:58 am	Leo	Fire	Barren	1st
13 Thu	Leo	Fire	Barren	1st
14 Fri 12:26 pm	Virgo	Earth	Barren	1st
15 Sat	Virgo	Earth	Barren	1st
16 Sun 9:19 pm	Libra	Air	Semi-fruitful	2nd 1:24 pm
17 Mon	Libra	Air	Semi-fruitful	2nd
18 Tue	Libra	Air	Semi-fruitful	2nd
19 Wed 2:38 am	Scorpio	Water	Fruitful	2nd
20 Thu	Scorpio	Water	Fruitful	2nd
21 Fri 4:31 am	Sagittarius	Fire	Barren	2nd
22 Sat	Sagittarius	Fire	Barren	2nd
23 Sun 4:08 am	Capricorn	Earth	Semi-fruitful	Full 7:32 am
24 Mon	Capricorn	Earth	Semi-fruitful	3rd
25 Tue 3:27 am	Aquarius	Air	Barren	3rd
26 Wed	Aquarius	Air	Barren	3rd
27 Thu 4:32 am	Pisces	Water	Fruitful	3rd
28 Fri	Pisces	Water	Fruitful	3rd
29 Sat 9:07 am	Aries	Fire	Barren	3rd
30 Sun	Aries	Fire	Barren	4th 12:54 am

June Aspectarian/Favorable & Unfavorable Days

Date	Sun	Mercury	Venus	Mars	Jupiter	Saturn	Uranus	Neptune	Pluto
1					Q				
2		Q	Q	X					Q
3	X						C		
4			X		X	O		X	
5		X							T
6									
7				C				X	Q
8	C								
9					C	T		T	
10		C	C					Q	O
11									
12				X		Q			
13	X							T	
14					X	X		O	
15			X	Q					T
16	Q	X			Q				
17				T				O	Q
18	T	Q	Q		T				
19						C		T	X
20		T	T						
21									Q
22			O					T	
23	O				O	X	Q	X	C
24		O	O						
25						Q	X		
26				T					
27	T				T	T		C	X
28		T		Q					
29			T		Q				
30	Q							C	Q

Date	Aries	Taurus	Gemini	Cancer	Leo	Virgo	Libra	Scorpio	Sagittarius	Capricorn	Aquarius	Pisces
1		f	u	f		U		f	u	f		F
2	F		f	u	f		U		f	u	f	
3	F		f	u	f		U		f	u	f	
4		F		f	u	f		U		f	u	f
5		F		f	u	f		U		f	u	f
6		F		f	u	f		U		f	u	f
7	f		F		f	u	f		U		f	u
8	f		F		f	u	f		U		f	u
9	f		F		f	u	f		U		f	u
10	u	f		F		f	u	f		U		f
11	u	f		F		f	u	f		U		f
12	f	u	f		F		f	u	f		U	
13	f	u	f		F		f	u	f		U	
14	f	u	f		F		f	u	f		U	
15		f	u	f		F		f	u	f		U
16		f	u	f		F		f	u	f		U
17	U		f	u	f		F		f	u	f	
18	U		f	u	f		F		f	u	f	
19		U		f	u	f		F		f	u	f
20		U		f	u	f		F		f	u	f
21	f		U		f	u	f		F		f	u
22	f		U		f	u	f		F		f	u
23	u	f		U		f	u	f		F		f
24	u	f		U		f	u	f		F		f
25	f	u	f		U		f	u	f		F	
26	f	u	f		U		f	u	f		F	
27		f	u	f		U		f	u	f		F
28		f	u	f		U		f	u	f		F
29	F		f	u	f		U		f	u	f	
30	F		f	u	f		U		f	u	f	

July Moon Table

Date	Sign	Element	Nature	Phase
1 Mon 5:43 pm	Taurus	Earth	Semi-fruitful	4th
2 Tue	Taurus	Earth	Semi-fruitful	4th
3 Wed	Taurus	Earth	Semi-fruitful	4th
4 Thu 5:21 am	Gemini	Air	Barren	4th
5 Fri	Gemini	Air	Barren	4th
6 Sat 6:14 pm	Cancer	Water	Fruitful	4th
7 Sun	Cancer	Water	Fruitful	4th
8 Mon	Cancer	Water	Fruitful	New 3:14 am
9 Tue 6:48 am	Leo	Fire	Barren	1st
10 Wed	Leo	Fire	Barren	1st
11 Thu 6:12 pm	Virgo	Earth	Barren	1st
12 Fri	Virgo	Earth	Barren	1st
13 Sat	Virgo	Earth	Barren	1st
14 Sun 3:41 am	Libra	Air	Semi-fruitful	1st
15 Mon	Libra	Air	Semi-fruitful	2nd 11:18 pm
16 Tue 10:24 am	Scorpio	Water	Fruitful	2nd
17 Wed	Scorpio	Water	Fruitful	2nd
18 Thu 1:54 pm	Sagittarius	Fire	Barren	2nd
19 Fri	Sagittarius	Fire	Barren	2nd
20 Sat 2:39 pm	Capricorn	Earth	Semi-fruitful	2nd
21 Sun	Capricorn	Earth	Semi-fruitful	2nd
22 Mon 2:07 pm	Aquarius	Air	Barren	Full 2:16 pm
23 Tue	Aquarius	Air	Barren	3rd
24 Wed 2:22 pm	Pisces	Water	Fruitful	3rd
25 Thu	Pisces	Water	Fruitful	3rd
26 Fri 5:29 pm	Aries	Fire	Barren	3rd
27 Sat	Aries	Fire	Barren	3rd
28 Sun	Aries	Fire	Barren	3rd
29 Mon 12:43 am	Taurus	Earth	Semi-fruitful	4th 1:43 pm
30 Tue	Taurus	Earth	Semi-fruitful	4th
31 Wed 11:42 am	Gemini	Air	Barren	4th

July Aspectarian/Favorable & Unfavorable Days

Date	Sun	Mercury	Venus	Mars	Jupiter	Saturn	Uranus	Neptune	Pluto
1		Q		X	X				
2	X		Q			O		X	T
3		X							
4			X					Q	
5							X		
6				C	C				
7						T	Q	T	O
8	C	C							
9						Q			
10			C				T		
11				X					
12					X	X		O	T
13	X	X							
14				Q	Q				Q
15	Q	Q	X					O	
16				T	T	C		T	
17		T							X
18	T		Q					Q	
19							T		
20			T	O	O	X		X	
21		O						Q	C
22	O					Q			
23							X		
24			O			T		C	
25		T		T	T				X
26									
27	T	Q		Q	Q		C		Q
28									
29	Q		T	X	X	O		X	T
30		X							
31									Q

Date	Aries	Taurus	Gemini	Cancer	Leo	Virgo	Libra	Scorpio	Sagittarius	Capricorn	Aquarius	Pisces
1	F		f	u	f		U		f	u	f	
2		F		f	u	f		U		f	u	f
3		F		f	u	f		U		f	u	f
4	f		F		f	u	f		U		f	u
5	f		F		f	u	f		U		f	u
6	f		F		f	u	f		U		f	u
7	u	f		F		f	u	f		U		f
8	u	f		F		f	u	f		U		f
9	f	u	f		F		f	u	f		U	
10	f	u	f		F		f	u	f		U	
11	f	u	f		F		f	u	f		U	
12		f	u	f		F		f	u	f		U
13		f	u	f		F		f	u	f		U
14	U		f	u	f		F		f	u	f	
15	U		f	u	f		F		f	u	f	
16		U		f	u	f		F		f	u	f
17		U		f	u	f		F		f	u	f
18		U		f	u	f		F		f	u	f
19	f		U		f	u	f		F		f	u
20	f		U		f	u	f		F		f	u
21	u	f		U		f	u	f		F		f
22	u	f		U		f	u	f		F		f
23	f	u	f		U		f	u	f		F	
24	f	u	f		U		f	u	f		F	
25		f	u	f		U		f	u	f		F
26		f	u	f		U		f	u	f		F
27	F		f	u	f		U		f	u	f	
28	F		f	u	f		U		f	u	f	
29		F		f	u	f		U		f	u	f
30		F		f	u	f		U		f	u	f
31	f		F		f	u	f		U		f	u

August Moon Table

Date	Sign	Element	Nature	Phase
1 Thu	Gemini	Air	Barren	4th
2 Fri	Gemini	Air	Barren	4th
3 Sat 12:29 am	Cancer	Water	Fruitful	4th
4 Sun	Cancer	Water	Fruitful	4th
5 Mon 12:58 pm	Leo	Fire	Barren	4th
6 Tue	Leo	Fire	Barren	New 5:51 pm
7 Wed 11:57 pm	Virgo	Earth	Barren	1st
8 Thu	Virgo	Earth	Barren	1st
9 Fri	Virgo	Earth	Barren	1st
10 Sat 9:08 am	Libra	Air	Semi-fruitful	1st
11 Sun	Libra	Air	Semi-fruitful	1st
12 Mon 4:18 pm	Scorpio	Water	Fruitful	1st
13 Tue	Scorpio	Water	Fruitful	1st
14 Wed 9:04 pm	Sagittarius	Fire	Barren	2nd 6:56 am
15 Thu	Sagittarius	Fire	Barren	2nd
16 Fri 11:25 pm	Capricorn	Earth	Semi-fruitful	2nd
17 Sat	Capricorn	Earth	Semi-fruitful	2nd
18 Sun	Capricorn	Earth	Semi-fruitful	2nd
19 Mon 12:07 am	Aquarius	Air	Barren	2nd
20 Tue	Aquarius	Air	Barren	Full 9:45 pm
21 Wed 12:43 am	Pisces	Water	Fruitful	3rd
22 Thu	Pisces	Water	Fruitful	3rd
23 Fri 3:13 am	Aries	Fire	Barren	3rd
24 Sat	Aries	Fire	Barren	3rd
25 Sun 9:13 am	Taurus	Earth	Semi-fruitful	3rd
26 Mon	Taurus	Earth	Semi-fruitful	3rd
27 Tue 7:08 pm	Gemini	Air	Barren	3rd
28 Wed	Gemini	Air	Barren	4th 5:35 am
29 Thu	Gemini	Air	Barren	4th
30 Fri 7:33 am	Cancer	Water	Fruitful	4th
31 Sat	Cancer	Water	Fruitful	4th

August Aspectarian/Favorable & Unfavorable Days

Date	Sun	Mercury	Venus	Mars	Jupiter	Saturn	Uranus	Neptune	Pluto
1	X	Q					X		
2									
3					C	T		T	O
4			X	C				Q	
5		C						Q	
6	C					T			
7									
8					X	X		O	T
9			C	X					
10		X							
11	X			Q	Q		O		Q
12									
13		Q			T	C		T	X
14	Q		X	T					
15		T						T	Q
16	T								
17		Q			O	X	Q	X	C
18						O			
19		T					Q	X	
20	O	O							
21					T	T		C	X
22			T						
23		O							Q
24				Q		C			
25	T	T		Q		O		X	
26					X				T
27			X						
28	Q	Q					X	Q	
29		T							
30	X					T		T	
31		X	Q		C		Q		O

Date	Aries	Taurus	Gemini	Cancer	Leo	Virgo	Libra	Scorpio	Sagittarius	Capricorn	Aquarius	Pisces
1	f		F		f	u	f		U		f	u
2	f		F		f	u	f		U		f	u
3	u	f		F		f	u	f		U		f
4	u	f		F		f	u	f		U		f
5	u	f		F		f	u	f		U		f
6	f	u	f		F		f	u	f		U	
7	f	u	f		F		f	u	f		U	
8		f	u	f		F		f	u	f		U
9		f	u	f		F		f	u	f		U
10	U		f	u	f		F		f	u	f	
11	U		f	u	f		F		f	u	f	
12	U		f	u	f		F		f	u	f	
13		U		f	u	f		F		f	u	f
14		U		f	u	f		F		f	u	f
15	f		U		f	u	f		F		f	u
16	f		U		f	u	f		F		f	u
17	u	f		U		f	u	f		F		f
18	u	f		U		f	u	f		F		f
19	f	u	f		U		f	u	f		F	
20	f	u	f		U		f	u	f		F	
21		f	u	f		U		f	u	f		F
22		f	u	f		U		f	u	f		F
23	F		f	u	f		U		f	u	f	
24	F		f	u	f		U		f	u	f	
25		F		f	u	f		U		f	u	f
26		F		f	u	f		U		f	u	f
27		F		f	u	f		U		f	u	f
28	f		F		f	u	f		U		f	u
29	f		F		f	u	f		U		f	u
30	u	f		F		f	u	f		U		f
31	u	f		F		f	u	f		U		f

September Moon Table

Date	Sign	Element	Nature	Phase
1 Sun 8:01 pm	Leo	Fire	Barren	4th
2 Mon	Leo	Fire	Barren	4th
3 Tue	Leo	Fire	Barren	4th
4 Wed 6:43 am	Virgo	Earth	Barren	4th
5 Thu	Virgo	Earth	Barren	New 7:36 am
6 Fri 3:12 pm	Libra	Air	Semi-fruitful	1st
7 Sat	Libra	Air	Semi-fruitful	1st
8 Sun 9:44 pm	Scorpio	Water	Fruitful	1st
9 Mon	Scorpio	Water	Fruitful	1st
10 Tue	Scorpio	Water	Fruitful	1st
11 Wed 2:36 am	Sagittarius	Fire	Barren	1st
12 Thu	Sagittarius	Fire	Barren	2nd 1:08 pm
13 Fri 5:56 am	Capricorn	Earth	Semi-fruitful	2nd
14 Sat	Capricorn	Earth	Semi-fruitful	2nd
15 Sun 8:05 am	Aquarius	Air	Barren	2nd
16 Mon	Aquarius	Air	Barren	2nd
17 Tue 9:58 am	Pisces	Water	Fruitful	2nd
18 Wed	Pisces	Water	Fruitful	2nd
19 Thu 12:58 pm	Aries	Fire	Barren	Full 7:13 am
20 Fri	Aries	Fire	Barren	3rd
21 Sat 6:33 pm	Taurus	Earth	Semi-fruitful	3rd
22 Sun	Taurus	Earth	Semi-fruitful	3rd
23 Mon	Taurus	Earth	Semi-fruitful	3rd
24 Tue 3:34 am	Gemini	Air	Barren	3rd
25 Wed	Gemini	Air	Barren	3rd
26 Thu 3:24 am	Cancer	Water	Fruitful	4th 11:55 pm
27 Fri	Cancer	Water	Fruitful	4th
28 Sat	Cancer	Water	Fruitful	4th
29 Sun 3:57 am	Leo	Fire	Barren	4th
30 Mon	Leo	Fire	Barren	4th

September Aspectarian/Favorable & Unfavorable Days

Date	Sun	Mercury	Venus	Mars	Jupiter	Saturn	Uranus	Neptune	Pluto
1									
2			C			Q	T		
3		X							
4						X		O	T
5	C				X				
6		C							
7					X	Q		O	Q
8			C						
9					Q	C		T	X
10	X					T			
11		X			T			T	Q
12	Q								
13		Q	X			X		X	C
14	T				O		Q		
15		Q				Q			
16		T		O				X	
17		T					C		
18						T	T		X
19	O								
20		O		T	Q		C		Q
21									
22			O		O			X	T
23					Q	X			
24	T							Q	
25					X			X	
26	Q	T						T	
27						T	Q		O
28		T			C				
29	X	Q					Q		
30					C		T		

Date	Aries	Taurus	Gemini	Cancer	Leo	Virgo	Libra	Scorpio	Sagittarus	Capricorn	Aquarius	Pisces
1	u	f		F		f	u	f		U		f
2	f	u	f		F		f	u	f		U	
3	f	u	f		F		f	u	f		U	
4		f	u	f		F		f	u	f		U
5		f	u	f		F		f	u	f		U
6		f	u	f		F		f	u	f		U
7	U		f	u	f		F		f	u	f	
8	U		f	u	f		F		f	u	f	
9		U		f	u	f		F		f	u	f
10		U		f	u	f		F		f	u	f
11	f		U		f	u	f		F		f	u
12	f		U		f	u	f		F		f	u
13	u	f		U		f	u	f		F		f
14	u	f		U		f	u	f		F		f
15	f	u	f		U		f	u	f		F	
16	f	u	f		U		f	u	f		F	
17		f	u	f		U		f	u	f		F
18		f	u	f		U		f	u	f		F
19		f	u	f		U		f	u	f		F
20	F		f	u	f		U		f	u	f	
21	F		f	u	f		U		f	u	f	
22		F		f	u	f		U		f	u	f
23		F		f	u	f		U		f	u	f
24	f		F		f	u	f		U		f	u
25	f		F		f	u	f		U		f	u
26	f		F		f	u	f		U		f	u
27	u	f		F		f	u	f		U		f
28	u	f		F		f	u	f		U		f
29	f	u	f		F		f	u	f		U	
30	f	u	f		F		f	u	f		U	

October Moon Table

Date	Sign	Element	Nature	Phase
1 Tue 2:52 pm	Virgo	Earth	Barren	4th
2 Wed	Virgo	Earth	Barren	4th
3 Thu 10:59 pm	Libra	Air	Semi-fruitful	4th
4 Fri	Libra	Air	Semi-fruitful	New 8:35 pm
5 Sat	Libra	Air	Semi-fruitful	1st
6 Sun 4:33 am	Scorpio	Water	Fruitful	1st
7 Mon	Scorpio	Water	Fruitful	1st
8 Tue 8:21 am	Sagittarius	Fire	Barren	1st
9 Wed	Sagittarius	Fire	Barren	1st
10 Thu 11:17 am	Capricorn	Earth	Semi-fruitful	1st
11 Fri	Capricorn	Earth	Semi-fruitful	2nd 7:02 pm
12 Sat 2:00 pm	Aquarius	Air	Barren	2nd
13 Sun	Aquarius	Air	Barren	2nd
14 Mon 5:06 pm	Pisces	Water	Fruitful	2nd
15 Tue	Pisces	Water	Fruitful	2nd
16 Wed 9:18 pm	Aries	Fire	Barren	2nd
17 Thu	Aries	Fire	Barren	2nd
18 Fri	Aries	Fire	Barren	Full 7:38 pm
19 Sat 3:27 am	Taurus	Earth	Semi-fruitful	3rd
20 Sun	Taurus	Earth	Semi-fruitful	3rd
21 Mon 12:14 pm	Gemini	Air	Barren	3rd
22 Tue	Gemini	Air	Barren	3rd
23 Wed 11:36 pm	Cancer	Water	Fruitful	3rd
24 Thu	Cancer	Water	Fruitful	3rd
25 Fri	Cancer	Water	Fruitful	3rd
26 Sat 12:12 pm	Leo	Fire	Barren	4th 7:40 pm
27 Sun	Leo	Fire	Barren	4th
28 Mon 11:45 pm	Virgo	Earth	Barren	4th
29 Tue	Virgo	Earth	Barren	4th
30 Wed	Virgo	Earth	Barren	4th
31 Thu 8:22 am	Libra	Air	Semi-fruitful	4th

October Aspectarian/Favorable & Unfavorable Days

Date	Sun	Mercury	Venus	Mars	Jupiter	Saturn	Uranus	Neptune	Pluto
1	X	Q						O	
2						X			T
3			X	X					
4	C							O	Q
5				X	Q				
6		C				C		T	X
7					T				
8			C	Q				Q	
9	X							T	
10				T				X	
11	Q	X			O	X	Q		C
12									
13		Q	X			Q	X		
14	T			O			C		
15		T	Q			T			X
16						T			
17			T					C	Q
18	O				Q				
19				T				X	T
20	O				X	O			
21				Q				Q	
22			O				X		
23									
24	T				X		Q	T	O
25		T				C	T		
26	Q								
27		Q					Q	T	
28			T						
29	X				C			O	T
30		X	Q		X	X			
31									

Date	Aries	Taurus	Gemini	Cancer	Leo	Virgo	Libra	Scorpio	Sagittarius	Capricorn	Aquarius	Pisces
1	f	u	f		F		f	u	f		U	
2		f	u	f		F		f	u	f		U
3		f	u	f		F		f	u	f		U
4	U		f	u	f		F		f	u	f	
5	U		f	u	f		F		f	u	f	
6		U		f	u	f		F		f	u	f
7		U		f	u	f		F		f	u	f
8	f		U		f	u	f		F		f	u
9	f		U		f	u	f		F		f	u
10	u	f		U		f	u	f		F		f
11	u	f		U		f	u	f		F		f
12	u	f		U		f	u	f		F		f
13	f	u	f		U		f	u	f		F	
14	f	u	f		U		f	u	f		F	
15		f	u	f		U		f	u	f		F
16		f	u	f		U		f	u	f		F
17	F		f	u	f		U		f	u	f	
18	F		f	u	f		U		f	u	f	
19		F		f	u	f		U		f	u	f
20		F		f	u	f		U		f	u	f
21		F		f	u	f		U		f	u	f
22	f		F		f	u	f		U		f	u
23	f		F		f	u	f		U		f	u
24	u	f		F		f	u	f		U		f
25	u	f		F		f	u	f		U		f
26	u	f		F		f	u	f		U		f
27	f	u	f		F		f	u	f		U	
28	f	u	f		F		f	u	f		U	
29		f	u	f		F		f	u	f		U
30		f	u	f		F		f	u	f		U
31	U		f	u	f		F		f	u	f	

November Moon Table

Date	Sign	Element	Nature	Phase
1 Fri	Libra	Air	Semi-fruitful	4th
2 Sat 1:35 pm	Scorpio	Water	Fruitful	4th
3 Sun	Scorpio	Water	Fruitful	New 7:50 am
4 Mon 3:14 pm	Sagittarius	Fire	Barren	1st
5 Tue	Sagittarius	Fire	Barren	1st
6 Wed 4:44 pm	Capricorn	Earth	Semi-fruitful	1st
7 Thu	Capricorn	Earth	Semi-fruitful	1st
8 Fri 6:30 pm	Aquarius	Air	Barren	1st
9 Sat	Aquarius	Air	Barren	1st
10 Sun 9:36 pm	Pisces	Water	Fruitful	2nd 12:57 am
11 Mon	Pisces	Water	Fruitful	2nd
12 Tue	Pisces	Water	Fruitful	2nd
13 Wed 2:39 am	Aries	Fire	Barren	2nd
14 Thu	Aries	Fire	Barren	2nd
15 Fri 9:49 am	Taurus	Earth	Semi-fruitful	2nd
16 Sat	Taurus	Earth	Semi-fruitful	2nd
17 Sun 7:07 pm	Gemini	Air	Barren	Full 10:16 am
18 Mon	Gemini	Air	Barren	3rd
19 Tue	Gemini	Air	Barren	3rd
20 Wed 6:23 am	Cancer	Water	Fruitful	3rd
21 Thu	Cancer	Water	Fruitful	3rd
22 Fri 6:56 pm	Leo	Fire	Barren	3rd
23 Sat	Leo	Fire	Barren	3rd
24 Sun	Leo	Fire	Barren	3rd
25 Mon 7:11 am	Virgo	Earth	Barren	4th 2:28 pm
26 Tue	Virgo	Earth	Barren	4th
27 Wed 5:00 pm	Libra	Air	Semi-fruitful	4th
28 Thu	Libra	Air	Semi-fruitful	4th
29 Fri 11:03 pm	Scorpio	Water	Fruitful	4th
30 Sat	Scorpio	Water	Fruitful	4th

November Aspectarian/Favorable & Unfavorable Days

Date	Sun	Mercury	Venus	Mars	Jupiter	Saturn	Uranus	Neptune	Pluto
1					Q		O		Q
2		X						T	
3	C	C		X	T	C			X
4								Q	
5					Q		T		
6		X	C					X	
7	X				T	X	Q		C
8		Q				O			
9							Q	X	
10	Q								
11		T	X			T		C	X
12	T					O	T		
13			Q					C	Q
14								Q	
15		O						X	
16		T	T			O			T
17	O					X			
18							X	Q	
19			Q						
20								T	
21		T	O		C	T	Q		O
22	T			X					
23		Q						T	
24								Q	
25	Q								O
26		X	T			X	X		T
27					C				
28	X							O	Q
29			Q		Q				
30								T	X

Date	Aries	Taurus	Gemini	Cancer	Leo	Virgo	Libra	Scorpio	Sagittarius	Capricorn	Aquarius	Pisces
1	U		f	u	f		F		f	u	f	
2	U		f	u	f		F		f	u	f	
3		U		f	u	f		F		f	u	f
4		U		f	u	f		F		f	u	f
5	f		U		f	u	f		F		f	u
6	f		U		f	u	f		F		f	u
7	u	f		U		f	u	f		F		f
8	u	f		U		f	u	f		F		f
9	f	u	f		U		f	u	f		F	
10	f	u	f		U		f	u	f		F	
11		f	u	f		U		f	u	f		F
12		f	u	f		U		f	u	f		F
13	F		f	u	f		U		f	u	f	
14	F		f	u	f		U		f	u	f	
15		F		f	u	f		U		f	u	f
16		F		f	u	f		U		f	u	f
17		F		f	u	f		U		f	u	f
18	f		F		f	u	f		U		f	u
19	f		F		f	u	f		U		f	u
20	u	f		F		f	u	f		U		f
21	u	f		F		f	u	f		U		f
22	u	f		F		f	u	f		U		f
23	f	u	f		F		f	u	f		U	
24	f	u	f		F		f	u	f		U	
25		f	u	f		F		f	u	f		U
26		f	u	f		F		f	u	f		U
27		f	u	f		F		f	u	f		U
28	U		f	u	f		F		f	u	f	
29	U		f	u	f		F		f	u	f	
30		U		f	u	f		F		f	u	f

157

December Moon Table

Date	Sign	Element	Nature	Phase
1 Sun	Scorpio	Water	Fruitful	4th
2 Mon 1:31 am	Sagittarius	Fire	Barren	New 7:22 pm
3 Tue	Sagittarius	Fire	Barren	1st
4 Wed 1:49 am	Capricorn	Earth	Semi-fruitful	1st
5 Thu	Capricorn	Earth	Semi-fruitful	1st
6 Fri 1:53 am	Aquarius	Air	Barren	1st
7 Sat	Aquarius	Air	Barren	1st
8 Sun 3:34 am	Pisces	Water	Fruitful	1st
9 Mon	Pisces	Water	Fruitful	2nd 10:12 am
10 Tue 8:06 am	Aries	Fire	Barren	2nd
11 Wed	Aries	Fire	Barren	2nd
12 Thu 3:40 pm	Taurus	Earth	Semi-fruitful	2nd
13 Fri	Taurus	Earth	Semi-fruitful	2nd
14 Sat	Taurus	Earth	Semi-fruitful	2nd
15 Sun 1:40 am	Gemini	Air	Barren	2nd
16 Mon	Gemini	Air	Barren	2nd
17 Tue 1:17 pm	Cancer	Water	Fruitful	Full 4:28 am
18 Wed	Cancer	Water	Fruitful	3rd
19 Thu	Cancer	Water	Fruitful	3rd
20 Fri 1:48 am	Leo	Fire	Barren	3rd
21 Sat	Leo	Fire	Barren	3rd
22 Sun 2:19 pm	Virgo	Earth	Barren	3rd
23 Mon	Virgo	Earth	Barren	3rd
24 Tue	Virgo	Earth	Barren	3rd
25 Wed 1:17 am	Libra	Air	Semi-fruitful	4th 8:48 am
26 Thu	Libra	Air	Semi-fruitful	4th
27 Fri 8:58 am	Scorpio	Water	Fruitful	4th
28 Sat	Scorpio	Water	Fruitful	4th
29 Sun 12:37 pm	Sagittarius	Fire	Barren	4th
30 Mon	Sagittarius	Fire	Barren	4th
31 Tue 1:01 pm	Capricorn	Earth	Semi-fruitful	4th

December Aspectarian/Favorable & Unfavorable Days

Date	Sun	Mercury	Venus	Mars	Jupiter	Saturn	Uranus	Neptune	Pluto
1		C	X	X	T	C			
2	C					T	Q		
3				Q					
4							Q	X	C
5			C		O	X			
6		X		T			X		
7	X					Q			
8		Q						C	X
9	Q				T	T			
10			X	O			C		
11	T	T			Q				Q
12			Q					X	
13									T
14			T		X	O			
15			T				X	Q	
16		O							
17	O			Q				T	
18							Q		O
19			O		C	T			
20				X			T		
21						Q			
22	T	T						O	
23									T
24			T		X	X			
25	Q	Q		C			O		Q
26					Q				
27	X	X	Q					T	
28					T	C			X
29			X					Q	
30				X			T		
31			T						

Date	Aries	Taurus	Gemini	Cancer	Leo	Virgo	Libra	Scorpio	Sagittarus	Capricorn	Aquarius	Pisces
1		U		f	u	f		F		f	u	f
2	f		U		f	u	f		F		f	u
3	f		U		f	u	f		F		f	u
4	u	f		U		f	u	f		F		f
5	u	f		U		f	u	f		F		f
6	f	u	f		U		f	u	f		F	
7	f	u	f		U		f	u	f		F	
8	f	u	f		U		f	u	f			F
9	f	u	f		U		f	u	f			F
10	F		f	u	f		U		f	u	f	
11	F		f	u	f		U		f	u	f	
12	F		f	u	f		U		f	u	f	
13		F		f	u	f		U		f	u	f
14		F		f	u	f		U		f	u	f
15	f		F		f	u	f		U		f	u
16	f		F		f	u	f		U		f	u
17	f		F		f	u	f		U		f	u
18	u	f		F		f	u	f		U		f
19	u	f		F		f	u	f		U		f
20	f	u	f		F		f	u	f		U	
21	f	u	f		F		f	u	f		U	
22	f	u	f		F		f	u	f		U	
23		f	u	f		F		f	u	f		U
24		f	u	f		F		f	u	f		U
25	U		f	u	f		F		f	u	f	
26	U		f	u	f		F		f	u	f	
27		U		f	u	f		F		f	u	f
28		U		f	u	f		F		f	u	f
29		U		f	u	f		F		f	u	f
30	f		U		f	u	f		F		f	u
31	f		U		f	u	f		F		f	u

2013 Retrograde Planets

Planet	Begin	Eastern	Pacific	End	Eastern	Pacific
Saturn	02/18/13	12:02 pm	9:02 am	07/07/13		10:12 pm
				07/08/13	1:12 am	
Mercury	02/23/13	4:41 am	1:41 am	03/17/13	4:03 pm	1:03 pm
Pluto	04/12/13	3:34 pm	12:34 pm	09/20/13	11:29 am	7:29 am
Neptune	06/07/13	4:24 am	1:24 am	11/13/13	1:42 pm	10:42 am
Mercury	06/26/13	9:08 am	6:08 am	07/20/13	2:22 pm	11:22 am
Uranus	07/17/13	1:20 pm	10:20 am	12/17/13	12:40 pm	9:40 am
Mercury	10/21/13	6:29 am	3:29 am	11/10/13	4:12 pm	1:12 pm
Jupiter	11/06/13		9:03 pm	03/06/14	5:42 am	2:42 am
	11/07/13	12:03 am				
Venus	12/21/13	4:53 pm	1:53 pm	01/31/14	3:49 pm	12:49 pm

Eastern Time in plain type, **Pacific Time in bold type**

	Dec 12	Jan 13	Feb	Mar	Apr	May	Jun	Jul	Aug	Sep	Oct	Nov	Dec	Jan 14
☿				▓			▓				▓			
♀														▓
♂														
♃												▓	▓	▓
♄			▓	▓	▓	▓								
♅							▓	▓	▓	▓	▓			
♆							▓	▓	▓	▓	▓			
♇				▓	▓	▓	▓	▓	▓					

Egg-Setting Dates

To Have Eggs by this Date	Sign	Qtr.	Date to Set Eggs
Jan 14, 5:49 am–Jan 16, 11:07 am	Pisces	1st	Dec 24, 2012
Jan 18, 8:36 pm–Jan 21, 9:04 am	Taurus	2nd	Dec 28, 2012
Jan 23, 10:00 pm–Jan 26, 9:20 am	Cancer	2nd	Jan 02, 2013
Feb 10, 4:20 pm–Feb 12, 8:51 pm	Pisces	1st	Jan 20
Feb 15, 5:08 am–Feb 17, 4:50 pm	Taurus	1st	Jan 25
Feb 20, 5:45 am–Feb 22, 5:12 pm	Cancer	2nd	Jan 30
Mar 11, 3:51 pm–Mar 12, 7:17 am	Pisces	1st	Feb 18
Mar 14, 3:08 pm–Mar 17, 2:09 am	Taurus	1st	Feb 21
Mar 19, 2:55 pm–Mar 22, 2:50 am	Cancer	2nd	Feb 26
Mar 26, 5:32 pm–Mar 27, 5:27 am	Libra	2nd	Mar 05
Apr 10, 11:22 pm–Apr 13, 10:13 am	Taurus	1st	Mar 20
Apr 15, 10:49 pm–Apr 18, 11:13 am	Cancer	1st	Mar 25
Apr 23, 3:25 am–Apr 25, 6:25 am	Libra	2nd	Apr 02
May 9, 8:28 pm–May 10, 5:21 pm	Taurus	1st	Apr 18
May 13, 5:57 am–May 15, 6:38 pm	Cancer	1st	Apr 22
May 20, 1:07 pm–May 22, 4:55 pm	Libra	2nd	Apr 29
Jun 9, 12:16 pm–Jun 12, 12:58 am	Cancer	1st	May 19
Jun 16, 9:19 pm–Jun 19, 2:38 am	Libra	2nd	May 26
Jul 8, 3:14 am–Jul 9, 6:48 am	Cancer	1st	Jun 17
Jul 14, 3:41 am–Jul 16, 10:24 am	Libra	1st	Jun 23
Aug 10, 9:08 am–Aug 12, 4:18 pm	Libra	1st	Jul 20
Sep 6, 3:12 pm–Sep 8, 9:44 pm	Libra	1st	Aug 16
Sep 17, 9:58 am–Sep 19, 7:13 am	Pisces	2nd	Aug 27
Oct 4, 8:35 pm–Oct 6, 4:33 am	Libra	1st	Sep 13
Oct 14, 5:06 pm–Oct 16, 9:18 pm	Pisces	2nd	Sep 23
Nov 10, 9:36 pm–Nov 13, 2:39 am	Pisces	2nd	Oct 20
Nov 15, 9:49 am–Nov 17, 10:16 am	Taurus	2nd	Oct 25
Dec 8, 3:34 am–Dec 10, 8:06 am	Pisces	1st	Nov 17
Dec 12, 3:40 pm–Dec 15, 1:40 am	Taurus	2nd	Nov 21

Dates to Hunt and Fish

Date	Quarter	Sign
Jan 6, 1:09 am–Jan 8, 3:28 am	4th	Scorpio
Jan 14, 5:49 am–Jan 16, 11:07 am	1st	Pisces
Jan 23, 10:00 pm–Jan 26, 9:20 am	2nd	Cancer
Feb 2, 7:02 am–Feb 4, 10:45 am	3rd	Scorpio
Feb 10, 4:20 pm–Feb 12, 8:51 pm	1st	Pisces
Feb 20, 5:45 am–Feb 22, 5:12 pm	2nd	Cancer
Mar 1, 12:33 pm–Mar 3, 4:11 pm	3rd	Scorpio
Mar 3, 4:11 pm–Mar 5, 7:14 pm	3rd	Sagittarius
Mar 10, 1:19 am–Mar 12, 7:17 am	4th	Pisces
Mar 19, 2:55 pm–Mar 22, 2:50 am	2nd	Cancer
Mar 28, 8:53 pm–Mar 30, 11:13 pm	3rd	Scorpio
Mar 30, 11:13 pm–Apr 2, 1:35 am	3rd	Sagittarius
Apr 6, 9:00 am–Apr 8, 3:02 pm	4th	Pisces
Apr 15, 10:49 pm–Apr 18, 11:13 am	1st	Cancer
Apr 25, 6:25 am–Apr 27, 7:32 am	2nd	Scorpio
Apr 27, 7:32 am–Apr 29, 8:21 am	3rd	Sagittarius
May 3, 2:25 pm–May 5, 9:03 pm	4th	Pisces
May 13, 5:57 am–May 15, 6:38 pm	1st	Cancer
May 22, 4:55 pm–May 24, 5:49 pm	2nd	Scorpio
May 24, 5:49 pm–May 26, 5:28 pm	2nd	Sagittarius
May 30, 8:30 pm–Jun 2, 2:33 am	3rd	Pisces
Jun 9, 12:16 pm–Jun 12, 12:58 am	1st	Cancer
Jun 19, 2:38 am–Jun 21, 4:31 am	2nd	Scorpio
Jun 21, 4:31 am–Jun 23, 4:08 am	2nd	Sagittarius
Jun 27, 4:32 am–Jun 29, 9:07 am	3rd	Pisces
Jun 29, 9:07 am–Jul 1, 5:43 pm	3rd	Aries
Jul 6, 6:14 pm–Jul 9, 6:48 am	4th	Cancer
Jul 16, 10:24 am–Jul 18, 1:54 pm	2nd	Scorpio
Jul 18, 1:54 pm–Jul 20, 2:39 pm	2nd	Sagittarius
Jul 24, 2:22 pm–Jul 26, 5:29 pm	3rd	Pisces
Jul 26, 5:29 pm–Jul 29, 12:43 am	3rd	Aries
Aug 3, 12:29 am–Aug 5, 12:58 pm	4th	Cancer
Aug 12, 4:18 pm–Aug 14, 9:04 pm	1st	Scorpio
Aug 14, 9:04 pm–Aug 16, 11:25 pm	2nd	Sagittarius
Aug 21, 12:43 am–Aug 23, 3:13 am	3rd	Pisces
Aug 23, 3:13 am–Aug 25, 9:13 am	3rd	Aries
Aug 30, 7:33 am–Sep 1, 8:01 pm	4th	Cancer
Sep 8, 9:44 pm–Sep 11, 2:36 am	1st	Scorpio
Sep 17, 9:58 am–Sep 19, 12:58 pm	2nd	Pisces
Sep 19, 12:58 pm–Sep 21, 6:33 pm	3rd	Aries
Sep 26, 3:24 pm–Sep 29, 3:57 am	3rd	Cancer
Oct 6, 4:33 am–Oct 8, 8:21 am	1st	Scorpio
Oct 14, 5:06 pm–Oct 16, 9:18 pm	2nd	Pisces
Oct 16, 9:18 pm–Oct 19, 3:27 am	2nd	Aries
Oct 23, 11:36 pm–Oct 26, 12:12 pm	3rd	Cancer
Nov 2, 1:35 pm–Nov 4, 3:14 pm	4th	Scorpio
Nov 10, 9:36 pm–Nov 13, 2:39 am	2nd	Pisces
Nov 13, 2:39 am–Nov 15, 9:49 am	2nd	Aries
Nov 20, 6:23 am–Nov 22, 6:56 pm	3rd	Cancer
Nov 29, 11:03 pm–Dec 2, 1:31 am	4th	Scorpio
Dec 8, 3:34 am–Dec 10, 8:06 am	1st	Pisces
Dec 10, 8:06 am–Dec 12, 3:40 pm	2nd	Aries
Dec 17, 1:17 pm–Dec 20, 1:48 am	3rd	Cancer
Dec 27, 8:58 am–Dec 29, 12:37 pm	4th	Scorpio

Dates to Destroy Weeds and Pests

From		To		Sign	Qtr.
Jan 8	3:28 am	Jan 10	3:54 am	Sagittarius	4th
Jan 26	11:38 pm	Jan 28	6:27 pm	Leo	3rd
Jan 28	6:27 pm	Jan 31	1:36 am	Virgo	3rd
Feb 4	10:45 am	Feb 6	12:55 pm	Sagittarius	4th
Feb 8	2:16 pm	Feb 10	2:20 am	Aquarius	4th
Feb 25	3:26 pm	Feb 27	8:02 am	Virgo	3rd
Mar 3	4:11 pm	Mar 4	4:53 pm	Sagittarius	3rd
Mar 4	4:53 pm	Mar 5	7:14 pm	Sagittarius	4th
Mar 7	10:01 pm	Mar 10	1:19 am	Aquarius	4th
Mar 30	11:13 pm	Apr 2	1:35 am	Sagittarius	3rd
Apr 4	4:41 am	Apr 6	9:00 am	Aquarius	4th
Apr 8	3:02 pm	Apr 10	5:35 am	Aries	4th
Apr 27	7:32 am	Apr 29	8:21 am	Sagittarius	3rd
May 1	10:20 am	May 2	7:14 am	Aquarius	3rd
May 2	7:14 am	May 3	2:25 pm	Aquarius	4th
May 5	9:03 pm	May 8	6:09 am	Aries	4th
May 25	12:25 am	May 26	5:28 pm	Sagittarius	3rd
May 28	5:48 pm	May 30	8:30 pm	Aquarius	3rd
Jun 2	2:33 am	Jun 4	11:53 am	Aries	4th
Jun 6	11:32 pm	Jun 8	11:56 pm	Gemini	4th
Jun 25	3:27 am	Jun 27	4:32 am	Aquarius	3rd
Jun 29	9:07 am	Jun 30	12:54 am	Aries	3rd
Jun 30	12:54 am	Jul 1	5:43 pm	Aries	4th
Jul 4	5:21 am	Jul 6	6:14 pm	Gemini	4th
Jul 22	2:16 pm	Jul 24	2:22 pm	Aquarius	3rd
Jul 26	5:29 pm	Jul 29	12:43 am	Aries	3rd
Jul 31	11:42 am	Aug 3	12:29 am	Gemini	4th
Aug 5	12:58 pm	Aug 6	5:51 pm	Leo	4th
Aug 20	9:45 pm	Aug 21	12:43 am	Aquarius	3rd
Aug 23	3:13 am	Aug 25	9:13 am	Aries	3rd
Aug 27	7:08 pm	Aug 28	5:35 am	Gemini	3rd
Aug 28	5:35 am	Aug 30	7:33 am	Gemini	4th
Sep 1	8:01 pm	Sep 4	6:43 am	Leo	4th
Sep 4	6:43 am	Sep 5	7:36 am	Virgo	4th
Sep 19	12:58 pm	Sep 21	6:33 pm	Aries	3rd
Sep 24	3:34 am	Sep 26	3:24 pm	Gemini	3rd
Sep 29	3:57 am	Oct 1	2:52 pm	Leo	4th
Oct 1	2:52 pm	Oct 3	10:59 pm	Virgo	4th
Oct 18	7:38 pm	Oct 19	3:27 am	Aries	3rd
Oct 21	12:14 pm	Oct 23	11:36 pm	Gemini	3rd
Oct 26	12:12 pm	Oct 26	7:40 pm	Leo	3rd
Oct 26	7:40 pm	Oct 28	11:45 pm	Leo	4th
Oct 28	11:45 pm	Oct 31	8:22 am	Virgo	4th
Nov 17	7:07 pm	Nov 20	6:23 am	Gemini	3rd
Nov 22	6:56 pm	Nov 25	7:11 am	Leo	3rd
Nov 25	7:11 am	Nov 25	2:28 pm	Virgo	3rd
Nov 25	2:28 pm	Nov 27	5:00 pm	Virgo	4th
Dec 2	1:31 am	Dec 2	7:22 pm	Sagittarius	4th
Dec 17	4:28 am	Dec 17	1:17 pm	Gemini	3rd
Dec 20	1:48 am	Dec 22	2:19 pm	Leo	3rd
Dec 22	2:19 pm	Dec 25	1:17 am	Virgo	3rd
Dec 29	12:37 pm	Dec 31	1:01 pm	Sagittarius	4th

Time Zone Map

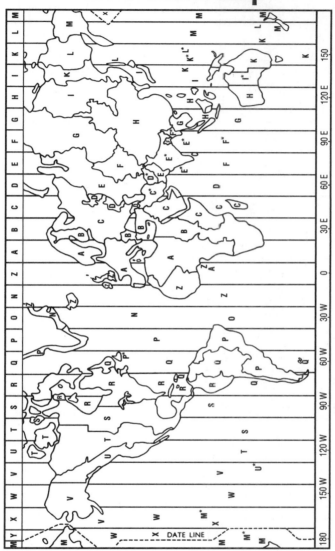

Time Zone Conversions

(R) EST—Used in book
(S) CST—Subtract 1 hour
(T) MST—Subtract 2 hours
(U) PST—Subtract 3 hours
(V) Subtract 4 hours
(V*) Subtract 4½ hours
(U*) Subtract 3½ hours
(W) Subtract 5 hours
(X) Subtract 6 hours
(Y) Subtract 7 hours
(Q) Add 1 hour
(P) Add 2 hours
(P*) Add 2½ hours
(O) Add 3 hours
(N) Add 4 hours
(Z) Add 5 hours
(A) Add 6 hours
(B) Add 7 hours
(C) Add 8 hours
(C*) Add 8½ hours

(D) Add 9 hours
(D*) Add 9½ hours
(E) Add 10 hours
(E*) Add 10½ hours
(F) Add 11 hours
(F*) Add 11½ hours
(G) Add 12 hours
(H) Add 13 hours
(I) Add 14 hours
(I*) Add 14½ hours
(K) Add 15 hours
(K*) Add 15½ hours
(L) Add 16 hours
(L*) Add 16½ hours
(M) Add 17 hours
(M*) Add 18 hours
(P*) Add 2½ hours

Important!

All times given in the *Moon Sign Book* are set in Eastern Time. The conversions shown here are for standard times only. Use the time zone conversions map and table to calculate the difference in your time zone. You must make the adjustment for your time zone and adjust for Daylight Saving Time where applicable.

Weather, Economic & Lunar Forecasts

All we need is a meteorologist who has once been soaked to the skin without ill effect. No one can write knowingly of the weather who walks bent over on wet days.

~E. B. WHITE

Forecasting the Weather

By Kris Brandt Riske

Astrometeorology—astrological weather forecasting—reveals seasonal and weekly weather trends based on the cardinal ingresses (Summer and Winter Solstices, and Spring and Autumn Equinoxes) and the four monthly lunar phases. The planetary alignments and the longitudes and latitudes they influence have the strongest effect, but the zodiacal signs are also involved in creating weather conditions.

The components of a thunderstorm, for example, are heat, wind, and electricity. A Mars-Jupiter configuration generates the necessary heat and Mercury adds wind and electricity. A severe thunderstorm, and those that produce tornados, usually involve Mercury, Mars, Uranus, or Neptune. The zodiacal signs add their energy to the planetary mix to increase or decrease the chance of weather phenomena and their severity.

In general, the fire signs (Aries, Leo, Sagittarius) indicate heat and dryness, both of which peak when Mars, the planet with a similar nature, is in these signs. Water signs (Cancer, Scorpio, Pisces) are conducive to precipitation, and air signs (Gemini, Libra, Aquarius) to cool temperatures and wind. Earth signs (Taurus, Virgo, Capricorn) vary from wet to dry, heat to cold. The signs and their prevailing weather conditions are listed here:

Aries: Heat, dry, wind
Taurus: Moderate temperatures, precipitation
Gemini: Cool temperatures, wind, dry
Cancer: Cold, steady precipitation
Leo: Heat, dry, lightning
Virgo: Cold, dry, windy
Libra: Cool, windy, fair
Scorpio: Extreme temperatures, abundant precipitation
Sagittarius: Warm, fair, moderate wind
Capricorn: Cold, wet, damp
Aquarius: Cold, dry, high pressure, lightning
Pisces: Wet, cool, low pressure

Take note of the Moon's sign at each lunar phase. It reveals the prevailing weather conditions for the next six to seven days. The same is true of Mercury and Venus. These two influential weather planets transit the entire zodiac each year, unless retrograde patterns add their influence.

Planetary Influences

People relied on astrology to forecast weather for thousands of years. They were able to predict drought, floods, and temperature variations through interpreting planetary alignments. In recent years there has been a renewed interest in astrometeorology. A weather forecast can be composed for any date—tomorrow, next week, or a thousand years in the future. According to astrometeorology, each planet governs certain weather phenomena. When certain planets are aligned with other planets, weather—precipitation, cloudy or clear skies, tornados, hurricanes, and other conditions—are generated.

Sun and Moon

The Sun governs the constitution of the weather and, like the Moon, it serves as a trigger for other planetary configurations that result in weather events. When the Sun is prominent in a cardinal ingress or lunar phase chart, the area is often warm and sunny. The Moon can bring or withhold moisture, depending upon its sign placement.

Mercury

Mercury is also a triggering planet, but its main influence is wind direction and velocity. In its stationary periods, Mercury reflects high winds, and its influence is always prominent in major weather events, such as hurricanes and tornadoes, when it tends to lower the temperature.

Venus

Venus governs moisture, clouds, and humidity. It brings warming trends that produce sunny, pleasant weather if in positive aspect to other planets. In some signs—Libra, Virgo, Gemini, Sagittarius—Venus is drier. It is at its wettest when placed in Cancer, Scorpio, Pisces, or Taurus.

Mars

Mars is associated with heat, drought, and wind, and can raise the temperature to record-setting levels when in a fire sign (Aries, Leo, Sagittarius). Mars is also the planet that provides the spark that generates thunderstorms and is prominent in tornado and hurricane configurations.

Jupiter

Jupiter, a fair-weather planet, tends toward higher temperatures when in Aries, Leo, or Sagittarius. It is associated with high-pressure systems and is a contributing factor at times to dryness. Storms are often amplified by Jupiter.

Saturn

Saturn is associated with low-pressure systems, cloudy to overcast skies, and excessive precipitation. Temperatures drop when Saturn is involved. Major winter storms always have a strong Saturn influence, as do storms that produce a slow, steady downpour for hours or days.

Uranus

Like Jupiter, Uranus indicates high-pressure systems. It reflects descending cold air and, when prominent, is responsible for a jet stream that extends far south. Uranus can bring drought in winter, and it is involved in thunderstorms, tornados, and hurricanes.

Neptune

Neptune is the wettest planet. It signals low-pressure systems and is dominant when hurricanes are in the forecast. When Neptune is strongly placed, flood danger is high. It's often associated with winter thaws. Temperatures, humidity, and cloudiness increase where Neptune influences weather.

Pluto

Pluto is associated with weather extremes, as well as unseasonably warm temperatures and drought. It reflects the high winds involved in major hurricanes, storms, and tornadoes.

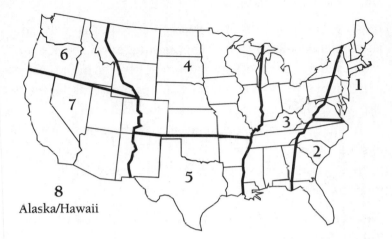

Weather Forecast for 2013

By Kris Brandt Riske

Winter 2013

Cloudy skies will be more the norm than the exception across much of the country this winter. Zone 1 will experience periods of very cold weather, and precipitation will be average to below. Similar conditions but with more seasonal temperatures will be the norm in zone 2, which will see storm fronts moving into northern and central areas from the northwest. Southern areas of zone 3 could see strong thunderstorms during warmer weeks, and although cloudiness and wind will be factors there and in western and central northern areas, temperatures will range from seasonal to above. Northeastern areas of zone 3, however, will be quite cold at times.

Zones 6 and 7 can expect fewer sunny days than usual along with periods of heavy precipitation. The same is true of central areas of zones 4 and 5, which will see major storms that descend from the Pacific Northwest, crossing western parts of the zones and bringing cold temperatures. Eastern areas of zones 4 and 5 will be more seasonal overall and windy, with the most precipitation in more southern areas; however, these parts of the country also will experience periods of very cold weather.

In zone 8, Alaska will be cloudy with an above-average number of storms moving in from the west, bringing precipitation across the state. Hawaii can expect seasonal albeit windy conditions with precipitation ranging from average to below.

December 28, 2012–January 3, 2013, Full Moon

Zone 1: The zone is cold and fair to partly cloudy.

Zone 2: Northern areas are variably cloudy and seasonal with warmer temperatures central and south, where strong thunderstorms are possible.

Zone 3: Variably cloudy skies prevail with increasing clouds central and east that bring precipitation and possibly strong storms in southern areas; temperatures are seasonal.

Zone 4: Western areas are cold, while central and eastern parts of the zone are more seasonal; central areas are cloudy with precipitation, and eastern areas are fair to partly cloudy.

Zone 5: Temperatures range from seasonal to below, and much of the zone is fair with partly cloudy skies in eastern areas.

Zone 6: The zone is cloudy with precipitation, which is heaviest east as a front moves through the zone with temperatures ranging from seasonal to below.

Zone 7: Western and central skies are windy, eastern skies are fair to partly cloudy, and northern coastal areas see precipitation later in the week; temperatures are seasonal to below.

Zone 8: Central areas of Alaska are cold with precipitation, western areas are mostly fair and seasonal, and eastern areas are windy with precipitation and seasonal temperatures. Hawaiian temperatures range from seasonal to below under cloudy, windy skies that bring precipitation.

January 4–10, Fourth Quarter Moon

Zone 1: The zone is fair to partly cloudy and cold with scattered precipitation in northern areas.

Zone 2: Much of the zone is cloudy with precipitation and stormy conditions in some areas.

Zone 3: Western skies are fair to partly cloudy, central and eastern areas are windy and cloudy with precipitation, and temperatures are seasonal.

Zone 4: Western areas see precipitation that moves into central parts of the zone, skies are fair to partly cloudy in eastern areas, and temperatures are seasonal to below.

Zone 5: Temperatures range from seasonal to above with variable cloudiness central and east, western parts of the zone see precipitation, and central areas are windy with possible thunderstorms.

Zone 6: The zone is cloudy with precipitation, and temperatures seasonal to below.

Zone 7: Northern coastal areas see precipitation that moves into central and eastern parts of the zone with stormy conditions in the mountains; temperatures are seasonal to below.

Zone 8: Western Alaska is fair and cold, central and eastern areas are variably cloudy with scattered precipitation east, and temperatures are seasonal. Hawaii is fair to partly cloudy, seasonal, and windy with showers followed by cooler temperatures in central parts of the state.

January 11–17, New Moon

Zone 1: Scattered precipitation accompanies variable cloudiness and seasonal temperatures.

Zone 2: Temperatures are seasonal to above with variable cloudiness and precipitation in northern and central areas.

Zone 3: The zone is variably cloudy with scattered precipitation east and winds west; temperatures are seasonal to above.

Zone 4: Western areas are variably cloudy and seasonal, and central and eastern parts of the zone are stormy with abundant downfall in some areas as a front moves through.

Zone 5: Eastern areas see more cloudiness and wind with precipitation, while western and central parts of the zone are variably cloudy with a chance for precipitation.

Zone 6: The zone is mostly fair and seasonal with partly cloudy skies in eastern areas.

Zone 7: Windy skies are partly cloudy west and fair in central and eastern areas; temperatures are seasonal to above.

Zone 8: Precipitation moves across western and central Alaska, which is variably cloudy with seasonal temperatures. Hawaii is fair to partly cloudy, seasonal, and windy with showers later in the week in western and central areas.

January 18–25, Second Quarter Moon

Zone 1: The zone is cloudy and windy with precipitation (some abundant in the south), and temperatures are seasonal to below.

Zone 2: Northern areas are cloudy with precipitation, while central and southern parts of the zone see scattered precipitation; temperatures are seasonal, and much of the zone is cloudy.

Zone 3: Variable cloudiness prevails across the zone along with precipitation and temperatures seasonal to below; eastern areas are windy with abundant precipitation.

Zone 4: Temperatures are seasonal to below under mostly fair to partly cloudy skies with wind and increasing clouds as precipitation moves from western areas into central parts of the zone.

Zone 5: Much of the zone is variably cloudy and windy with precipitation and temperatures seasonal to below.

Zone 6: Western and central areas are fair to partly cloudy, eastern areas are fair and windy, and temperatures are seasonal.

Zone 7: Skies are partly cloudy and windy in western parts of the zone with precipitation later in the week; eastern areas are fair under a high-pressure system; temperatures are seasonal to below.

Zone 8: Eastern Alaska sees abundant precipitation, western and central areas are windy and fair, and temperatures are seasonal. Hawaii is windy with scattered showers under fair to partly cloudy skies; temperatures range from seasonal to above.

January 26–February 2, Full Moon

Zone 1: The zone is windy with mostly fair skies and temperatures seasonal to below.

Zone 2: Central and southern areas see precipitation, northern areas are fair and windy, and temperatures are seasonal.

Zone 3: Skies are variably cloudy, and eastern areas are windy with precipitation; temperatures are seasonal but colder west.

Zone 4: The zone is variably cloudy, and the eastern Plains see scattered precipitation; windy conditions and seasonal to below temperatures prevail.

Zone 5: Western and central parts of the zone are windy with precipitation in central areas later in the week; eastern parts of the zone are windy, cloudy, and cold with precipitation.

Zone 6: The zone is windy and cloudy with a chance for precipitation in western and central areas; eastern areas are windy with more cloudiness and precipitation.

Zone 7: Precipitation in northern coastal areas moves into central parts of the zone, southern coastal areas are mostly fair, and eastern areas are cloudy and windy with precipitation; temperatures are seasonal.

Zone 8: Central Alaska is cloudy with abundant precipitation and then clearing and colder, and western and eastern areas are seasonal with precipitation later in the week. Hawaii is variably cloudy, seasonal, and windy with scattered precipitation.

February 3–9, Fourth Quarter Moon

Zone 1: The zone is seasonal and cloudy with precipitation.

Zone 2: Seasonal temperatures accompany fair to partly cloudy skies with a chance for precipitation later in the week.

Zone 3: Thunderstorms are possible in western areas, and eastern parts of the zone see scattered precipitation later in the week; skies are fair to partly cloudy with temperatures seasonal to above.

Zone 4: Western and central areas are windy in advance of a storm front that arrives later in the week, bringing abundant precipitation to some areas; temperatures are seasonal, and eastern areas are fair to partly cloudy.

Zone 5: Thunderstorms and tornadoes are possible in southern areas later in the week, and much of the zone sees precipitation; temperatures are seasonal to above.

Zone 6: Western areas are cloudy with precipitation (some abundant), and central and eastern areas are mostly fair; temperatures are seasonal to below.

Zone 7: Northern coastal areas see precipitation (some abundant), and much of the zone is fair with seasonal temperatures.

Zone 8: Central Alaska is cold, other parts of the state are more seasonal and windy, and central and eastern areas see precipitation later in the week. Hawaii is mostly fair and seasonal with a chance for scattered showers in some areas.

February 10–16, New Moon

Zone 1: The zone is windy, partly cloudy, and seasonal with scattered precipitation.

Zone 2: Mostly fair to partly cloudy and seasonal, the zone is also windy with a chance for precipitation.

Zone 3: Windy conditions west could contribute to strong thunderstorms with tornado potential in western areas; central and eastern areas are mostly fair to partly cloudy with precipitation in the east.

Zone 4: Western areas are cold with temperatures in the seasonal range in central and eastern parts of the zone; a low-pressure system could bring significant precipitation to some central parts of the zone before moving east; northwestern parts of the zone also see precipitation.

Zone 5: Strong thunderstorms with tornado potential are possible in eastern parts of the zone, central areas see more clouds, and western areas are fair; temperatures are seasonal to above.

Zone 6: Western skies are fair, central and eastern areas see precipitation (some locally heavy in central parts of the zone), and temperatures are seasonal to below.

Zone 7: The zone is variably cloudy with precipitation in southern coastal areas that moves across the zone with increasing cloudiness, and central mountain areas see the heaviest downfall; temperatures are seasonal.

Zone 8: Alaska is cold and windy with precipitation. Hawaii is seasonal and windy with showers and thunderstorms.

February 17–24, Second Quarter Moon

Zone 1: The zone is seasonal with variable cloudiness, scattered precipitation, and seasonal temperatures.

Zone 2: Seasonal temperatures and partly cloudy skies prevail across the zone with precipitation central and south.

Zone 3: Western areas are stormy, including potential for severe thunderstorms and tornadoes in southern parts of the zone, and eastern areas are variably cloudy with scattered precipitation; temperatures are seasonal.

Zone 4: The zone is variably cloudy, windy west, and seasonal but colder east with precipitation.

Zone 5: Variable cloudiness prevails with precipitation; temperatures are seasonal, and western areas are windy.

Zone 6: The zone is variably cloudy and seasonal with precipitation in western areas; wind and precipitation move into the eastern parts of the zone.

Zone 7: The zone is fair to partly cloudy with temperatures ranging from seasonal to above; eastern areas are windy.

Zone 8: Alaska is windy with precipitation central and west, fair skies east, and seasonal temperatures. Eastern Hawaii is cloudy with precipitation, temperatures are seasonal, and central and western areas are fair.

February 25–March 3, Full Moon

Zone 1: The zone is partly cloudy to cloudy with windy skies and precipitation in northern areas; temperatures are seasonal.

Zone 2: Skies are variably cloudy and windy with a chance for precipitation, and temperatures are seasonal.

Zone 3: Much of the zone is partly cloudy and windy with scattered precipitation and temperatures seasonal to below.

Zone 4: Western and eastern parts of the zone are cloudy with precipitation, and central areas of the zone are fair to partly cloudy with increasing clouds and precipitation later in the week; temperatures are seasonal to below.

Zone 5: The zone is partly cloudy with precipitation possible, and temperatures are seasonal to below.

Zone 6: The zone is variably cloudy and windy with precipitation (heaviest in central and eastern areas), followed by clearing and colder temperatures.

Zone 7: Increasing cloudiness brings precipitation to western and

2012 © Brian Finestone. Image from BigStockPhoto.com

central parts of the zone, eastern areas are windy with precipitation, and temperatures are seasonal.

Zone 8: Seasonal temperatures prevail in Alaska, which is windy in central areas, fair west, and cloudy with precipitation in eastern parts of the state. Hawaii is fair to partly cloudy and seasonal with winds in central and eastern areas.

March 4–10, Fourth Quarter Moon

Zone 1: Much of the zone is windy with seasonal temperatures and precipitation.

Zone 2: Precipitation accompanies windy, cloudy skies, and temperatures are seasonal to below.

Zone 3: Western areas are cloudy with precipitation, central and eastern areas are fair to partly cloudy with scattered precipitation east, and temperatures are seasonal to below.

Zone 4: Much of the zone is cloudy with precipitation and temperatures ranging from seasonal to below; the heaviest precipitation and windy conditions are in western areas.

Zone 5: Western areas are fair to partly cloudy, eastern and central areas see precipitation (heaviest in central parts of the zone), and temperatures are seasonal to below.

Zone 6: Temperatures are seasonal to below under partly cloudy to cloudy skies with precipitation across much of the zone.

Zone 7: The zone is fair to partly cloudy with scattered precipitation in northern coastal and central areas; temperatures are seasonal to above.

Zone 8: Alaska is windy with precipitation and seasonal temperatures. Central and eastern areas of Hawaii see showers, western areas are fair, and temperatures are seasonal.

March 11–18, New Moon

Zone 1: The zone is windy with precipitation (especially north), and temperatures are seasonal to below.

Zone 2: Skies are variably cloudy with precipitation in northern areas, and temperatures are seasonal.

Zone 3: Western and central areas are fair to partly cloudy, eastern areas see more cloudiness with precipitation later in the week, and temperatures are seasonal.

Zone 4: Western areas are windy with precipitation, central and eastern parts of the zone are fair to partly cloudy with scattered precipitation east, and temperatures are seasonal to below.

Zone 5: Windy conditions prevail in western and central parts of the zone, and skies are fair to partly cloudy in eastern areas; temperatures are seasonal to below.

Zone 6: Increasing clouds bring precipitation with seasonal temperatures.

Zone 7: The zone is variably cloudy with precipitation in southern coastal and central parts of the zone moving into eastern areas, which are windy; temperatures are seasonal.

Zone 8: Western and central parts of Alaska are windy and cloudy, eastern areas are fair, and temperatures are seasonal to below. Hawaii is cloudy with precipitation and seasonal temperatures.

Spring 2013

Cloudy skies will continue to be a factor during the spring season, and some areas will see strong thunderstorms with potential for an above-average number of tornadoes, particularly in the Plains states. Zone 1 will continue to be cold with potential for major storms, but conditions will be more seasonal in zone 2 with average to above-average precipitation in northern and central areas. Southern areas of zone 3 will also be prone to thunderstorms and tornadoes, while northern areas will see more cloudiness and precipitation.

Nearly all of zones 4 and 5 will experience strong thunderstorms with tornado potential throughout the season; the greatest concentration will be in central and eastern areas. Temperatures in these zones will be average overall, and eastern areas of zone

5 will see more precipitation and possibly flooding in the lower Mississippi River valley. Temperatures will range from average to below in zones 6 and 7 with storm systems moving into these areas from the Pacific. Mountainous areas will be particularly prone to major storms, and although the desert Southwest will also experience more cloudiness, temperatures there are likely to be above average under the influence of high-pressure systems.

In zone 8, central Alaska will be cold with a greater number of storms, and the remainder of the state will be mostly seasonal with above-average precipitation in western areas. Temperatures in Hawaii will range from seasonal to above with periods of dryness alternating with strong thunderstorms; much of the state will be windy.

March 19–26, Second Quarter Moon
Zone 1: The zone is seasonal and partly cloudy to cloudy, and northern areas are windy with precipitation.
Zone 2: Strong thunderstorms with tornado potential are possible in central and southern areas of the zone, which are cloudy, while northern areas are partly cloudy; temperatures are seasonal.
Zone 3: Temperatures are seasonal, eastern areas see precipitation, and strong thunderstorms with tornado potential are possible in western and central parts of the zone.
Zone 4: Strong thunderstorms with tornado potential are possible across the zone, along with locally heavy precipitation; temperatures are seasonal.
Zone 5: Much of the zone sees precipitation and cloudy skies with seasonal temperatures, and strong thunderstorms with tornado potential are possible in western areas.
Zone 6: Western areas are cloudy with precipitation that moves into central areas of the zone, while eastern areas are partly cloudy with scattered precipitation; temperatures are seasonal to below.
Zone 7: Northern coastal areas see precipitation, southern coastal

areas have a chance for precipitation, and the zone is windy with temperatures seasonal to above under a high-pressure system.

Zone 8: Stormy conditions in western Alaska move into central areas, and the state is windy with temperatures seasonal to below. Hawaii is seasonal and windy with thunderstorms (some strong) in western and central areas.

March 27–April 2, Full Moon

Zone 1: The zone is fair to partly cloudy and seasonal with a chance for showers.

Zone 2: Central and southern areas are windy with showers, and northern areas are fair to partly cloudy; temperatures are seasonal.

Zone 3: Windy conditions in western areas accompany potential for strong thunderstorms and locally heavy precipitation in western parts of the zone, eastern areas are fair to partly cloudy with scattered precipitation, and temperatures are seasonal.

Zone 4: Much of the zone is cloudy with precipitation, temperatures are seasonal, and central and eastern areas are windy with potential for strong thunderstorms.

Zone 5: The zone is variably cloudy and seasonal with precipitation in central and eastern areas, including possible strong thunderstorms.

Zone 6: Western and central areas of the zone are partly cloudy, and eastern areas are cloudy with precipitation; temperatures are seasonal across the zone.

Zone 7: Eastern areas see more cloudiness with precipitation, northern areas are windy, and western and central parts of the zone are fair to partly cloudy; temperatures are seasonal.

Zone 8: Eastern and western Alaska see precipitation, central areas are fair, and temperatures are seasonal. Hawaii is windy, fair, and seasonal.

April 3–9, Fourth Quarter Moon

Zone 1: The zone is seasonal and fair to partly cloudy with precipitation in northern areas.

Zone 2: Conditions are seasonal under partly cloudy skies.

Zone 3: Western and central parts of the zone see showers with cloudy skies, and eastern areas are partly cloudy.

Zone 4: Scattered thunderstorms and showers (some locally heavy) prevail in western parts of the zone with fair to partly cloudy skies in eastern areas; temperatures are seasonal but cooler in the east, which is windy.

Zone 5: The zone is seasonal and variably cloudy with scattered showers and thunderstorms, some locally heavy.

Zone 6: Western and central areas are fair to partly cloudy, eastern areas are windy with precipitation, and temperatures are seasonal to below.

Zone 7: Northern coastal and central areas of the zone see showers, while fair to partly cloudy skies prevail in the remainder of the zone under temperatures seasonal to above.

Zone 8: Western Alaska is stormy with precipitation moving into central areas of the zone, and temperatures are seasonal to below. Hawaii is seasonal with showers under windy, cloudy skies in central and eastern areas; western parts of the state are fair to partly cloudy.

April 10–17, New Moon

Zone 1: The zone is partly cloudy and seasonal with scattered precipitation.

Zone 2: Conditions are seasonal under partly cloudy skies with scattered precipitation.

Zone 3: Fair to partly cloudy skies prevail across the zone with possible strong storms and tornado potential in southern areas.

Zone 4: Western skies are fair, and central and eastern areas are cloudy with showers and possible strong thunderstorms with tornado potential; temperatures are seasonal to above.

Zone 5: Strong thunderstorms with tornado potential are possible in central and eastern parts of the zone, and western areas are mostly fair; temperatures are seasonal.

Zone 6: Western areas are cloudy with precipitation, and central and eastern parts of the zone are windy with showers and storms.

Zone 7: Northern coastal areas are cloudy with precipitation, the remainder of the zone is windy and fair to partly cloudy, and temperatures are seasonal.

Zone 8: Alaskan temperatures are seasonal to below with precipitation. Hawaii is fair to partly cloudy and seasonal.

April 18–24, Second Quarter Moon

Zone 1: The zone is generally fair and seasonal.

Zone 2: Central and southern areas are cloudy and windy with locally heavy precipitation, including possible strong thunderstorms with tornado potential; northern areas are partly cloudy with a chance for precipitation.

Zone 3: Western areas could see strong storms with tornado potential, precipitation could be abundant in northeastern parts of the zone with flood potential, and eastern areas are mostly fair with precipitation later in the week; temperatures are seasonal.

Zone 4: Western skies are fair to partly cloudy, while central and eastern areas could see strong thunderstorms with tornado potential; temperatures are seasonal.

Zone 5: Strong storms with tornado potential and abundant precipitation are possible in some eastern areas, western and central parts of the zone are partly cloudy, and temperatures are seasonal.

Zone 6: Western areas are mostly fair, and central and eastern parts of the zone see showers and thunderstorms with strong winds, especially at higher elevations; temperatures are seasonal.

Zone 7: Western and central parts of the zone see showers and thunderstorms, and eastern areas are partly cloudy with showers, thunderstorms, and high winds later in the week; temperatures are seasonal.

Zone 8: Central and eastern areas of Alaska see precipitation (some abundant), and western skies are fair to partly cloudy;

temperatures are seasonal. Temperatures in Hawaii are seasonal, precipitation in eastern areas could be significant, and central and western parts of the state are partly cloudy.

April 25–May 1, Full Moon

Zone 1: Temperatures are seasonal, and the zone is cloudy and windy with showers and thunderstorms.

Zone 2: Northern areas see scattered thunderstorms, southern areas are mostly fair with a chance for precipitation, and temperatures are seasonal to above.

Zone 3: Showers and strong storms with tornado potential are possible in western areas, while eastern parts of the zone see scattered showers and thunderstorms; temperatures are seasonal.

Zone 4: Precipitation across much of the zone is locally heavy in some locations with thunderstorms and tornado potential in central and eastern areas; temperatures are seasonal.

Zone 5: Western areas are mostly fair and windy with scattered precipitation, and eastern areas could see abundant precipitation with strong thunderstorms and tornado potential.

Zone 6: Western and central parts of the zone could see strong winds, stormy conditions, and abundant precipitation later in the week, while eastern areas see showers and then clearing, warmer conditions.

Zone 7: Much of the zone sees precipitation, with the heaviest in northern coastal areas and the central mountains; temperatures are seasonal, and skies are partly cloudy to cloudy.

Zone 8: Eastern and central Alaska see precipitation, while western areas are mostly fair and windy; temperatures are seasonal. Hawaii is variably cloudy with showers in central and eastern parts of the state.

May 2–8, Fourth Quarter Moon

Zone 1: The zone is cloudy, windy, and seasonal with precipitation south and fair skies north.

Zone 2: Much of the zone sees showers and thunderstorms (some strong) under windy skies and seasonal temperatures.

Zone 3: Western areas are partly cloudy, while central and eastern parts of the zone see precipitation; temperatures range from seasonal to below.

Zone 4: Temperatures are seasonal, eastern skies are fair, and western and central parts of the zone see showers and thunderstorms, some strong with tornado potential.

Zone 5: High winds accompany thunderstorms in western areas, central parts of the zone are partly cloudy with a chance for precipitation, and eastern skies are cloudy with showers.

Zone 6: Western areas are windy and cloudy with scattered precipitation, central areas are windy and partly cloudy, and eastern parts of the zone see abundant precipitation and windy conditions; temperatures are seasonal.

Zone 7: Northern coastal areas are cloudy with precipitation; southern coastal, central, and eastern parts of the zone are fair to partly cloudy and windy with eastern areas seeing showers later in the week; temperatures are seasonal to above.

Zone 8: Western and central Alaska are windy with precipitation, eastern parts of the state are fair, and temperatures are seasonal to below. Hawaii sees showers, clouds, and seasonal temperatures.

May 9–17, New Moon

Zone 1: Temperatures are seasonal to below, and the zone is variably cloudy with showers and scattered thunderstorms; locally heavy precipitation is possible in southern areas.

Zone 2: Much of the zone is cloudy with showers, temperatures are seasonal to below, and some areas see heavy precipitation.

Zone 3: Temperatures range from seasonal to below across the zone, which sees precipitation, some abundant in eastern areas.

Zone 4: Western areas are cloudy with showers, central and eastern areas see thunderstorms (some strong with tornado potential), and temperatures are seasonal to above.

Zone 5: Much of the zone is windy and cloudy with thunder-storms (some strong with tornado potential), and temperatures are seasonal to above.

Zone 6: Western areas see showers, and central and eastern areas are fair to partly cloudy; temperatures are seasonal.

Zone 7: The zone is fair to partly cloudy with increasing cloudiness west that brings showers later in the week; temperatures are seasonal to above.

Zone 8: Western Alaska sees precipitation, and central and eastern areas are fair to partly cloudy with scattered precipitation; temperatures are seasonal. Much of Hawaii is cloudy with showers and seasonal temperatures.

May 18–24, Second Quarter Moon

Zone 1: Temperatures are seasonal to above, and the zone sees scattered thunderstorms.

Zone 2: Northern and inland areas of central parts of the zone see scattered thunderstorms, coastal areas are dry, and temperatures are seasonal to above.

Zone 3: Temperatures are seasonal to below with scattered showers and thunderstorms across the zone; eastern areas are windy.

Zone 4: Much of the zone sees showers and thunderstorms with more cloudiness east and strong thunderstorms and tornado potential west; temperatures are seasonal to below.

Zone 5: The zone is seasonal and variably cloudy with scattered showers and more precipitation in western areas.

Zone 6: Central and eastern parts of the zone are windy with showers and thunderstorms (some strong with high winds), western areas are partly cloudy with scattered precipitation, and temperatures are seasonal to below.

Zone 7: The zone is windy with showers and thunderstorms west and central and a chance for precipitation in eastern areas later in the week; temperatures are seasonal to above.

Zone 8: Alaskan temperatures are seasonal to below with precipitation central and east and windy conditions west. Hawaii is windy and seasonal to below with precipitation.

May 25–30, Full Moon

Zone 1: Southern areas see scattered thunderstorms, temperatures are seasonal, and northern parts of the zone are partly cloudy with scattered showers.

Zone 2: Temperatures are seasonal, and much of the zone sees scattered thunderstorms (some strong).

Zone 3: The zone is variably cloudy with showers and thunderstorms in eastern areas and scattered thunderstorms west; temperatures are seasonal.

Zone 4: Most of the zone is fair to partly cloudy with showers and thunderstorms in central areas and more cloudiness and precipitation (some abundant) east; temperatures are seasonal to below.

Zone 5: Western and central parts of the zone see scattered showers and thunderstorms, and precipitation and cloudiness centers in eastern areas; temperatures are seasonal.

Zone 6: Western areas are fair to partly cloudy with showers and thunderstorms in central and eastern areas (some with locally heavy precipitation); temperatures are seasonal.

Zone 7: Temperatures are seasonal to above, eastern areas are humid and partly cloudy, and western and central areas are fair.

Zone 8: Central Alaska sees abundant precipitation, western areas are fair, and eastern parts of the zone see precipitation; temperatures are seasonal. Hawaii is seasonal and fair to partly cloudy with scattered showers.

May 31–June 7, Fourth Quarter Moon

Zone 1: Much of the zone is very windy with precipitation and storm potential, and temperatures are seasonal to below.

Zone 2: Humidity and seasonable temperatures trigger showers and thunderstorms, some strong in central and southern areas with potential for tornados.

Zone 3: Western and central parts of the zone are cloudy with showers, eastern areas are party cloudy with scattered precipitation, and temperatures are seasonal.

Zone 4: Western and central areas are fair and dry, while eastern areas see more cloudiness with showers later in the week; temperatures are seasonal to above.

Zone 5: Temperatures are seasonal to above, western and central areas are mostly fair and dry, and eastern parts of the zone are partly cloudy with scattered showers later in the week.

Zone 6: Eastern and central areas see strong thunderstorms with tornado potential and locally heavy precipitation that could result in flooding, and western areas are partly cloudy with precipitation later in the week.

Zone 7: Eastern parts of the zone are fair to partly cloudy and humid with a chance for thunderstorms later in the week, and western and central areas see scattered showers and thunderstorms; temperatures are seasonal.

Zone 8: Western and central Alaska see precipitation, while eastern areas are fair with increasing cloudiness and precipitation (some abundant) later in the week; temperatures are seasonal to below. Hawaii is partly cloudy, seasonal, and windy with showers.

June 8–15, New Moon

Zone 1: The zone is variably cloudy with temperatures ranging from seasonal to above and scattered showers and thunderstorms.

Zone 2: Northern areas see showers and thunderstorms, while central and southern areas could experience strong storms with tornado potential; humidity accompanies seasonal temperatures.

Zone 3: Much of the zone is humid and fair to partly cloudy, with more cloudiness east and scattered showers and thunderstorms across the zone; temperatures are seasonal.

Zone 4: Cloudy western and central skies yield precipitation, eastern areas are partly cloudy with scattered showers and thunderstorms, and temperatures are seasonal to below.

Zone 5: Western and central areas are humid, and skies across the zone are variably cloudy with scattered showers and thunderstorms west and central and a chance for precipitation east.

Zone 6: Fair skies prevail in eastern parts of the zone, central areas are cloudy with scattered precipitation, and western areas are stormy.

Zone 7: Western areas are windy with showers, central and eastern areas are fair to partly cloudy, and temperatures range from seasonal to above.

Zone 8: Alaska is fair to partly cloudy. Western Hawaii is humid with showers, central and eastern areas are cloudy and windy with scattered precipitation, and temperatures are seasonal.

June 16–22, Second Quarter Moon

Zone 1: The zone is fair and humid with temperatures seasonal to above and a chance for thunderstorms.

Zone 2: A chance for thunderstorms accompanies temperatures seasonal to above.

Zone 3: Temperatures are seasonal, and skies are variably cloudy with showers and scattered thunderstorms across the zone.

Zone 4: Scattered showers and thunderstorms across much of the zone could produce locally heavy precipitation in western and central areas; eastern areas see more cloudiness, and temperatures are seasonal to above.

Zone 5: Western areas are humid, and much of the zone sees scattered storms with temperatures ranging from seasonal to above.

Zone 6: Temperatures are seasonal, central and eastern areas are partly cloudy, and western parts of the zone see showers.

Zone 7: The zone is windy and partly cloudy with scattered thunderstorms in eastern areas; temperatures are seasonal to above.

Zone 8: Central and eastern Alaska see precipitation, western areas are fair, and temperatures are seasonal. Hawaii is mostly fair with scattered thunderstorms and temperatures ranging from seasonal to above.

Summer 2013

Cloudy skies will remain a factor during the summer months, and there will be fewer periods of high temperatures. Strong thunderstorms with tornado potential will continue to be a factor, and hurricanes will be more likely to affect the Gulf states. Zone 1 will be cloudy with more precipitation and temperatures ranging from seasonal to below. Although temperatures will be more seasonal, cloudiness will be a factor in zone 2 with tropical storms and hurricanes more likely to affect the northern and Panhandle areas of Florida and southern Georgia. Eastern Florida and other coastal areas in this zone will experience dryness at times. Western areas of zone 3 will also see strong thunderstorms, central parts of this zone are likely to experience higher temperatures and dryness along with periodic strong storms, and eastern areas will see more clouds and average to above-average levels of precipitation with strong thunderstorms.

Zones 4 and 5, especially the central Plains, will see an abundance of precipitation at times, and severe thunderstorms with tornado potential are greatest in eastern areas of both zones; the greatest precipitation will be in eastern parts of zone 5. Low-pressure systems will enter the Pacific Northwest in zone 6, which will experience above-average cloudiness and cooler temperatures. To the south, northern coastal areas of zone 7 will see above-average precipitation, while central and southern areas of California will be dryer with increased fire potential, as will central parts of the zone. Eastern areas of zone 7 could see more cloudiness and fronts moving in from the northwest, but monsoon season in eastern Arizona/western New Mexico is likely to be average at best.

In Zone 8, Alaskan temperatures will range from seasonal to below with eastern and central areas seeing above-average precipitation; western areas will be more seasonal. Temperatures in Hawaii will fluctuate more than usual and tend toward the high side; dryness will also be a factor at times.

June 23–29, Full Moon

Zone 1: The zone is humid with temperatures ranging from seasonal to above along with a chance for scattered thunderstorms.

Zone 2: Humidity and temperatures ranging from seasonal to above accompany partly cloudy skies and a chance for storms.

Zone 3: The zone is humid and fair to partly cloudy with a chance for showers and storms; temperatures are seasonal to above.

Zone 4: Western areas have a chance for showers, eastern and central areas see scattered thunderstorms (some strong with tornado potential), and temperatures are seasonal to above.

Zone 5: Temperatures are seasonal to above with scattered showers and thunderstorms, some of which could be strong.

Zone 6: Much of the zone has a chance for showers and thunderstorms, but eastern areas are cloudy with showers and storms while other parts of the zone are fair to partly cloudy; temperatures range from seasonal to above.

Zone 7: Western areas are windy, eastern areas are humid, the entire zone is variably cloudy with a chance for showers and thunderstorms (primarily east), and temperatures range from seasonal to above.

Zone 8: Eastern Alaska is windy with precipitation (some abundant), western and central areas are mostly fair, and temperatures are seasonal. Temperatures in Hawaii range from seasonal to above; the state is partly cloudy and humid, and eastern areas see showers.

June 30–July 7, Fourth Quarter Moon

Zone 1: Temperature are seasonal to above, conditions are humid, and the zone sees scattered showers and thunderstorms.

Zone 2: The zone is partly cloudy to cloudy with scattered thunderstorms and showers and temperatures that range from seasonal to above.

Zone 3: Temperatures range from seasonal to above, western and central areas see showers and thunderstorms, and eastern areas are partly cloudy to cloudy with showers.

Zone 4: Western parts of the zone are windy with scattered thunderstorm and showers, central and eastern areas see more precipitation, including potential for strong tornado-producing thunderstorms; temperatures are seasonal to above.

Zone 5: Temperatures are seasonal to above and much of the zone sees thunderstorms, some strong with tornado potential, especially in eastern areas.

Zone 6: Western and central areas are windy and much of the zone sees precipitation, some abundant in eastern areas; temperatures are seasonal.

Zone 7: The zone is windy and partly cloudy to cloudy with humidity and strong storms with locally heavy precipitation in eastern and northern mountain areas; temperatures are seasonal.

Zone 8: Central Alaska is very windy with precipitation, eastern areas are cloudy with precipitation, western parts of the state are mostly fair, and temperatures range from seasonal to above. Hawaii is humid with temperatures seasonal to above, eastern areas are windy with precipitation, and western and central parts of the state see scattered showers and thunderstorms.

July 8–14, New Moon

Zone 1: The zone is mostly fair to partly cloudy and seasonal with a chance for showers in southern areas.

Zone 2: Much of the zone is cloudy and windy with showers and thunderstorms; temperatures range from seasonal to above.

Zone 3: Western and central areas are cloudy with showers, and eastern areas could see strong thunderstorms; conditions are humid with mostly seasonal temperatures.

Zone 4: Temperatures are seasonal to above, western areas are windy and humid with showers, central areas are mostly fair, and eastern parts of the zone are cloudy with scattered showers.

Zone 5: Western areas of the zone are humid with showers, central and eastern parts of the zone are fair to partly cloudy, and temperatures are seasonal to above.

Zone 6: Much of the zone is cloudy with scattered showers and thunderstorms and temperatures ranging from seasonal to above.

Zone 7: The zone is variably cloudy and humid with temperatures ranging from seasonal to above; central and eastern areas are windy with scattered showers and thunderstorms.

Zone 8: Much of Alaska is cloudy with precipitation, which is abundant in central areas, where conditions are windy; eastern areas are mostly fair; and temperatures are seasonal. Western Hawaii is windy with showers, central and eastern areas see showers (some locally heavy), and temperatures are seasonal.

July 15–21, Second Quarter Moon

Zone 1: Temperatures are seasonal to above, and the zone sees strong thunderstorms with locally heavy precipitation, especially in the north.

Zone 2: Fair to partly cloudy skies and seasonal temperatures accompany scattered thunderstorms north and a chance for precipitation in central and southern areas.

Zone 3: The zone is variably cloudy with scattered showers and thunderstorms, mostly fair east, and with seasonal temperatures; strong thunderstorms are possible in western areas.

Zone 4: Western areas are windy with thunderstorms, some with locally heavy precipitation and tornado potential; eastern areas are windy with scattered precipitation; and conditions are humid with temperatures ranging from seasonal to above.

Zone 5: Tornadoes are possible with showers and thunderstorms across much of the zone along with humidity and temperatures seasonal to above; eastern areas are fair to partly cloudy.

Zone 6: The zone is windy with strong thunderstorms in central areas, showers east, and scattered precipitation west; temperatures are seasonal under variably cloudy skies.

Zone 7: Showers and thunderstorms (some strong) prevail across much of the zone with variably cloudy skies and temperatures ranging from seasonal to above.

Zone 8: Western and central Alaska see precipitation, some abundant in central areas; eastern parts of the state are partly cloudy; and temperatures are seasonal to below. Hawaii is windy with showers and thunderstorms, and temperatures are seasonal to above before the state becomes much cooler.

July 22–28, Full Moon

Zone 1: Seasonal temperatures accompany scattered thunderstorms across the zone.

Zone 2: The zone is fair to partly cloudy, seasonal, and humid with a chance for precipitation.

Zone 3: Western and central parts of the zone are cloudy with potential for abundant precipitation, possibly from a tropical storm or hurricane; northern and eastern areas are windy with scattered thunderstorms.

Zone 4: Much of the zone sees precipitation as the week unfolds with the heaviest in eastern areas, possibly from a tropical storm or hurricane; the zone is variably cloudy and humid.

Zone 5: The zone is humid with potential for abundant precipitation, possibly from a tropical storm or hurricane.

Zone 6: Tornadoes are possible along with high winds and strong thunderstorms in central and eastern areas, temperatures are seasonal, and western parts of the zone are fair to partly cloudy.

Zone 7: Much of the zone sees thunderstorms, with the strongest in central areas along with high winds; temperatures range from seasonal to above.

Zone 8: Central and eastern Alaska are cloudy with precipitation, western areas are windy, temperatures are seasonal, and eastern parts of the state are mostly fair. Much of Hawaii sees showers (some with locally heavy precipitation) and cloudy skies with humidity and seasonal temperatures.

July 29–August 5, Fourth Quarter Moon

Zone 1: The zone is seasonal with fair to partly cloudy skies.

Zone 2: Northern areas are partly cloudy; central and southern areas are cloudy with precipitation (some abundant), possibly from a tropical storm or hurricane; and temperatures are seasonal to below.

Zone 3: Western parts of the zone are partly cloudy, central areas are cloudy with showers, and eastern parts of the zone see scattered thunderstorms; temperatures are seasonal.

Zone 4: Humidity accompanies seasonal temperatures, central and eastern areas are partly cloudy with a chance for showers, and western areas are windy with strong thunderstorms.

Zone 5: The zone is seasonal, fair to partly cloudy, and humid with scattered precipitation.

Zone 6: Western skies are fair and central and eastern areas are cloudy with scattered thunderstorms, some strong with tornado potential.

Zone 7: Temperatures range from seasonal to above, the zone is variably cloudy, central areas see scattered thunderstorms, and strong storms in eastern areas are accompanied by high winds.

Zone 8: Central and eastern Alaska are windy with showers, some locally heavy, and western parts of the state are fair to partly cloudy; temperatures are seasonal. Hawaii is windy with scattered showers and thunderstorms and temperatures ranging from seasonal to above.

August 6–13, New Moon

Zone 1: The zone is cloudy and windy with precipitation, which is heaviest in northern areas; temperatures are seasonal.

Zone 2: Much of the zone is humid with scattered precipitation under variably cloudy and windy skies in northern areas.

Zone 3: Western and central parts of the zone see thunderstorms (some possibly strong), while eastern areas are variably cloudy and windy; temperatures are seasonal with humidity.

Zone 4: Western areas are fair, and central and eastern areas are cloudy with showers and thunderstorms, some strong with tornado potential in the eastern third of the zone; temperatures are mostly seasonal.

Zone 5: Seasonal temperatures accompany windy skies with variable cloudiness west and central, while eastern areas see scattered showers and thunderstorms, some possibly strong.

Zone 6: Temperatures are seasonal, and much of the zone sees precipitation with more cloudiness in western areas.

Zone 7: The zone is variably cloudy and seasonal with scattered showers and thunderstorms; eastern areas see more precipitation.

Zone 8: Increasing cloudiness brings precipitation to western and central parts of Alaska, eastern areas are mostly fair, and temperatures are seasonal to below. Hawaii is variably cloudy and seasonal as showers move across the state.

August 14–19, Second Quarter Moon

Zone 1: Seasonal temperatures accompany partly cloudy skies with scattered precipitation.

Zone 2: Temperatures range from seasonal to above, and northern and central parts of the zone see scattered showers and thunderstorms.

Zone 3: The zone is variably cloudy with precipitation in western and central areas, and scattered precipitation falls under fair to partly cloudy skies in eastern parts of the zone; temperatures are seasonal.

Zone 4: Temperatures range from seasonal to above, western parts of the zone are humid with scattered precipitation, and central and eastern areas see more cloudiness with precipitation (some abundant in central areas).

Zone 5: The zone is variably cloudy and humid with temperatures seasonal to above and a chance for precipitation.

Zone 6: Eastern parts of the zone are partly cloudy, western and central areas see showers, and temperatures are seasonal.

Zone 7: Western and central areas are partly cloudy to cloudy with possible strong thunderstorms in southern coastal and central parts of the zone; eastern areas are humid and fair to partly cloudy; and temperatures are seasonal to above.

Zone 8: Alaska is seasonal, windy with precipitation in central and eastern areas, and partly cloudy west. Eastern Hawaii sees precipitation (some abundant), temperatures are seasonal to above, and western parts of the state are partly cloudy.

August 20–27, Full Moon

Zone 1: Skies are partly cloudy to cloudy with abundant precipitation later in the week, possibly from a tropical storm or hurricane; temperatures are seasonal.

Zone 2: Northern areas see abundant precipitation, possibly from a tropical storm or hurricane, while central and southern areas are humid with precipitation under partly cloudy to cloudy skies.

Zone 3: Western parts of the zone are windy and mostly fair, eastern areas are cloudy and windy with precipitation, some abundant, possibly from a tropical storm or hurricane; temperatures are seasonal.

Zone 4: Skies are fair to partly cloudy west with strong thunderstorms and tornado potential, central and eastern parts of the zone are mostly fair with precipitation later in the week, and temperatures are seasonal.

Zone 5: Western areas see scattered thunderstorms, central and eastern areas are fair to partly cloudy, and temperatures range from seasonal to above.

Zone 6: Much of the zone is windy under partly cloudy to cloudy skies with precipitation, which is heaviest central and east, and temperatures are seasonal.

Zone 7: The zone is partly cloudy to cloudy with showers and thunderstorms, some strong in eastern areas with locally heavy precipitation; eastern areas are humid; and temperatures range from seasonal to above.

Zone 8: Central and eastern Alaska are windy with precipitation, some abundant in central areas, and temperatures are seasonal; increasing cloudiness in western areas brings precipitation later in the week. Hawaii is seasonal, windy, and fair to partly cloudy with scattered precipitation.

August 28–September 4, Fourth Quarter Moon

Zone 1: Mostly fair skies accompany seasonal temperatures.

Zone 2: The zone is fair to partly cloudy and windy with temperatures seasonal to above.

Zone 3: Thunderstorms with tornado potential are possible in western parts of the zone, central areas are cloudy with showers, eastern areas are fair to partly cloudy, and temperatures are seasonal to below.

Zone 4: Western areas are cloudy with precipitation (some abundant) that moves into central parts of the zone, while eastern areas are cloudy with showers and thunderstorms and tornado potential; the zone is humid with temperatures ranging from seasonal to above.

Zone 5: Western and central skies are partly cloudy to cloudy with showers, temperatures are seasonal to above, and eastern parts of the zone are windy with scattered thunderstorms and tornado potential.

Zone 6: The zone is partly cloudy to cloudy, temperatures are seasonal to above, and eastern areas see showers and thunderstorms, some strong with tornado potential.

Zone 7: Much of the zone is fair to partly cloudy with scattered showers and thunderstorms and temperatures ranging from seasonal to above.

Zone 8: Eastern Alaska sees precipitation, western and central parts of the state are variably cloudy with scattered precipitation, and temperatures are seasonal. Hawaii is seasonal, windy, and fair to partly cloudy.

September 5–11, New Moon

Zone 1: Northern areas are fair, temperatures are seasonal, and southern areas are windy and cloudy with precipitation.

Zone 2: Windy conditions accompany precipitation in northern areas, and central and southern areas are partly cloudy to cloudy with showers; temperatures are seasonal.

Zone 3: The zone is variably cloudy with showers and scattered thunderstorms, eastern areas are windy, and temperatures are seasonal.

Zone 4: Western areas are fair to partly cloudy, temperatures are seasonal, and central and eastern parts of the zone see more cloudiness with scattered precipitation and more downfall in northern areas.

Zone 5: Temperatures are seasonal, western areas see scattered precipitation, and central and eastern parts of the zone could experience strong thunderstorms with tornado potential and locally heavy precipitation.

Zone 6: Western skies are cloudy and stormy, central and eastern areas are mostly fair with a chance for scattered precipitation, and temperatures range from seasonal to below.

Zone 7: Northern coastal areas are cloudy with precipitation, eastern areas are windy, and the remainder of the zone is fair to partly cloudy; temperatures are seasonal.

Zone 8: Central and eastern Alaska see precipitation, western areas are windy with precipitation later in the week, and temperatures are seasonal. Much of Hawaii is windy as a front moves through with precipitation followed by cooler temperatures.

September 12–18, Second Quarter Moon

Zone 1: Temperatures are seasonal, and the zone is partly cloudy to cloudy with precipitation.

Zone 2: Skies are partly cloudy to cloudy across the zone with precipitation north, scattered precipitation in other areas, and seasonal temperatures.

Zone 3: Western and southern parts of the zone could experience abundant precipitation and strong thunderstorms, possibly as a result of a tropical storm; much of the remainder of the zone also sees precipitation.

Zone 4: Western areas are windy with precipitation later in the week, while eastern areas see more clouds that bring precipitation (some abundant) and thunderstorms with tornado potential; temperatures are seasonal.

Zone 5: Central and eastern areas are windy with precipitation (some abundant) and thunderstorms with tornado potential, possibly from a tropical storm; western areas are partly cloudy, and temperatures are seasonal.

Zone 6: Temperatures are seasonal to below, western and central parts of the zone see precipitation (some abundant), and eastern areas are partly cloudy.

Zone 7: Precipitation prevails in much of the zone (some abundant), and temperatures are seasonal to above; eastern areas are partly cloudy and windy with a chance for precipitation.

Zone 8: Much of Alaska is windy with precipitation, and temperatures range from seasonal to below. Hawaii is windy, fair to partly cloudy, and seasonal.

Autumn 2013

Autumn will bring stormy weather in many parts of the country, cloudiness will be a factor, and several areas will see abundant precipitation. Zone 1 will see the greatest downfall throughout the season, along with temperatures ranging from seasonal to below. Zone 2 will also see some of these influences, although not as severe. Nevertheless, northern and central areas of zone 2 will see stormy conditions at times, while southern areas will tend toward dryness. Zone 3 will also experience periods of cold weather, along with strong thunderstorms and tornado potential in southern areas of both zones 3 and 5.

Much of California in zone 7 will be dry with temperatures ranging from seasonal to above. Central and eastern areas of the zone will also experience periods of warm, dry weather; California could see an unusually high number of fires this year. The same influence will be a factor in the western areas of zone 6 at times, but this zone will also be the site of strong weather systems that enter the continental United States. These weather systems will take a southeastern path through zones 4 and 5, both of which will see heavy precipitation, cloudy skies, and cold temperatures at times. Major low-pressure systems will form in the northeastern area of zone 4, bringing abundant precipitation.

In zone 8, central Alaska will see abundant precipitation, and weather patterns will be generally seasonal in eastern and western parts of the state. Far western areas, however, will experience abundant precipitation. Hawaii can expect more cloudiness as well as precipitation levels that range from average to above; temperatures will be generally seasonal.

September 19–25, Full Moon

Zone 1: The zone is seasonal and partly cloudy.

Zone 2: Northern skies are partly cloudy, temperatures are seasonal, and central and southern parts of the zone see more cloudiness and precipitation.

Zone 3: Temperatures are seasonal, eastern areas are partly cloudy to cloudy with scattered precipitation, and western parts of the zone are windy.

Zone 4: Western areas are cloudy with precipitation, central and eastern areas are partly cloudy and windy, and temperatures range from seasonal to above.

Zone 5: Temperatures range from seasonal to above, and the zone is windy and variably cloudy.

Zone 6: The zone is windy with temperatures that range from seasonal to below, western areas are cloudy with precipitation, and central and eastern parts of the zone are fair to partly cloudy.

Zone 7: Northern coastal areas are windy with scattered precipitation, as are eastern parts of the zone; temperatures are seasonal, and skies are mostly fair to partly cloudy.

Zone 8: Central and eastern Alaska are partly cloudy and windy with scattered precipitation, while western areas are mostly fair;

temperatures are seasonal to below. Hawaii is seasonal, very windy, and fair to partly cloudy.

September 26–October 3, Fourth Quarter Moon

Zone 1: Seasonal temperatures accompany variable cloudiness with a chance for precipitation.

Zone 2: The zone is seasonal and variably cloudy with a chance for showers.

Zone 3: Western areas are cloudy with precipitation (some abundant), temperatures are seasonal, and central and eastern parts of the zone are cloudy with scattered precipitation.

Zone 4: Western areas see precipitation, and central parts of the zone see increasing cloudiness with precipitation (some locally heavy) later in the week that moves into eastern areas; much of the zone is cloudy, and temperatures are seasonal.

Zone 5: Temperatures are seasonal, and western areas are cloudy with precipitation that moves east as the week unfolds.

Zone 6: Western and central parts of the zone are windy and partly cloudy, while eastern areas are also windy with more clouds and precipitation later in the week; temperatures are seasonal.

Zone 7: Temperatures are seasonal, western and central areas are partly cloudy with a chance for precipitation, and eastern areas see more cloudiness; clouds are also abundant in northern areas.

Zone 8: Western parts of Alaska are mostly fair to partly cloudy and windy, while central and eastern areas see precipitation; temperatures are seasonal. Hawaii is seasonal and humid with variable cloudiness and scattered showers.

October 4–10, New Moon

Zone 1: The zone is cloudy and seasonal with precipitation, which is abundant in northern areas.

Zone 2: Northern areas are windy with precipitation, and central and southern parts of the zone have a greater chance for precipitation later in the week; temperatures are seasonal.

Zone 3: Much of the zone sees showers and thunderstorms, along with seasonal temperatures and windy skies that are partly cloudy to cloudy.

Zone 4: The zone is variably cloudy with precipitation, and western and central areas are very windy with possibly strong thunderstorms; temperatures are seasonal.

Zone 5: Showers and thunderstorms prevail across much of the zone, which is partly cloudy to cloudy and seasonal; eastern areas see precipitation later in the week.

Zone 6: The zone is partly cloudy to cloudy and seasonal with precipitation west and scattered precipitation in other areas.

Zone 7: Temperatures are seasonal, and the zone is variably cloudy with precipitation in northern coastal areas and scattered precipitation central and east.

Zone 8: Alaska is windy and seasonal with precipitation in eastern and western areas, where downfall could be significant. Hawaii is fair to partly cloudy and seasonal.

October 11–17, Second Quarter Moon

Zone 1: The zone is fair to partly cloudy and seasonal with scattered precipitation.

Zone 2: Strong thunderstorms with locally heavy precipitation and tornado potential are possible in central and southern parts of the zone; northern areas are partly cloudy with a chance for precipitation.

Zone 3: Much of the zone sees precipitation under windy skies that are partly cloudy to cloudy with temperatures that range from seasonal to below.

Zone 4: The zone is partly cloudy to cloudy and windy with scattered precipitation central and east and seasonal temperatures.

Zone 5: Scattered precipitation prevails across much of the zone, which is windy central and east with variably cloudiness and seasonal temperatures.

Zone 6: Precipitation under cloudy skies in western parts of the zone moves into central areas, with a chance for precipitation east; temperatures are seasonal.

Zone 7: Northern coastal areas see precipitation that advances into central parts of the zone, which are variably cloudy; eastern areas also have a chance for precipitation, and temperatures are seasonal.

Zone 8: Alaska is generally fair to partly cloudy and seasonal, and eastern areas are windy with precipitation. Hawaii is fair to partly cloudy and seasonal with scattered showers.

October 18–25, Full Moon

Zone 1: Northern areas are cloudy with precipitation, southern areas are partly cloudy with scattered precipitation, and temperatures range from seasonal to below.

Zone 2: The zone is mostly fair to partly cloudy with scattered precipitation and seasonal temperatures.

Zone 3: Strong thunderstorms are possible in southern areas, and the zone is mostly fair to partly cloudy with a chance for precipitation in northern areas; temperatures are seasonal to above.

Zone 4: Much of the zone sees precipitation, especially west and northwest, where stormy conditions could prevail; the zone is windy with temperatures that range from seasonal to below.

Zone 5: Much of the zone sees precipitation with possible strong thunderstorms and tornadoes, and temperatures are seasonal.

Zone 6: The zone is partly cloudy and seasonal with more cloudiness east and scattered precipitation.

Zone 7: Partly cloudy to cloudy skies prevail with scattered precipitation and a greater chance for downfall in eastern areas; temperatures are seasonal.

Zone 8: Central Alaska is windy, eastern and western parts of the state are partly cloudy, and temperatures are seasonal. Hawaii is windy and fair to partly cloudy with temperatures seasonal to below.

October 26–November 2, Fourth Quarter Moon

Zone 1: Cloudy, windy skies prevail along with precipitation, some abundant in southern areas; temperatures are seasonal.

Zone 2: Northern areas are cloudy, southern and central areas are variably cloudy, and much of the zone sees precipitation, including the possibility of thunderstorms and locally heavy downfall.

Zone 3: The zone is variably cloudy with precipitation, some abundant in eastern areas, and temperatures are seasonal.

Zone 4: Skies in central areas are partly cloudy to cloudy with precipitation, including possible thunderstorms; temperatures are seasonal to above.

Zone 5: Temperatures are seasonal to above, and skies are variably cloudy with precipitation in much of the zone; strong thunderstorms are possible.

Zone 6: The zone is generally partly cloudy, eastern areas are windy with precipitation later in the week, and temperatures are seasonal to below.

Zone 7: Scattered precipitation and winds accompany partly cloudy to cloudy skies and seasonal temperatures.

Zone 8: Alaska is variably cloudy, windy east and west with precipitation, and temperatures range from seasonal to below. Eastern Hawaii sees precipitation, some locally heavy, and the remainder of the state is fair to partly cloudy; temperatures are seasonal.

November 3–9, New Moon

Zone 1: Seasonal temperatures accompany windy, cloudy skies, and precipitation.

Zone 2: Northern areas are windy, and central and southern areas see precipitation (some abundant) under partly cloudy to cloudy skies with temperatures ranging from seasonal to above.

Zone 3: Much of the zone is partly cloudy to cloudy and windy with precipitation, which could be locally heavy in eastern areas;

temperatures are seasonal to below.

Zone 4: Western parts of the zone are windy with abundant precipitation that moves into central areas, eastern areas are partly cloudy with scattered precipitation, and temperatures are seasonal to below.

Zone 5: Much of the zone sees precipitation, with the greatest downfall in western and central areas; skies are partly cloudy to cloudy, and temperatures are seasonal to below.

Zone 6: The zone is partly cloudy and seasonal with a chance of precipitation.

Zone 7: Skies are fair to partly cloudy with a chance for precipitation, and temperatures are seasonal to above.

Zone 8: Alaska is windy, partly cloudy to cloudy, and seasonal with precipitation. Hawaii is seasonal, partly cloudy, and windy.

November 10–16, Second Quarter Moon
Zone 1: Temperatures are seasonal to below under fair to partly cloudy skies with precipitation later in the week.

Zone 2: Much of the zone is cloudy with scattered precipitation and seasonal temperatures.

Zone 3: Central and western skies are partly cloudy to cloudy with precipitation, and eastern areas see abundant downfall; temperatures are seasonal to below.

Zone 4: The zone is partly cloudy to cloudy with the most clouds in central areas and precipitation across much of the zone; temperatures range from seasonal to below.

Zone 5: Skies are partly cloudy to cloudy and windy with scattered precipitation and seasonal temperatures.

Zone 6: Variable cloudiness across the zone brings precipitation to many areas; temperatures are seasonal.

Zone 7: The zone is fair to partly cloudy and windy in eastern areas, and temperatures are seasonal to above.

Zone 8: Alaska is cloudy, windy, and seasonal with precipitation.

Hawaiian temperatures are seasonal to above under windy skies that are fair to partly cloudy.

November 17–24, Full Moon

Zone 1: The zone is partly cloudy and windy with scattered precipitation and temperatures ranging from seasonal to below.

Zone 2: Seasonal temperatures accompany fair to partly cloudy skies.

Zone 3: Western and central areas are partly cloudy followed by increasing cloudiness and precipitation; eastern areas are fair to partly cloudy and windy; and temperatures are seasonal.

Zone 4: Western and eastern areas of the zone are partly cloudy, central areas are cloudy with precipitation, and temperatures are seasonal to below.

Zone 5: Eastern areas of the zone see precipitation, while western and central areas are partly cloudy and windy; temperatures are seasonal.

Zone 6: The zone is windy and seasonal with partly cloudy to cloudy skies and scattered precipitation.

Zone 7: Temperatures are seasonal, eastern areas are windy and mostly fair, and western and central parts of the zone are windy and partly cloudy to cloudy.

Zone 8: Central Alaska is windy with precipitation that moves into eastern areas, temperatures are seasonal, and western areas are partly cloudy. Hawaii is windy and seasonal with scattered precipitation.

November 25–December 1, Fourth Quarter Moon

Zone 1: The zone is partly cloudy and windy with precipitation in southern areas and temperatures seasonal to below.

Zone 2: Much of the zone is windy with precipitation later in the week as temperatures range from seasonal to below.

Zone 3: Western areas are windy with a chance for thunderstorms; the zone is fair to partly cloudy with temperatures seasonal to above but cooler in eastern areas.

Zone 4: Temperatures are seasonal to above under windy and fair to partly cloudy skies with precipitation later in the week.

Zone 5: Thunderstorms are possible in southern areas, skies are fair to partly cloudy, and temperatures are seasonal to above.

Zone 6: Western skies are fair to partly cloudy, central and eastern areas see increasing cloudiness with precipitation (some abundant), and temperatures are seasonal.

Zone 7: The zone is partly cloudy to cloudy with the greatest downfall west and central and then in eastern areas, primarily north; temperatures are seasonal.

Zone 8: Precipitation and wind in central parts of Alaska move into eastern areas, while western areas are fair; temperatures are seasonal. Much of Hawaii sees showers under variably cloudy skies that accompany seasonal temperatures.

December 2–8, New Moon

Zone 1: Much of the zone is windy with some areas receiving abundant precipitation, and temperatures are seasonal to below.

Zone 2: Temperatures ranging from seasonal to below accompany windy skies that are partly cloudy to cloudy with precipitation.

Zone 3: Eastern areas are windy with precipitation, while western and central parts of the zone are fair to partly cloudy; temperatures are seasonal to below.

Zone 4: Abundant precipitation is possible in western and central parts of the zone, which are cloudy, while eastern areas are partly cloudy; temperatures range from seasonal to below.

Zone 5: Temperatures are seasonal, eastern areas are partly cloudy, and western and central areas are cloudy with precipitation.

Zone 6: The zone is partly cloudy to cloudy with scattered precipitation (some abundant), western areas are windy, and temperatures are seasonal to below.

Zone 7: Much of the zone is windy with precipitation under partly cloudy to cloudy skies with seasonal temperatures.

Zone 8: Alaska is windy with temperatures seasonal to below, western and central areas are fair to partly cloudy, and eastern parts of the state see precipitation. Hawaii is seasonal to below and mostly fair and windy.

December 9–16, Second Quarter Moon

Zone 1: Temperatures are seasonal to below under partly cloudy to cloudy skies with scattered precipitation.

Zone 2: Northern areas are fair to partly cloudy, and central and southern parts of the zone are cloudy with precipitation; temperatures are seasonal to below.

Zone 3: Western and central parts of the zone are fair to partly cloudy, while eastern areas see more cloudiness; temperatures are seasonal to below.

Zone 4: Partly cloudy to cloudy skies prevail in eastern parts of the zone, and western and central areas are cloudy; temperatures range from seasonal to below.

Zone 5: The zone is variably cloudy; precipitation in western and central areas moves into eastern parts of the zone later in the week; temperatures are seasonal.

Zone 6: Western areas are windy with scattered precipitation, and the remainder of the zone is fair to partly cloudy; temperatures are seasonal to below.

Zone 7: Eastern areas see more cloudiness and scattered precipitation, western and central areas are fair to partly cloudy, and temperatures are seasonal to below.

Zone 8: Central and eastern Alaska see precipitation (some abundant), skies are partly cloudy in western parts of the state, and temperatures are seasonal. Eastern Hawaii sees showers, and the state is variably cloudy and windy with seasonal temperatures.

December 17–24, Full Moon

Zone 1: Temperatures are seasonal under cloudy skies that bring precipitation (some abundant).

Zone 2: Much of the zone is windy with precipitation, and strong thunderstorms with tornado potential are possible in southern areas; temperatures are seasonal to below.

Zone 3: The zone is cloudy with precipitation (some abundant), and temperatures range from seasonal to below.

Zone 4: Western areas see precipitation (some abundant), while central parts of the zone are variably cloudy with scattered precipitation, and eastern areas are cloudy with precipitation; temperatures are seasonal.

Zone 5: The zone is variably cloudy and windy with scattered precipitation across much of the zone; eastern areas see more downfall, possibly abundant; temperatures are seasonal.

Zone 6: Western areas are windy with possibly stormy conditions, and central and eastern parts of the zone are partly cloudy to cloudy with potential for abundant downfall in eastern areas; temperatures are seasonal to below.

Zone 7: Much of the zone is cloudy with scattered precipitation,

eastern areas are fair to partly cloudy, and temperatures are seasonal to below.

Zone 8: Central and eastern areas of Alaska see precipitation, some locally heavy, eastern areas are windy with scattered precipitation, and temperatures are seasonal to below. Hawaii is seasonal and windy.

December 25–31, Fourth Quarter Moon

Zone 1: The zone is cloudy with precipitation and temperatures seasonal to below.

Zone 2: Temperatures range from seasonal to below under cloudy skies with precipitation.

Zone 3: Variable cloudiness with scattered precipitation prevails across much of the zone with more cloudiness and precipitation in eastern areas; temperatures are seasonal.

Zone 4: Skies are partly cloudy to cloudy across the zone with precipitation (abundant in eastern areas), and temperatures are seasonal.

Zone 5: The zone is variably cloudy with scattered precipitation west and central; stormy conditions and abundant downfall are possible in eastern parts of the zone; temperatures are seasonal to below.

Zone 6: Temperatures are seasonal to below, eastern areas are stormy, and western and central areas are variably cloudy.

Zone 7: Western and central parts of the zone are partly cloudy to cloudy with precipitation that moves into eastern areas along with high winds; temperatures range from seasonal to below.

Zone 8: Central and eastern Alaska are cloudy with precipitation (some abundant), and western skies are partly cloudy; temperatures are seasonal. Much of Hawaii is windy with precipitation and temperatures ranging from seasonal to below.

About the Author

Kris Brandt Riske is the executive director and a professional member of the American Federation of Astrologers (AFA), the oldest U.S. astrological organization, founded in 1938; and a member of the National Council for Geocosmic Research (NCGR). She has a master's degree in journalism and a certificate of achievement in weather forecasting from Penn State.

Kris is the author of several books, including Llewellyn's Complete Book of Astrology: The Easy Way to Learn Astrology; Mapping Your Money; Mapping Your Future; *and she is coauthor of* Mapping Your Travels and Relocation *and* Astrometeorology: Planetary Powers in Weather Forecasting. *Her newest book is* Llewellyn's Complete Book of Predictive Astrology. *She also writes for astrology publications and does the annual weather forecast for* Llewellyn's Moon Sign Book.

In addition to astrometeorology, she specializes in predictive astrology. Kris is an avid NASCAR fan, although she'd rather be a driver than a spectator. In 2011 she fulfilled her dream when she drove a stock car for twelve fast laps. She posts a weather forecast for each of the thirty-six race weekends (qualifying and race day) for NASCAR drivers and fans. Visit her at www.pitstopforecasting.com. Kris also enjoys gardening, reading, jazz, and her three cats.

Economic Forecast for 2013

By Bill Meridian

This year, 2013, is likely to be a vital one for the economy and the global financial structure. I can shed some light on the situation by describing a meeting that I had with the dean of the school that I graduated from. He asked me how astrological cycles can be used to make projections. I explained that there were cycles of varying lengths that tended to mark turning points in the economy. If several cycles all showed turning points in a given year, that year was likely to be an important one, as was 2007. I went on to explain to him that this method can be utilized to predict events many years in advance. As the time period approaches, signs of the impending crisis become obvious to the trained eye. For example, it was obvious that real estate values were at unsustainable levels as the Saturn-Neptune opposition of 2007 neared. I was able to predict that the opposition would coincide with a pop in the real estate bubble. The dean and I then attended a lecture by a professor who began with a graph showing the enormous amount of debt that is due for payment in 2013 and 2014. I leaned over to the dean and said that this debt would lead to the next crisis in 2013. So the news may be grim, but there are ways to navigate the downturn. Let us see what the planets can tell us about developments in the coming year.

I conducted a study of the US economy about fifteen years ago, and its results are in my book *Planetary Economic Forecasting*. The data was obtained in the 1980s, and the study began in 1998. This study was done on two levels: The first was quantitative, comparing sidereal and synodic astrological cycles to a monthly index of industrial production. Thus, the reader is able to determine the influence that planets (Jupiter and Saturn, in particular) have on production at any point in their synodic cycle or at any degree of the zodiac as the planet transits.

The second level was qualitative. Charts showing the chronological placement of financial crises relative to synodic and sidereal cycles were constructed. In this way, one can see the astrological and economic events that manifested at any point in a cycle. For example, one can scan down a graph showing Saturn 270 degrees to Neptune. The vertical axis lists all crises that occurred when those planets were in that angular relationship. This takes the guesswork out of economic projection through planetary influences.

The Methodology
The first level described above requires some explanation, namely

the "composite cycle." This approach involves measuring the effect that a pair of planets has on business activity. This is done by measuring the percentage change in business activity from conjunction to conjunction. The business activity index was obtained from an analysis done by some innovative economists in a bank in the Midwestern United States. The result is an oscillator that fluctuates around a level that represents a "normal" level of production (100). It is important to remember that the index is a histogram that fluctuates around a normal long-term trend. The original index usually fluctuated +20 to –20. During the Great Depression, the index fell –51, followed by a rise of +50 during the boom of World War II. A rise from 100 to 110 represents a 10 percent increase in business activity.

So the business activity index might be 100 at the conjunction and may rise to 103 at the 30-degree separation between the pair of planets chosen. This is a 3 percent rise. This measurement is done degree by degree until the next conjunction is reached, which completes the first cycle. The first cycle is then added to the next cycle until all past cycles are summed. Then an average is calculated. By using historical economic and astrological information, we can see the effect that any pair of planets has had on US business activity from 1780 to the present. The same can be done for planets as they transit through the signs. The planets that were most reliable in describing past business activity are:

Jupiter through the Signs (in a square with Saturn in 2013)
Neptune-Node[1]
Pluto-Node
Saturn-Pluto
Saturn through the Signs (not described in this article)
Saturn-Neptune

---

1. All references to "Node" indicate the north lunar node. A planet's node occurs where its orbit crosses the ecliptic path of the Sun.

I will go through these important indicators one by one to explore their historical facts and how they might activate in the 2013 economy.

Jupiter through the Signs

The study shows that Jupiter and Saturn add value to the economy primarily at conjunction and at opposition. Other aspects and phases were not as useful as traditional astrology would lead us to believe. Mundane astrologers contend that the Jupiter-Saturn conjunction horoscopes set the political—and perhaps the economic—tone for the following twenty years. There is some truth to this, but this also raises questions. In 1920, there was a Jupiter-Saturn conjunction during the little-known depression of that time. In response, US President Coolidge simply cut the size of government by two-thirds and let the natural entrepreneurial spirit of the American people take over. The Roaring Twenties followed only to end in the Great Depression of the 1930s. How can one horoscope—that of the 1920 conjunction—describe both a decade of the great prosperity and a decade of great loss?

In 1931, the government instituted policies that turned a recession into a depression just as Jupiter opposed Saturn. This raised the idea that horoscopes set for the moment of the *opposition* better describe the following decade, not horoscopes based on the *conjuntion* from ten years earlier. There were three relevent oppositions. In the 1930 chart, the Jupiter-Saturn opposition is square to the Uranian planet Hades. (The Uranian system was developed in Hamburg between the world wars. It utilizes eight additional bodies that are theorized to exist beyond Pluto, including Hades.) Hades symbolizes want and poverty, which is very descriptive of that period. In fact, Hades was conjunct another Uranian planet, Admetos (and therefore square to the Jupiter-Saturn opposition), in 1933, the worst year of the Great Depression.

Why bring this up now? The Jupiter-Saturn oppositions of

2010 and 2011(May 23 and August 16, 2010, and March 28, 2011) also made a square with Hades. Beginning in 1931, the federal government enacted New Deal legislation that actually *prolonged* the Great Depression. Looking back, researchers see that the states that received the most aid actually experienced the slowest growth rates in subsequent years. In other states, people were forced to innovate in order to overcome the hard times. Such states turned toward manufacturing and away from agriculture, kickstarting themselves into prosperity. In addition, Americans had to comply with many rules to recieve aid, which inhibited growth. Eventually, World War II ended the New Deal and thus ended the Great Depression.

Origins of the Crisis

Just as the 1930s politicians adopted the wrong strategies, so have those in recent years. Part of the crisis originated with the 2007 real estate bubble and subsequent decline. This bubble began on October 12, 1977, when President Carter signed the Community Reinvestment Act (CRA). The intention was to prevent banks from "red-lining" communities by not making mortgages available in those areas. They may have done so because loans there are more risky than in other areas, but some people in government called this racism. Unfortunately, Carter signed this legislation on the day of a total solar eclipse. Actions commenced within one week of an eclipse take on a higher degree of importance. Actions taken in the week before eclipses have a fated quality, while those taken on the day of an eclipse are the most fated, taking on a life of their own.[2] The CRA was relatively benign until 1994–1995, when the Clinton administration forced banks to make such loans to an extreme. Banks were even given a CRA rating to monitor their compliance. These loans were very risky, and the risk

---

2. The effects of actions taken in the days around eclipses were enumerated by Charles Jayne in *The Predictive Power of Eclipse Paths*.

was increased when these mortgages were rolled into securities, repackaged, and sold around the globe. Risk was raised yet again when the loans were insured, meaning someone stood to gain if they failed. Easy credit and lending terms fueled a boom until Saturn opposed Neptune in 2007, and we all know what happened then: the housing crisis.

The proposed solutions to the current crisis are simply continuations of past policies that caused the crisis. This is like trying to fight a fire with gasoline. The federal government has been on a hiring binge, and debt has been accumulating rather than being reduced. Some US representatives are pushing plans to extend more credit or relief from mortgage payments to homeowners. In 2011, the administration pushed for tax increases. Pennsylvania and the Dakotas are benefiting from gas drilling, but the state of New York has banned this industry. California could solve many of their difficulties by drilling for oil offshore, but they refuse to do so. The Environmental Protection Agency (EPA) continues to issue rules that are costly to implement, which inhibits business and adds to costs. All these practices create what has been termed "regime uncertainty." This means that businesses are restrained from expansion because they are uncertain what the government may do next in terms of rules and regulations. Until this uncertainty ends, entrepreneurs will continue to keep their future plans under wraps and their cash in their pockets.

The Natural Solution

The economy, wages, and prices move in a cycle—a natural manner of expansion and contraction—but the periods of expansion can be artificially extended by the excessive issuance of credit. In ancient times, precious metals were money. These cannot be duplicated or counterfeited, but they can be clipped. (That is, shaving off a few grams of gold or silver from many coins.) When paper replaced coins, the temptation to issue more and

more paper money became very great. The excessive issuance of credit over and above the demand for money is the definition of *inflation*. This makes periods of growth into bubbles, and bubbles eventually burst. The excess credit or money supply also depresses interest rates. Thus, many projects are undertaken that would not be started if rates were at a higher, more realistic level. When the cycle turns down, these bubble businesses or projects go bust. The Jupiter-Saturn opposition suggests that a natural recovery is unlikely until the conjunction at the end of the decade (December 2020).

Neptune-Node

This potent pair will be about 130 degrees apart in 2013. The last such contacts occurred near the crisis that took place when the Russian and Thai currencies dropped in 1998. This specific angular separation is usually connected to currency crises. Business activity is thus typically flat during such times.

Pluto-Node

This cycle will have less effect in 2013 than the other cycles. Crises sometimes do occur near this angle, such as the BCCI (Bank of

Credit and Commerce International) collapse in 1991. Business activity has historically been flat around this cycle.

The sign that the node transits in this year is Scorpio. Crises do tend to occur during this transit. In the mid-1990s, we saw the Mexican peso crisis, the bankruptcy of Orange County, and the collapse of Barings Bank connected to this astrological event.

Saturn-Pluto

This pair will be about 300 degrees apart all year. Historically, there have not been many crises when these planets are in this relationship; industrial production generally rises. But the sign transited by Saturn is telling. There have been crises in each of Saturn's Scorpio transits since 1790. The last transit brought the Mexican peso crisis of 1982–1983. Often industrial production suddenly plummets and then suddenly recovers during this event. Thus there may be gains to be had in the industrial sectors if you buy in a low period and sell in a high one.

Saturn-Neptune

The history of Saturn and Neptune is one of deflation. Neptune rules credit. Credit is accepted as money, but it is not *real* money. Thus there is a difference between hard (cash and real assets) and soft money. Some aspects between these two planets, such as the square, tend to remove credit from the system.

This can be done by the central bank reducing the amount of money in circulation, as President Reagan and Paul Volcker did in 1982. Or, it can occur after a period of rapid monetary contraction through bankruptcies, as it did in the 1930s. The 1970s period of inflation ended on such a square when the attempted corner of the silver market by the Hunt Brothers collapsed in March 1980. The series of Saturn-Neptune oppositions from 2006 to 2007 coincided with the top of the real estate market. The last opposition in late June 2007 was the beginning of the sub-prime meltdown.

In 2013, this pair will be about 240 degrees apart. Tracing financial history back to 1763, there have been seven episodes of panic or crisis near this angular separation. Wise folks will hold on to their hats this year and be prepared for further credit losses.

Other Factors

The Uranus-Pluto Squares

There are squares between Uranus and Pluto on May 20 and on November 1 this year. These are the third and fourth such aspects between the two planets in a series of seven.

There are two ways to assess the effect of planetary influences upon current conditions. One can trace the effect historically or determine the effect through the intrinsic nature of the planets involved in the event. There have been too few Uranus-Pluto squares for me to make a historical judgment; thus we combine the meanings of the planets. This pair can bring sudden and radical change. In personal horoscopes, this square can represent sudden changes in financial position. The effect on society can be to polarize and send factions to extremes. The gap between those who support big government and socialism and those who support individual freedom will be at its widest, making agreement on major issues very difficult. As Charles Jayne wrote many years ago, Pluto is the planet of government. It is the power, or the glue, that holds government together. Uranus is likely to fracture or splinter that power. Pluto can also be seen in its Scorpionic link to debt. That is, if one is in debt heavily enough, one loses control to the creditor. And, Jayne taught, Pluto transits always bring shifts in power.

One important feature of this square is the degrees that are being transited. Uranus is in Aries and Pluto is in Capricorn. Many dynamic individuals and powerful nations have planets in the cardinal degrees in their horoscope charts. (A nation's horoscope chart is calculated using it's date of independence or other significant establishment.) There are specific degrees that I call the power points in the zodiac:

0° of the cardinal signs (and 15° fixed);

10° Cancer, the north node of Jupiter;

13–14° Cancer and Capricorn, the invariable plane;

20° Cancer, the north node of Pluto; and

24° Cancer, the north node of Saturn.

Many major political entities have important points near these cardinal degrees in their charts. This includes the United States' Sun in Cancer, the USSR's Sun opposite it in Capricorn, imperial Japan's Sun in Capricorn, and China's Sun in a square from Libra. Given these positions, it's possible for one transit to hit all four nations!

Basic astrology sometimes teaches that Americans born with planets near the United States' Cancer Sun will likely prosper because they are in tune with the country's light. But look at it another way: could it be that America is wealthy because its Jupiter and Sun are conjunct to the north Jupiter node? The drive and ambition conferred by this axis seems to explain the clustering of planets in important world horoscopes in Cancer and Capricorn.

The Invariable Plane

Charles Jayne worked with the invariable plane, which was discovered by the French astronomer LaPlace. It is the average plane of the solar system. Each of the planets has an orbit that traces out a plane. If an average is found that takes into account the masses of the planets, we have the invariable plane. Think of it like a teeter-totter: as some planets increase eccentricity and inclination, others reduce theirs. It all works in a mind-boggling three-dimensional balancing act to keep the invariable plane in place.

Many of the great powers are so because they tap into the energy that streams from this stable axis of 13–14 degrees Cancer-Capricorn. In the 1970s, I began to notice that people who were born with planets along the invariable plane tend to feel that they are caught between opposing forces. That is, that they must maintain a balance to hold a situation together. A chart drawn based on the date of the U.S. Declaration of Independence shows the Sun at 13 degrees Cancer—right on the invariable plane. If my description of the plane is correct, then it's no wonder that America acts as the world's policeman, holding opposing forces at bay.

Russia and the USSR also have many significant planetary positions at 17–18 degrees Cancer or Capricorn. The July 11, 1991, solar eclipse at 19 degrees Cancer preceded the Gorbachev "coup" by one month. This event certainly drew the globe's attention. Future activity at these degrees will shift power once again, with Pluto's transit of 17 degrees Capricorn looming as a major change in 2014.

The horoscope for imperial restoration in Japan (set for January 3, 1868) has the Sun and Mars at 12 degrees Capricorn, Uranus at 11 degrees Cancer, and the Moon and Neptune at 10–12 degrees Aries. (Note the aspects to the United States' chart positions.) Many entities have a national day or have begun on January 1, when the Sun is at 10 degrees Capricorn. Many more, like the Philippines, have their national day near that of the United States' July 4, when the Sun is in early Cancer.

Jayne said that "Breadth is essential in mundane astrology." Once a country's history has been studied and a series of horoscopes had been collected, the connections between the charts will emphasize certain degrees of the zodiac. In other words, one discovers that planets around a certain degree coincide with major events on a consistent basis. This is a vital concept, because future stimulation of these degrees will likely lead to major events.

The major countries of the world have many planets in the cardinal degrees and in the zodiac power grid. In 1989–1990, Jupiter, Saturn, and Neptune on the Cancer/Capricorn axis saw the fall of the Berlin Wall. Pluto on the axis ushered in the Great Depression and the origins of World War II in the 1930s.

As Jayne used to write, Pluto transits always bring shifts in power. Pluto activity along the invariable axis will shift power once again. It is highly likely that the debt and budget crises worldwide will spin out of control. Pluto will stir up market forces that are beyond control. Uranus tells us that these forces will strike suddenly. Citizens (as symbolized by Uranus) will resist the changes that their governments demand. We will likely see rioting as we saw in the UK in 2011. Those riots did take place during a Mars-Uranus-Pluto square. We only need to look at history and at recent developments in US states as a guide. When governments run out of cash, they can resort to scrip—paper that serves as an IOU. Some areas will adopt sane market solutions; that is, they will balance budgets and drop unnecessary programs and projects. Other areas will look to the federal government to bail them out. This difference in opinion and course of action will likely be the great divide in 2013.

We can use the degrees of the Uranus-Pluto squares to pinpoint the countries where the stress or crisis is likely to manifest first. The first Uranus-Pluto square of 2013 (May 20) is at 11 degrees of the cardinal signs Capricorn and Aries, which directly ties into the horoscope of Japan. Look for Japanese markets to be rocked during the spring.

The square will take place about 2 degrees short of forming a t-square with the United States' natal Sun in Cancer. I predict that a financial crisis will force US leadership to alter its course, and extreme measures will be adopted. Pluto was in Capricorn 1516–1532 and 1762–1778, and will be there again 2008–2024. During the 1762–1778 period, the colonies struggled to free themselves from the rule of the British crown. During the current transit, the American people will resist efforts to force upon them beliefs and institutions that are unsuited to their spirit. In the 1770s, the people fought the English king; now they form the Tea Party to resist unwanted political efforts and policy changes.

Here Comes International Big MAC

When Pluto moved over New York City's Jupiter in the 1970s, there was a budget crisis. The Municipal Assistance Corporation, or Big MAC, was established to take control of the city's budget. I expect the same solution to be proposed for the US by the international community.

Pluto now opposes the Cancer planets in the United States' chart. This implies that a solution will be imposed on the country from outside of its borders. Already in 2011, the Russian and Chinese leaders stated that the US debt is a problem for the world economy. Most of the political leaders in the world are not in agreement with the American way of life. Other countries favor increased government role in social issues like health care, retirement, and welfare systems. For the last several years, many Americans have opposed increasing government control that is steering the country in that direction. It is likely that internationalists will establish an international Big MAC to manage US debt. And whenever a bank moves in to manage a debt-laden company, that new bank sets the rules and guidelines. The same is likely to occur in the US by 2015, with a new organization making rules for the American economy.

Hades at 0 Cancer

The Uranian planet Hades moves at a slow rate of about 1 degree annually. Thus, it requires about 360 years to complete one transit of the zodiac. Hades represents the lower part of the human nature, the lower self. This is the least-educated part of the human soul. It is the most distant from the light, and therefore the least able to understand or obey the laws of the universe. In a mundane sense, Hades symbolizes want, poverty, lack, and general deprivation. Hades brings deterioration.

In 2009, I looked back at previous transits of this hypothetical body over 0 degrees Cancer. In the early 1300s, there was excessive rain in Europe, and crops rotted in the fields. Food prices rose, living conditions fell, and people rioted against their governments. This particularly strong Hades transit led to the Black Plague and the Mongol invasion. In the 1600s, food prices again rose and living standards fell. Governments were too large and too expensive, and again, people rebelled. Conditions were so severe that even the normally calm folks in Switzerland rebelled during the Peasant's Revolt of 1653.

Since Hades first reached 0 Cancer in 2011, we have seen rising food prices. Weather has been a bit more unpredictable than usual. Human behavior is returning to a more base mode; that is, the slow economy has caused people to focus more upon base needs like food and shelter. It also, unfortunately, lowers the morals of society. People are less prone to hide the lower part of their nature during this transit, and they are less ashamed. This results in incidents such as the London and Illinois riots of 2011. Hades impels people to simply take what they want or to act out any whim. The misuse of the Internet to solicit sex and sexting scandals are also signs of Hades' transit. Look for general lack and deterioation due to financial disruptions. This transit reinforces the effect of the Jupiter-Saturn opposition square to Hades.

China in 2013

There have been concerns that the Chinese economy would slow down and perhaps crash. Many observers see China as being the engine of world growth. The current chart for the People's Republic of China (set for October 1, 1949) has a grouping of planets in Libra, so the exit of Saturn from this sign in late 2012 is a relief. The chart of the original republic (set for January 1, 1912) has the Sun in Capricorn, so this chart is also benefiting from Saturn's move. Neither chart is very afflicted in 2013. The November Uranus-Pluto square comes very close to the Suns of both charts, but the aspect is now separating. Thus, there may be some rumbling of debt problems in November this year, but it does not appear that this red dragon will be the center of a crisis.

Commodities in 2013

I have conducted the same study on commodities as was conducted on business activity. An index that extends back to 1250 was used. The strongest cycles are: Saturn-Neptune, Pluto-Node, Jupiter through Signs, Saturn through Signs, Jupiter-Neptune, and Jupiter-Node.

I won't go into the level of detail I did for the business activity cycles, but the sum of these cycles also points downward in 2013. A decline in commodities will be beneficial to some and a bane to others. Commodity prices are costs to many producers, so a decline could lead to lower prices for many consumers, which may revive retail sales to some degree.

On the other hand, many commodity-producing countries have borrowed with the expectation of earning higher prices for their goods. For example, the Gulf states have borrowed excessively in the recent past, so despite the high price of oil, they continue to carry significant debt. A drop in commodity prices will likely leave these states in a difficult situation. The banks that loaned money to them will be under new stress as another bubble bursts, so watch out for banking busts.

The Bottom Line

The composite cycle of business activity hit a high in 2007–2008 and then fell into 2011. After that point, many cycles are cancelling each other out. That is to say, when some cycles turn up, others turn down. The net result is a flat line and no or low growth. But take heart: the predictors show that business activity rises strongly in 2017 and 2018, as it did in 2007 and 2008. The above graph of business activity index according to astrological factors was first produced in 2001. Note the rise in activity

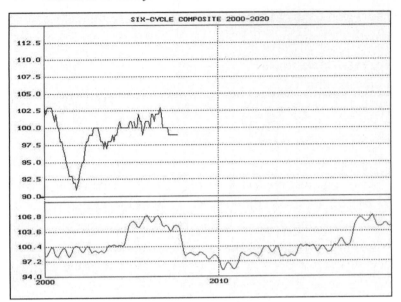

around 2005–2008, followed by the sharp decline. Note also the coming rise in the late 2010s.

This is another sign that there will be no strong recovery just yet. The crises that we are in now will likely terminate in 2015. The key is whether the American government will embrace free enterprise or move toward central planning.

About the Author

Bill Meridian began to study astrology in 1972 as he entered Wall Street. Bill began applying computers to financial astrology in 1983, eventually designing the AstroAnalyst. He contributed the efficiency test, first-trade charts, composite cycles, and other useful tools to the Market Trader program. Bill has authored three books. His Cycles Research service was ranked number one in stock and gold market timing by Timer Digest. He has written Dell Horoscope's mundane astrology column since 1990.

2012 © Alistair Cotton. Image from BigStockPhoto.com

New and Full Moon Forecasts

By Sally Cragin

For years I've presented astrology workshops that focus on the details of personal horoscopes, the advantages of understanding how Sun sign compatibilities operate, and the tension or harmony that plays out in people's personal charts. And I always talk about the phases of the Moon during these seminars. I try to schedule appearances at libraries or educational centers at a time when the Moon is increasing, so people are open to learning about new ideas.

Knowing what phase the Moon is in is a huge help in all aspects of your life. If you're in a job that's got high-pressure deadlines, see if people aren't more crazed around the Full Moon. If you're in the health care or education professions, make observations.

Are patients or students more frazzled around the time of the Full Moon? If you're in sales, look at your sales records and see if the New Moon is a time of low sales. No one wants to buy anything when the Moon is waning—but it's a fine time to look for bargains.

Yes, even in an era of incandescent, LED, and other nighttime illumination, what's going on with Luna hanging out in the night sky makes a difference in our lives. We're just less in tune with the Moon because our world has changed. Not long ago, we lived in a world where we had to make our own illumination at night, either by lighting candles or an oil lamp. Nowadays, the click of a switch gets you lumens aplenty.

We have actually created fake "Full Moon" conditions around the clock. I don't think this is necessarily healthy, especially for people who live in cities and may not have total darkness in the room where they sleep. Remember, our species is only six or so generations separated from the invention of Thomas Edison's lightbulb. That's not much time for the brain and eyes to develop coping mechanism for living in a fully lit world.

The result is that the idea of the "work week" is completely mixed up. We live in a world of 24/7 information—we have in our cellphones as much technology (or more) than NASA had to get all those rockets to the Moon and back. Sure, we're more efficient—watch my PC spit out pages of manuscript it would have taken me hours to type on my beloved, now-disused IBM Selectric. But is this progress healthy?

I leave it to you, reader, to decide. But here is some lunar information and New and Full Moon forecasts to help you plan your life and career over the next twelve months. It is this point in the conversation that my astrology students or clients usually cock their heads like little birds, as if to say, "What does that mean?"

To start, take a field trip. Go outside at night. Look at the Moon. Observe its shape. How can you tell if it's waxing (getting larger) or waning (getting smaller)? Look for the shadow of the Earth on the Moon. The shadow will be on the left if the Moon is waxing. It's on the right if the Moon is waning.

The Moon goes from new to second quarter to full to fourth quarter to new again in about 29.5 days. Thus we call the quarter Moon the "quarter" not for its shape (since half the Moon is visible, not just a quarter of it), but for the length of the phase. Each of those lunar phases takes about a week—plenty of time to launch a project or relationship or to wind something down. When you see these phases represented on a calendar, usually the New Moon is represented by a black circle, and the Full Moon is show as a circle outline. If you want to get more precise, here are some increasing terms: New Moon, first quarter, waxing crescent, second quarter, gibbous Moon, and Full Moon. The waning (decreasing) phases are this: Full Moon, third quarter, fourth quarter, Balsamic, waning crescent, dark of the Moon (the day before the New Moon), and New Moon.

Full and New Moon FAQ

Over the years that I've spoken to many, many clients, I've heard lots of questions about how to "understand" the lunar phases. People ask, "What should I do now?" and "Is this a good time to take action?" I decided to collect some of these FAQs for you!

Why are the phases important?

Follow the folklore. Every culture has mythology about the Moon, usually based on agricultural principles. Farmers plant when the Moon is just past new, in the waxing phase. They cull plantings, weed, or harvest when the Moon is waning. Fishermen find the fish tend to bite more when the Moon is waxing and close to the Full Moon than when the Moon is waning.

I advise clients to start projects during the waxing phase, and end projects during the waning phase. The quarter Moons can represent a turning point (for projects, relationships, plans, events, and so on). During the quarter Moon period, you might be able to look backward and forward with equal wisdom and insight and thus make decisions more easily. If you are like some folks I know (most often Libra, Gemini, Pisces, and Cancer Sun signs), you may waffle over decisions. If you're chronically indecisive, think about using the Moon phases to your advantage.

I feel kind of crazy—is it a Full Moon?

It could be. However, my experience with female clients is that anxiety and depressive tendencies can be linked to a wide variety of stimuli, including health in general and menstrual cycles (if applicable) as well as lunar cycles. If you feel like you don't know what to do next or what move to make, do some analysis of the phase of the Moon. Yes, the Full Moon is associated with literal *lunacy* and *lunatic* behavior or emotions. However, I've found that the fourth quarter Moon, the days that follow, and the day before the New Moon can be the most challenging, personally. If I talk to clients at that point, chances are they're willing to spill the beans on their problems—and shake the jar to make sure no beans remain!

I feel kind of sad—how does the Moon affect this?

Some people get overwhelmed if there is too much going on (hustle and bustle, raised voices, and busyness that can come during the Full Moon). Others may find themselves aimless and vulnerable to thoughts of unworthiness, ambivalence, and other hallmarks of depression during the Full Moon. First, ask yourself if you're overtired, hungry, lonely, or angry about something you can't change. Then, if the Moon is waning, tell yourself this is a resting period and you shouldn't be making decisions or feeling like you have to make big changes in your life. That waning period is about summing things up—seeing what your options are—but it's not necessarily about taking action, unless the action is about wrapping up something.

Some people find the time of the Full Moon most uncomfortable; for others it's the New Moon. What I've found is that if my client was born around the time of the New Moon, they're really on edge during the Full Moon. Conversely, if they were born around the time of the Full Moon, they're happiest when there's a lot going on, or they have a job where they have to manage crises constantly. It's the time of the New Moon that makes my Full Moon–born clients nervous and stirred up.

I have a business and I am not getting many customers (or clients). Is there a good time for me to expand my business?

Absolutely! Keep it simple for yourself. If you are having an open house for clients or prospective customers, try to schedule it in the seond quarter Moon or Full Moon phase. Sometimes even a day or so after the Full Moon is a "flat" time—people don't feel the same urgency. However, if you have a business where you are the person doing the purchasing or getting the stock, the best time to buy will be during the waning Moon. Ask for discounts anytime from the fourth quarter Moon onward. It can't hurt to ask, and some vendors may feel that they may as well get rid of goods at that time.

I don't know anything about my chart except my Sun sign. Does it matter about the New and Full Moon?

Yes, because there are times when the sign and phase the Moon is in will definitely influence you through your Sun sign. Here are examples for all twelve natal Sun signs.

If you are an **Aries**, the New Moon in Aries is a time of great beginnings. The Full Moon in Aries could find you wanting to take some real chances, or you may need to show courage. Difficult lunar phases for you will be New and Full Moons in Cancer and Capricorn. When the Moon is new in Libra, you could feel squeezed or overwhelmed. When it's full in Libra, you could be impulsive—to your own detriment. Easy does it during those phases.

If you are a **Taurus**, the New Moon in Taurus is a time of reassessing your financial situation. The Full Moon in Taurus is excellent for improving your home, enjoying music, or being the center of attraction. Difficult lunar phases for you will be New and Full Moons in Leo and Aquarius. When the Moon is new in Scorpio, you may be fussy and difficult to please. When it's full in Scorpio, you could gossip to the wrong person or lash out (or have others perceive you're lashing out).

If you are a **Gemini**, the New Moon in Gemini is a time of starting communication or learning how to talk to someone differently. The Full Moon in Gemini makes you the star—the center of attention. Your opinion is sought out and you could be giddy with popularity. However, make time for yourself! Difficult lunar phases for you will be New and Full Moons in Virgo and Pisces. When the Moon is new in Sagittarius, you could be accident-prone. When it's full in Sagittarius, you could be careless or impulsive about important items.

If you are a **Cancer**, the New Moon in Cancer is a time of renewing commitment and making sure you're emotionally sus-

2012 © Yuri Arcurs. Image from BigStockPhoto.com

tained. The Full Moon in Cancer makes you super-sensitive, even psychic. Others are attracted to you because of your empathy, but be careful of letting the wrong people get too close—they could exhaust you. Difficult lunar phases for you will be New and Full Moons in Aries and Libra. When the Moon is new in Capricorn, you could be unintentionally cold to others. When it's full in Capricorn, you could be awkward or more blunt than you mean to be (and then wracked by guilt afterward).

If you are a **Leo**, the New Moon in Leo is a time of enjoying children and pleasures and finding new ways to relax. The Full Moon in Leo is excellent for gathering disparate groups of people together or finding something to celebrate. Difficult lunar phases for you will be New and Full Moons in Taurus and Scorpio. When the Moon is new in Aquarius, you could be frustrated if people aren't responsive to you. When it's full in Aquarius, you could commit to a project or event you have no real interest in.

If you are a **Virgo**, the New Moon in Virgo is a time of being very serious about your health and diet and exercise regimen. The Full Moon in Virgo is excellent for decluttering—you know you have hoarding tendencies! Difficult lunar phases for you will be New and Full Moons in Gemini and Sagittarius. When the Moon is new in Pisces, you will be impatient with others who are spacey or unreliable. When it's full in Pisces, you could be spacey or unreliable yourself.

If you are a **Libra**, the New Moon in Libra is a time of having new judgment on a person, event, project, or institution. This is helpful for indecisive Libra. The Full Moon in Libra makes you dynamic and attractive to others. Make more of an effort with grooming or clothing. Difficult lunar phases for you will be New and Full Moons in Cancer and Capricorn. When the Moon is new in Aries, you may feel lost (and irritable). When it's full in Aries, hold off on making decisions—you don't have all the information.

If you are a **Scorpio**, the New Moon in Scorpio is an amazing time of sensitivity and attractiveness. As the Moon diminishes, you may want to also diminish the hassles in your life. Be careful how you do this, as you may not be clearly communicating. The Full Moon in Scorpio is excellent for deepening relationships or delving further into education that makes you feel spiritually renewed. Difficult lunar phases for you will be New and Full Moons in Leo and Aquarius. When the Moon is new in Taurus, you could be impatient with those who lack imagination or a sense of adventure. When it's full in Taurus, you need to step back from the arena of responsibility for a little while.

If you are a **Sagittarius**, the New Moon in Sagittarius is excellent for taking your education seriously or reaching out to help a friend in need. The Full Moon in Sagittarius draws others to you—it's an "instant charisma" moment. Use this time wisely and spend it with people you're crazy about or who can help you in your career. Difficult lunar phases for you will be New and Full Moons in Virgo and Pisces. When the Moon is new in Gemini, you could be clumsy or bump into things. When it's full in Gemini, hold off on impulse purchases or journeys. Wait a moment and get more information.

If you are a **Capricorn**, the New Moon in Capricorn is a time of potential workaholism (that gives you oh-so-much pleasure!). The Full Moon in Capricorn gives you a boost of energy and enthusiasm. Others may wonder if you're taking special vitamins! Difficult lunar phases for you will be New and Full Moons in Aries and Libra. When the Moon is new in Cancer, you could be emotional without realizing you're feeling sensitive. When it's full in Cancer, you will not be seeing everything in front of you. Hold off big decisions, and don't be swayed by others' emotional outbursts.

If you are an **Aquarius**, the New Moon in Aquarius is a time of creativity and excitement, mind-expanding experiences, and adventures. The Full Moon in Aquarius is similar, times ten! This is a time when you could use your imagination in new ways or come up with brilliant new schemes. Difficult lunar phases for you will be New and Full Moons in Taurus and Scorpio. When the Moon is new in Leo, you could be surprised if others around you are passionate and wonder why you're not. When it's full in Leo, your judgment is mildly impaired. That would be a great time for a party—just make sure you have a ride home.

If you are a **Pisces**, the New Moon in Pisces is a time of intense spiritual searching. The Full Moon in Pisces is another excellent time for getting in touch with your sensitive side and also for standing up for those who can't stand up for themselves. Difficult lunar phases for you will be New and Full Moons in Gemini and Sagittarius. When the Moon is new in Virgo, you will be easily vexed if others want information from you that seems trivial or not pertinent. When it's full in Virgo, you should hold back on purchases and other major life decisions.

New and Full Moon Phases

Friday, January 11, New Moon in Capricorn

Happy New Year! The Moon, Mars, and Jupiter are making a grand trine in earth signs, which means today is excellent for long-term investment strategy. This is also a useful time for those in the building/contracting fields. Productive for Taurus, Virgo, Capricorn, Pisces, and Scorpio. Agitating for Libra, Cancer, and Aries. A neutral time for Gemini, Sagittarius, Leo, and Aquarius.

Saturday, January 26, Full Moon in Leo

The Winter Moon is an excellent night for a party or for getting in touch with your childish side. This is also good for sales; if you're a Taurus, Scorpio, or Aquarius, you could get talked into a purchase you really don't want. But if you're a Leo, Sagittarius, Aries, Libra, or Gemini, you'll be persuasive and winning. Capricorn,

Cancer, Virgo, and Pisces are on the fence and could be persuaded either way.

Sunday, February 10, New Moon in Aquarius

It's an excellent day for enjoying fantasy novels or science fiction. Today is also good for talking to large groups of people or dealing with electricity (is it time to get more environmentally friendly energy conservation lights?). Aquarius, Libra, Gemini, Aries, and Sagittarius could be humorous and good company, but Taurus, Leo, and Scorpio could be irritable, especially with others who change their mind or lack follow-through. Pisces, Virgo, Cancer, and Capricorn could go in either direction.

Monday, February 25, Full Moon in Virgo

This is the Trapper's Moon; are you the hunter or the quarry? The prey or the predator? Now Mars and the Moon are in lockstep, and those born under Virgo, Capricorn, Taurus, and (to a lesser extent) Cancer and Scorpio are in a take-no-prisoners mode. Not enjoyable for their friends, since these signs will be uncharacteristically intense. It's an awkward time for Gemini, Sagittarius, and Pisces (although Mercury favors Pisces, who could turn their woes into a song or poem). Aquarius, Leo, Libra, and Aries could take action in ways that surprise themselves.

Wednesday, March 11, New Moon in Pisces

It's a fine day for meetings or figuring out how to reach a larger audience, whatever that means for your career or business. Again, the Moon and Mars are at odds, so Gemini and Sagittarius could be feeling squeezed or have miscommunication issues. Photography is also favored, as is buying shoes. However, some tasks will take longer than anticipated. Virgo could be fussy. Pisces, Scorpio, Cancer, Capricorn, and Taurus will be crazily insightful. Leo, Aquarius, Libra, and Aries could experience low energy.

Wednesday, March 27, Full Moon in Libra

This is the Egg Moon, but with Mercury still retrograde, it might be the *scrambled egg* Moon, as messages are likely to be garbled. This is a good time for having creative discussions with partners or for seeing both sides of an issue. Some folks (Aries, Cancer, and Capricorn) could be needy in a way that surprises themselves. However, harmony should prevail for Libra, Aquarius, Gemini, Leo, and Sagittarius. Scorpio, Taurus, Virgo, and Pisces could be looking for direction from others rather than from themselves.

Wednesday, April 10, New Moon in Aries

New friends, new hats, new items for the barbecue—all these bring great joy. This New Moon is excellent for getting that fresh start and keeping some momentum going. Gemini, Sagittarius, Aries, Leo, and Aquarius are at their best, socializing gracefully and thinking strategically. Capricorn, Cancer, and Libra could feel energized, but in a diffuse way (as in, you want someone else to provide direction). Virgo, Pisces, Taurus, and Scorpio are open to different influences, and they could have temporary attention-deficit disorder.

Thursday, April 25, Full Moon in Scorpio

We had the Egg Moon last month and now we have the Milk Moon. The Moon and Jupiter are at odds, so don't count on the generosity of others (especially if you've been dependent). It's an excellent day for getting to the root of a problem or for getting the garden ready by turning over the soil, if you're in a warm climate. Some folks (Taurus, Leo, and Aquarius) could be sharper-tongued than usual. Others (Scorpio, Pisces, and Cancer) could be feeling sensitive to the point of vulnerability. A fine day for therapy, Libra, Aries, Sagittarius, and Gemini could be insightful yet mush-mouthed.

Thursday, May 9, New Moon in Taurus

Shopping, buying high-end merchandise, and other material investments are a good idea today. So is gardening; take a chance and consider planting a new flower or herb. Tenacity is also a theme, particularly for Taurus, Virgo, Capricorn, Pisces, and Cancer. Those signs have incredible follow-through, so if you want something done, knock on their door. Scorpio, Leo, and Aquarius should hold off on taking action, as they don't have all the information. Gemini, Sagittarius, Aries, and Libra will add zing to all social occasions.

Saturday, May 25, Full Moon in Sagittarius

This Full Moon brings out the travel bug. How long has it been since you've really gotten away? Planning a day trip or a longer voyage feels great for Sagittarius, Aquarius, Libra, and Leo. Absent-mindedness could be a theme for Virgo, Pisces, and Gemini. But the bottom line for all is to keep moving and stay interested in countries and cultures outside of your own. It's also a good time for humor, and Virgo, Pisces, Taurus, and Scorpio might need some lightening up.

Saturday, June 8, New Moon in Gemini

Fresh starts beckon, particularly if you enjoy writing. This New Moon is good for getting together with peers or siblings, and for buying a car. Some signs (Virgo, Pisces, and Sagittarius) will feel frazzled and will lack follow-through. Gemini, Libra, Aquarius,

2012 © Andy Dean. Image from BigStockPhoto.com

Aries, and Leo need to do something new, as the old will not suit. Cancer, Capricorn, Taurus, and Scorpio could say too much (yes, even circumspect Scorpio) and regret their comments later.

Sunday, June 23, Full Moon in Capricorn

The Honey Moon brings excellent ingredients for a sea-change. Jupiter has moved into Gemini, which increases our consumer need for communication technology. This Full Moon brings us back to basics: what do you have, what are you using, and can you be more careful in your actions? It's not a good time for getting people to see both sides of a situation, but Taurus, Virgo, Capricorn, Pisces, and Scorpio could be insightful. Cancer, Aries, and Libra may lack long-term planning and should hold off on decisions. Gemini, Sagittarius, Aquarius, and Leo could be more conservative than usual.

Monday, July 8, New Moon in Cancer

Emotions and presumptions are bubbling over. Look for evidence before you think someone is feeling a certain way. However, some signs (Scorpio, Cancer, Pisces, Virgo, and Taurus) are highly perceptive and sensitive now. This is a fine time to start enjoying your home again; do you have a place where you can relax? Clear the clutter! Capricorn, Aries, and Libra will be off-balance, but only temporarily (don't let others stir you up).

Monday, July 22, Full Moon in Aquarius

Friendships erupt between unlikely folks during this Full Moon, which makes a dynamic grand trine in the three air signs. This makes for stability and speed when it comes to communication. Aquarius, Gemini, Libra, Aries, and Sagittarius are communication wizards right now. However, Taurus, Leo, and Scorpio could be overwhelmed by too much information and not enough precision. Virgo, Pisces, Taurus, and Scorpio could be overextended.

Tuesday, August 6, New Moon in Leo

Childish concerns, festivities, and questions of rulership dominate this New Moon. It's a fine day for getting a new perspective on sales or marketing (and yes, you can count yourself as something to be marketed). Leo, Sagittarius, Aries, Libra, and Gemini could be brave in social situations. Taurus, Scorpio, and Aquarius may have a hard time being firm or getting others to see what they want. Virgo, Pisces, Cancer, and Capricorn could turn even a difficult encounter into a party.

Tuesday, August 20, Full Moon in Aquarius

Disruption is probably a good thing in the long run, and this Dog Days Moon makes everyone want to howl, particularly Taurus, Leo, and Scorpio. Fantasy fiction, movies, and the idea of escape is compelling—as is fooling around with electronics. Those in the groove include Aquarius, Gemini, Sagittarius, Libra, and Aries. Cancer, Capricorn, Pisces, and Virgo need to suspend any tendency toward repetition or routine. It's time to improvise!

Thursday, September 5, New Moon in Virgo

This New Moon is an excellent time for being meticulous or taking a second look at some fine print. Taking the initiative won't be comfortable, unless you're a Virgo, Taurus, Capricorn, Cancer, Scorpio. These folks will have excellent judgment for evaluating costs or materials. Pisces, Sagittarius, and Gemini: be wary of snap judgments. Crucial information may be missing, so your evaluation will be insufficient, though it's no fault of your own. Libra, Aries, Gemini, and Sagittarius could be impatient if others move slowly.

Thursday, September 19, Full Moon in Pisces

Take a closer look at spiritual matters. This could mean an established religion or freewheeling, do-it-yourself spirituality. It's a super day for photographers, filmmakers, getting a pedicure or buying shoes, or dealing with people who are incarcerated or in protected conditions. Pisces, Cancer, Scorpio, Taurus, and Capricorn get in touch with their quirky or empathetic side. Virgo, Sagittarius, and Gemini could procrastinate, no matter how efficient they think they are. Interruptions could bedevil Libra, Aries, Gemini, and Sagittarius.

Friday, October 4, New Moon in Libra

Activities with a partner are more successful than solitary forays during this New Moon. It's a fine day for bookkeeping and exercising your judgment. As this is the final week of Saturn's visit to Libra, a celebration about the end of long and difficult lessons is better than solo revelry. If you're in a mood to shop, don't hesitate. Taurus, Libra, Aquarius, Gemini, Sagittarius, and Leo may be most prone to consumerism. Aries, Cancer, and Capricorn may be touchy and should be on the move, versus stuck in one place.

Friday, October 18, Full Moon in Aries

Work on projects that can be finished quickly. How quickly? Like, *yesterday* quickly. It's a fine day for eating spicy foods or cooking on a barbeque. Even better, move that business meeting or get-together to the local home-cooking establishment. Relationships could be fraught for Cancer, Capricorn, and Libra—these folks may feel attacked if too many questions are asked. Aries, Leo, Sagittarius, Aquarius, and Gemini, on the other hand, will be energized and imaginative.

Sunday, November 3, New Moon in Scorpio

Scorpio makes for a provocative New Moon, and it's time to hear secrets or have unexpected sensual experiences. These Moons can be erotic or sensual to an unexpected degree. Interpret this as you will! Those who can go with the flow and convince others to join them: Scorpio, Cancer, Pisces, Virgo, Capricorn, and Sagittarius (who have Mars on their side). Libra, Aries, Gemini, Leo, Aquarius, and Taurus may play hard to get.

Sunday, November 17, Full Moon in Gemini

Folks will be chatty and open-minded during the Gemini Full Moon. This is a good day for sending a lot of messages or completing short errands. If you need to stop a habit (and talk about it) the aspects are good for all, particularly Gemini, Libra, Aquarius, Leo, and Aries. Taurus, Scorpio, Cancer, and Capricorn could be wary of the impulsive folks they know. Sagittarius, Virgo, and Pisces could be antsy and may need to "withdraw from the fray." (But will they? Not likely—they have too many people-pleasing urges after all.)

Monday, December 2, New Moon in Sagittarius

The Sun and Moon are in harmony for our last New Moon of the year. Plan a trip or purchase items that enable a really scary or adrenaline-inducing sport (half of the fun of which is, of course, scaring others when you tell them what you've done). Sagittarius, Leo, Aries, Libra, and Aquarius should trust their instincts. Gemini, Virgo, and Pisces should trust someone else's instincts! Taurus, Scorpio, Cancer, and Capricorn could be done in by impulsiveness.

2012 © Melinda Nagy. Image from BigStockPhoto.com

Tuesday, December 17, Full Moon in Cancer

This is the Long Night Moon. What a very interesting collection of stellar activity. Everyone should take time to enjoy the silence, stillness, and beauty of the night sky. Today is excellent for shopping for consumables, but it's even better for giving thanks that we now will have longer days with more light in the coming spring. It could be a day of social missteps for Aries, Libra, and Capricorn, who might act without having all the information. Cancer, Scorpio, Pisces, Virgo, and Taurus have insights into others during this time.

About the Author
Sally Cragin is a teacher and the author of Astrology on the Cusp *for people whose birthdays are at the end of one Sun sign or the beginning of the next. Her first book is* The Astrological Elements, *and both are published through Llewellyn Worldwide. She has written the astrological forecast "Moon Signs" for the* Boston Phoenix, *syndicated throughout New England. She also provides forecasts for clients, which are "cool, useful, and accurate." More at moonsigns. net.*

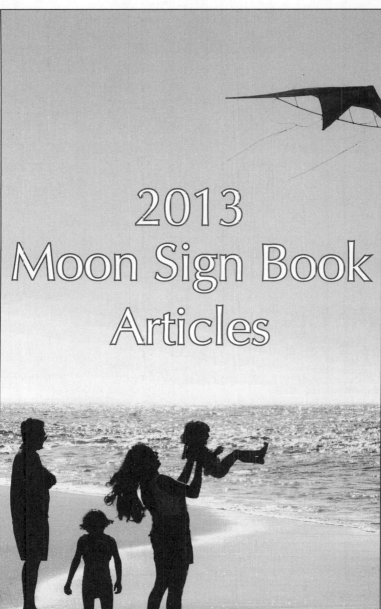

2013
Moon Sign Book
Articles

The History of the Moon

By Bruce Scofield

Our Moon is really something else. Think about it: It's huge, and it just keeps changing its shape—or at least the portion we can see is constantly changing shape. When it is full, you can watch the Moon rise in the east just as the Sun sets in the west. It appears big at that time, and we can see some of its features—craters and smooth areas, all in shades of gray. Over the course of the month, the Moon undergoes changes in rising time and in the amount of surface illuminated. Sometimes when it is full and positioned just right, the Moon moves into the shadow of Earth and becomes copper-colored. The Moon pulls the waters of Earth and causes the tides. Many marine animals live their lives in synch with the Moon, and many terrestrial animals use its movements as signals for breeding or migrating events. Without a doubt, the Moon has a more intimate relationship with Earth than any other solar system body, aside from the Sun.

For most of humanity's time on Earth, the Moon has been a timekeeper and a source of light at night. Calendars, including those of the Ancient Near East, have been based on its cycles. It has been seen as the embodiment of feminine mysteries, volatile emotions, and wide mood swings, all of which still have a place in the astrological interpretation of the Moon. Some Greeks and Romans thought the Moon was inhabited, and that the darker areas were great seas (the mares). In 1634 Johannes Kepler, astrologer and mathematician, wrote a short story called "Somnium" ("The Dream"), considered the very first science fiction novel! The story featured a trip to the Moon where the traveler encounters a strange collection of living things.

Just a few years later, with the help of the newly invented telescope, Galileo began the modern scientific project of discovering what the Moon really is. In this venture, instrumentation has made all the difference. With telescopes, computers, space flight, and actual rock samples taken from the Moon, we now have a new and mostly verifiable story about the Moon and how it got there.

The solar system was formed out of a massive dust cloud that was sent spinning by a disturbance thanks to a nearby exploding star. Over time, most of the dust aggregated toward the center of the cloud, and when this dust became extremely dense, nuclear fusion was triggered—and thus the Sun was born. The remaining dust congealed into small globs, which then formed larger and larger globs, until planet-sized bodies were formed. Gradually, these planets settled into their orbits, the denser ones—Mercury, Venus, Earth, and Mars—near to the Sun and the lighter bodies farther out. These big planets are the gas giants—Jupiter, Saturn, Uranus and Neptune. Smaller bodies were "captured" by the gravitational pull of larger bodies and became satellites, or moons. Our Moon is very large relative to its planet, and it is the fifth largest in the entire solar system with a diameter one-quarter that of Earth's. The moons of Jupiter and Saturn have masses less than one-thousandth of their planets, while the Moon's mass is closer to one-hundredth of the Earth. The Moon is also unusual in that its orbit is tilted relative to the Earth's orbit around the Sun.

Two hundred years ago, some scientists thought the Moon was formed at the same time of the Earth and the two formed a double planet system, this being called the "common condensation theory." Another later idea was that the Moon was spun off the Earth as it was formed when both were still molten. This is called the "fission theory." During the early twentieth century, another theory was proposed: that the Moon was a small planet orbiting at the same distance from the Sun as Earth. When the orbits of the two coincided, the smaller Moon was "captured" by Earth. However, this scenario presents some problems, as the Moon would have had to slow down considerably to be captured, possibly requiring a third celestial body or a very dense Earth atmosphere.

When NASA astronauts landed on the Moon in the late 1960s and early 1970s, they took detailed measurements, photos, and samples of Moon rock. Analysis found that the Moon was composed of the same materials and in similar proportion as those of the Earth's crust, except the Moon was found to be low in iron. This ruled out the common condensation theory, which would suggest a very different composition for the two bodies. The lack of a large iron core also rules out the fission theory, because a dividing planet would most likely share a similar proportion of materials, both dense and light.

It was then that a new theory of the Moon's formation was proposed. In the "big splat" theory, another planet crashed into the Earth and knocked crustal materials into orbit. These materials eventually consolidated to form the Moon. This event—thought to have occurred about 4.5 billion years ago and just 30–50 million years after the formation of the solar system—would explain why the Earth has a dense core and the Moon doesn't. It also explains why the Earth is tilted by 23.5 degrees, a factor that produces climatic and seasonal differences. This theory is still being tested, though at present it is accepted by a majority of scientists and has made its way into astronomy textbooks.

After the impact of this third celestial body, both Earth and Moon were essentially masses of molten rock. A crust was soon formed on the Moon, and for the next 600 million years—what lunar geologists call the Pre-Nectarian period—cooling continued. This period began about 4.55 billion years ago and ended with the Nectaris impact on the Moon, around 3.9 billion years ago.

Along with mountains and mares, such impact craters are major features on the Moon. Galileo was the first to use the word *crater* to describe these features—*crater* means "cup" in Latin. A steady bombardment of space debris of all sizes bombarded Earth and Moon for the first 500 million years of their existence. The Earth once had many craters, but these were worn down by wind and water long ago, though a few recent impacts remain, such as the Meteor Crater in Arizona. Craters of all sizes cover the Moon, and each will last for billions of years, as the erosional processes on the Moon are very slow. Between 4.1 and 3.8 billion years ago was a period called the Late Heavy Bombardment, a last blast of space debris. The surface of the Moon records this event, though evidence of it on Earth is scant. On the Moon, the Late Heavy Bombardment occurred toward the end of the Pre-Nectarian and during the Nectarian periods—what geologist call the Hadean period (4.5 to 3.8 billion years ago) on Earth.

The interior of the Moon was molten rock at first, melted by radioactivity. Debris that was left over after the Moon consolidated then began to bombard it, creating craters. Large objects hit the surface so hard that molten rock from the interior oozed up and coated portions of the lunar surface. These areas of molten basalt flooding are called maria (MAR-ee-a), the regions once thought to have been seas. These events all occurred during the Moon's first half-billion years, and by the end of this period, the Moon was cooling down and most of the debris had been absorbed. This decline of bombardment allowed the maria to remain relatively unmarred.

The Nectarian period (roughly 3.9 to 3.8 billion years ago) began with the Nectaris impact and ended with the formation of the Imbrium impact basin on the Moon. Apollo 16 was sent to investigate the geology of this particular impact basin. The Imbrian period then begins with the Imbrian impact and ends with the Orientale impact around 3.2 billion years ago, about the time when most of the early impact craters had been mostly worn down by later impacts and space weathering. During this period most of the basalt flooding that created the mares occurred. Next is the Eratosthian period, a long one, lasting from 3.2 to 1.1 billion years ago. This time is defined also by erosional processes. The most recent lunar period is the Copernican, from 1.1 billion years ago to the present. Rays extending out from certain craters, which are originally bright but fade over time, are used as the basis of this dating (though the impact crater Copernicus was not formed at the beginning of this period, as one might think).

Anyone with a small telescope or even binoculars can see craters on the Moon. These are classified according to a scheme that begins with ALC craters (defined by the crater Albategnius), which are less than 10 km in diameter and are cup-shaped, to TYC craters (defined by the crater Tycho), which are more than 50 km in diameter and have flat floors. The crater Tycho is a huge and easy to find crater on the southern hemisphere of the Moon. It is about 80 km in diameter and has distinct rays emanated from it that are still quite visible. This is a young crater, only about 108 million years old. Another easily seen crater is Copernicus, a bit

bigger than Tycho but about 800 million years old. It too has rays, but these are not as distinct as those radiating out from Tycho. Apollo 12 landed near one of these rays. The mare Imbrium (Latin for "Sea of Showers"), a huge impact basin that was flooded by lava and is used to date the Imbrium period, is just to the north of Copernicus. It is the second largest mare (the largest is Oceanus Procellarum) and its diameter is 1,146 km. It is surrounded by a ring of mountains, created by the original impact, that rise 7 km above the basin.

After the formation of the solar system and the Earth and Moon, the Moon orbited very close to Earth. Its appearance must have been striking, and its tidal effects probably made the early oceans move like water in a washing machine. The Earth rotated more rapidly then, a day lasting as little as five hours. Over time the Earth has slowed in rotation, and the Moon's orbit has receded at the rate of about 1 inch a year. The Moon and Earth became locked into synchronous rotation. The Moon's rotation now is exactly the same as its orbital period, so only one side faces the

Earth. The side that faces the Earth, the side we see, shows craters, but also extensive maria. The far side of the Moon, however, is almost completely pockmarked by craters with very little mare visible. This is due to the far side's exposure to deep space; the near side is protected to some extent by the much larger Earth. But even this state of affairs is not an absolute constant! A billion years from now, the rotation of the Earth and the Moon will become the same, making the Moon visible from only one half of the Earth. It's all part of the every-changing and ever-beautiful body we call the Moon.

Sources

NASA. "The Moon." http://nssdc.gsfc.nasa.gov/planetary/planets/moonpage.html

Arny, Thomas T. *Explorations: An Introduction to Astronomy*. Boston: McGraw-Hill/WCB, 1998.

Bakich, Michael E. *The Cambridge Planetary Handbook*. Cambridge, UK: Cambridge University Press, 2000.

Long, Kim. *The Moon Book*. Boulder, CO: Johnson Books, 1988.

About the Author

Bruce Scofield is a practicing astrologer who has maintained a private practice as an astrological consultant and conference speaker for over forty years. He is the author of seven books and hundreds of articles on astrology. He has served on the education committee of the National Council for Geocosmic Research since 1979 and was that organization's national education director between 1998 and 2003. He holds a master's degree in history and a Ph.D. in geosciences, and currently teaches at Kepler College and at the University of Massachusetts. Bruce Scofield and Barry Orr maintain a website, www.onereed.com, that contains articles and an online calculation program on Mesoamerican (Maya and Aztec) astrology.

Fourth House Natal Moon Sign and Your Ideal Home

By Amy Herring

The Moon in astrology represents your overall emotional needs and disposition, but its depth goes beyond simply what makes you happy or sad. The Moon represents the places in us that are soft and vulnerable, so its placement in your natal chart can reveal the kind of experiences and environments you require to feel safe and nurtured, to feel relaxed enough to be yourself and show that soft side.

The ultimate symbol of nurturing and shelter (besides good ol' mom herself) is the home. It's the place where we should be able to be our truest and most natural self, removed from all the fake smiles and social dances we all do to get along out there in the world. Your natal Moon can give insight into what your early home and childhood was like and the emotional tone of your family unit growing up. However, even if your childhood home wasn't the best fit, you can create an ideal home environment for yourself as an adult, and your Moon sign can provide valuable clues about what kind of home would be the most beneficial and nurturing for you.

In addition to the Moon and equal in relevance is the sign on the cusp of the fourth house in your natal chart, as well as any planets that fall inside the fourth house. The fourth house represents the "home and family" area of life, so the sign and planets in it can reveal much about the kind of environment you require to provide a personalized "home base" for yourself. Combining the meaning of your natal Moon with your fourth house sign can give you a more complete picture of how to create your perfect nest.

If your natal Moon is in **Aries**, or if your fourth house begins in Aries, you need room to move in your home, so a bit of a minimalist approach can be beneficial. Aries color schemes may incorporate warm reds and oranges, and bold bronze and black, although these colors may be best in accents rather than covering your entire home. Decorative elements and accessories such as wall hangings, lamps, or sculpture must convey a definitive and powerful statement, such as the ornate and rich style of certain Asian decorative elements or even a showcase of metal weaponry like antique shields and swords. Also look to the sign of your Natal Venus for further clues about what styles and colors appeal to you to bring into your home.

When sharing your home with roommates or family members, you tend to want to be the boss, or at least not be bossed around. You can get territorial with what's yours because you need freedom to do as you please, and sharing or checking in with others can feel limiting if excessive. Due to this need for freedom, you might prefer to rent to avoid being tied down in one place too long or having to deal with a constant stream of home repairs.

If your natal Moon is in **Taurus**, or if your fourth house begins
in Taurus, your home environment needs to feel homey and
casual. Overstuffed furniture and comfy blanket throws, with a
place to put your feet up are a must. While you may like things
to look nice, you aren't one for stuffiness or pretense, so the less
your home looks like a pristine museum and feels more inviting,
the better. If the rest of your chart supports the nature-loving part
of Taurus, you might especially like to bring nature into your
home, with plants and animal friends. You don't mind living with
two-legged friends and family, too, for the most part but while
you can be easy-going in many ways, you tend to like things the
way you like them. Therefore, people who bring too much chaos
into the home or personalities that lean more toward fussiness
might get to be too much to handle.

Taurus is an earth sign, so an earthy color palette that leans
toward the warm side is ideal. Also look to your Venus sign
for further clues about what styles and colors appeal to you to
bring into your home. Unless you have a lot of planets in the
mutable signs or houses, owning rather than renting may suit you
best, which will appeal to the Taurean desire for stability. Taurus
doesn't like a lot of hassle, so even if you rent, you may be one
who likes to stay in a place for a long time rather than moving
frequently.

If your natal Moon is in **Gemini**, or if your fourth house begins
in Gemini, you will enjoy a lot of activity in your home and won't
typically mind the comings and goings of roommates or family
members. To you they provide opportunity for conversation and
keep things interesting. Frequent mental stimulation is a must, so
you'll need lots of room for gadgets of all kinds to avoid boredom.
You may be one to pile up clutter, so lots of surfaces and cup-
boards to store media can be helpful, although unless you have
lots of planets in earth signs, you might not mind things being in

disarray as long as you can find what you need. Each room can have a little of everything in it: the sewing machine behind the treadmill with a television in the corner next to your collection of miniatures? Why not?! As a Gemini Moon once said, "My home needs to feel like a Chinese-style buffet: a little of everything, available all at once, to be enjoyed at a moment's notice."

Your decorating style is likely to be eclectic, with anything that you find interesting or clever in its style or function. Also look to your Venus sign for further clues about what styles and colors appeal to you. A lightless den isn't your style; your home will need to feel breezy and open, not a place to hibernate in dull isolation. As Gemini is a mutable sign, you might end up moving frequently unless you have a lot of planets in fixed signs or houses, because Gemini can be restless and bored with staying in one place for too long. You might prefer renting to give you that flexibility. Even if you stay in one place for a while, frequent rearranging of furniture can keep things interesting.

If your natal Moon is in **Cancer**, or if your fourth house begins in Cancer, your home isn't just a place to sleep and eat, it's a haven. The richness and comfort of homemade items, antiques, and things passed down from previous generations support your sense of emotional well-being—especially if enjoyed while wrapped in a hand-crocheted afghan on the couch in front of the fireplace! You may enjoy decorating your home with personal touches and memorabilia that remind you of places and people you love. Cancer's color scheme is anything that feels warm and inviting, from rosy pink and gentle lavender to beautiful (but not icy) blues. Also look to your Venus sign for further clues about what styles and colors appeal to you. There should be a mood of abundance in your home, whether it's a well-stocked fridge or a cozy room filled to the brim with much-loved items.

If the rest of your chart supports a more social personality, your home needs to be a place in which you can enjoy entertaining friends and family in a comfortable way. Whether you are married or single, with or without children, there is a nurturing side to you, so people, pets, and/or plants can provide a sense of joy and cohesion in your home. However, you'll need at least one room or place in your home that is your own personal space so you can retreat into your shell when you need time to process and relax. Like your opposite sign, Capricorn, you may prefer to own over renting, which feels more secure and rooted.

If your natal Moon is in **Leo**, or if your fourth house begins in Leo, your home is your castle, as the saying goes. It should be a place that you are proud of and can enjoy showing off to others when "holding court." The overall décor should have a tone of opulence, with sophisticated and rich-looking pieces. Even if you're on a budget, indulgent little touches and grand accessories can make you feel like a king or queen, such as a richly covered chair or a large mirror with an elegant frame. Color schemes should be warm, bright colors, such as ginger orange or rich reds and dark yellows with gold accents, or even royal purples and blues. Also look to your Venus sign for further clues about what styles and colors appeal to you to bring into your home. The tone of your home should be one that makes you feel special and deserving, with a hint of the dramatic.

Unless the rest of your chart disagrees, you tend to enjoy living with others, as you can be quite a social creature (lions typically live with other lions, of course, which is appropriately called a pride). It's important, though, that you have a sense of authority in your own home, even if you are sharing it with others, because respect for you, your things, and your space is imperative.

If your natal Moon is in **Virgo**, or if your fourth house begins in Virgo, you might have heard that you are supposed to be a clean freak, scrubbing the baseboards with a toothbrush and any number of such clichés. But it's the sense of order that Virgo most appreciates in the home. Sufficient and intelligent storage solutions can provide this order and are a must in a Virgo home. Virgo's motto could be "less is more," so rooms packed with wall-to-wall furniture and clutter can overwhelm. Virgo's color scheme is the range of earthy colors, such as greens and browns, in subtle and understated but crisp tones. Virgos can also be fans of mono-chromatic color schemes, which provide variety but are still in harmony with each other. Also look to your Venus sign for clues about what styles and colors appeal to you. Your home should feel elegant but simple, so avoid crazy patterns or mismatched furniture.

When sharing your home with others, especially if it's your family with whom schedules might collide, you are likely to prefer a clear schedule so you know what to expect and can feel in control. Something like a central bulletin board can maintain sanity. You expect others to clean up after themselves and take responsibility for their share of the workload to keep the home running smoothly.

If your natal Moon is in **Libra**, or if your fourth house begins in Libra, you want to incorporate a sense of balance into your home's décor, whether it's literal (such as matching chairs with matching end tables and matching table lamps on each end of the room) or more of an overall feel of balance and furnishings that give the room a symmetrical feel. You may benefit from arranging your home with guidance from the art of feng shui, which concen-trates on keeping a positive energy flow through the home. Your color scheme can vary as long as it is pleasant and not chaotic or clashing. Too much color and "stuff" in your home can feel over-powering, although you may enjoy collecting knick-knacks and accessories that can accumulate. Also look to your Venus sign for clues about what styles and colors appeal to you.

In some ways, sharing your home with roommates or family is second nature to you because you know how to get along with others and generally treat people fairly and with consideration; however, if you don't receive the same from housemates, things can get tense. You don't deal well with interpersonal tension in the home and can get tired of dealing with all the niceties of the world, so at home you need a place where you don't have to jump through hoops and can relax and trust those around you.

If your natal Moon is in **Scorpio**, or if your fourth house begins in Scorpio, you may enjoy décor that is dramatic and edgy with bold, deep colors such as blues, purples, or reds, offset by high contrast blacks and/or whites. Lighting and decorative elements that make a striking statement will appeal to you. You may like a little bit of a den feeling; not necessarily lightless. but perhaps dramatic lighting that highlights certain areas and casts interesting shadows to add to the drama and intensity. Also look to your Venus sign for further clues about what styles and colors appeal to you to bring into your home.

When sharing space with roommates or family members, privacy is going to be the key in being able to co-exist. Unless the rest of your chart reveals other influences, you don't mind telling it like it is and don't pull punches, but that doesn't mean you yourself are an open book, nor do you like people getting into your business or your stuff.

If your natal Moon is in **Sagittarius**, or if your fourth house begins in Sagittarius, you may enjoy a little of everything decorating your home. Souvenirs of any kind, whether they've been given to you or collected first-hand, can make your home that much more special. A Sagittarian color scheme is nearly every color in the rainbow with multiple colorful patterns. You can use your knack for combining colors and patterns to create an eclectic but cohesive environment. Carved tribal statues, tapestries, images of sailboats, photos of hiking in a foreign land—these can all provide very real inspiration and joy. Also look to your Venus sign for further clues about what styles and colors appeal to you to bring into your home.

Unless the rest of your chart says otherwise, you usually like a lot going on in your home. Whether it's entertaining guests or interacting with family members, you prefer a lively environment. You likely have the most easy-going attitude of all the zodiac signs about what goes on in your home. Sagittarius is a mutable sign, often restless and on the go, so you may prefer to rent rather than own, and in extreme cases, you may find yourself comfortable with your home in your backpack as you explore the world!

If your natal Moon is in **Capricorn**, or if your fourth house begins in Capricorn, you may enjoy a more traditional theme in your décor, with earthy, muted tones that feel sophisticated and thoughtfully coordinated. Timeless pieces and the look that "never goes out of style" are a good fit. Also look to your Venus sign for further clues about what styles and colors appeal to you to bring into your home. Anything you bring in, whether it's a piece of furniture or pots and pans for the kitchen, should be well-made to last a long time, even if it's used, such as a restored antique. Although things like this can be more expensive upfront, you know that in the long run it will pay off with having to replace things less often. You do best to think of your home and everything in it as an investment, rather than just something for the moment. Because of this attitude, you may prefer to own your home rather than to rent, whether it's an old but well-maintained cottage or a stylish downtown condo, so your monthly payment builds toward something long-lasting rather than simply the monthly use of living space.

One of the symbols for Capricorn is the hermit, and while there are plenty of Capricorns that have families and roommates, you may feel that you are most "at home" when you are on your own. Unless you have a more socially oriented chart, you typically don't feel the pangs of loneliness as much as some pecple do; you enjoy your self-sufficiency and autonomy. If you do share your home with roommates or family, independence is still important for your emotional well-being, and you need to carve out your own time and space for the solitude you need.

If your natal Moon is in **Aquarius**, or if your fourth house begins in Aquarius, you like an eclectic atmosphere in your home. You enjoy unique and weird decorative finds that can be conversation starters. For the most part, your style is functional, sleek, and modern, such as the look of chrome fixtures or black and white tile instead of flowered prints on the linoleum and farm animal kitchen towels. You probably won't enjoy the overstuffed chair and the fringed lampshade as much as you will the streamlined entertainment center, flat-screen television, and modern but comfortable couch. You may prefer monochromatic color schemes and/or high-contrast black and white. Also look to your Venus sign for further clues about what styles and colors appeal to you to bring into your home.

While roommates may occasionally be bothersome, you are generally pretty independent and come and go as you please. You will probably find it draining to live with people who are more emotionally clingy. Aquarius is a fixed sign, so you tend to like things how you like them and may find it difficult to make changes when requested by housemates. Although you don't like to feel tied down, you may still prefer owning to renting, unless you can find a low-stress landlord who takes care of things promptly but is flexible and stays out of your hair.

If your natal Moon is in **Pisces**, or if your fourth house begins in Pisces, you are very sensitive to the emotional and spiritual fluctuation of energy in your home, so you need a calming and peaceful space, but that doesn't mean boring! You have a vivid imagination and have a love of things mystical and fantastical, which you may enjoy incorporating into your décor. Dreamy colors, such as aquamarine, deep blues, and purples might suit you. Also look to your Venus sign for further clues about what styles and colors appeal to you to bring into your home. Wall hangings and framed art can incorporate this as well, such as fantasy fairy art, scenes of far-off places, celestial imagery, or paintings of ocean creatures. Along with Libra, you may especially benefit from the practice of feng shui, which is an ancient system that can be used to arrange your home in such a way that allows positive energy to flow and avoid trapping negative energy.

You are very giving and usually do well with the day-to-day realities of sharing space with family or roommates, as long as appropriate boundaries are maintained so you don't end up feeling taken advantage of or outvoted too many times on home or family issues. You also need to be careful that you don't share space with volatile or high-strung people if you can help it, which will end up draining your energy and stressing you out, not replenishing you as a home should.

About the Author

A graduate of Steven Forrest's Evolutionary Astrology program, Amy has been a professional astrologer for 15 years. Her book, **Astrology of the Moon,** *covers the natal and progressed moon relationship in detail and is available from Llewellyn. Visit http://heavenlytruth.com for personal readings and astrology study resources.*

A Moon Cycle's Gardening Journal

By Clea Danaan

New

New Moon in Leo, Sun in Leo. There's a fiery energy in the air, a sense of charging forward into new projects. Seed packets for fall planting wait by the back door: spinach, carrots, and chard. Their bright illustrations call me to transform a hot, dry, summer garden plot into the sweetness of a fall garden. I can just about feel the fresh green of autumn spinach salads splashed with the orange of baby carrots. I need a little pick-me-up—and so does my garden. The high heat of late summer has me down. The barren, scorched soil sucks the life out of my tomatoes, beans, and corn. The possibility of a shift into fall gives me hope.

At the Dark Moon, I turned the soil and fertilized, preparing the darkness to receive seeds. The New Moon is a time to plant and the soil is ready, yet something holds me back. The intense, dry heat of August will fry my seeds. Plus, Moon in Leo is a barren time, despite the growth of light. But I am so anxious to plant, to start anew, to move forward! I feel like ignoring the Moon sign and the heat, but past failures urge me to wait.

Colorado's late summer is so hot and parched that I find fall crops to be only partially successful. My desire to transform the tired garden and my own tired mood makes me impatient. I curse the climate, the heat, my inadequacies as a gardener. I visited a nearby farm recently, where the summer crop grew abundantly. Patches of carefully planned autumn crops had begun to sprout as well. I feel both inspired and inadequate. I know fall crops are possible here, so what have I done wrong? What do I need to transform my barren garden?

My corn plants curl against the drought no matter how much I water them. I planted them in a huglekultur bed this year, a permaculture technique that involves burying rotting logs under soil or compost, then planting in the raised, decomposing bed. The logs trap moisture while their decomposition slightly raises the temperature of the soil. I hoped to transform my tired and unproductive beds into vibrant patches of happy vegetables with this approach. My corn seemed to be appreciating the setup until just recently. Then monsoon rains hit during July and soaked into the spaces between logs as well as into the allegedly rotting wood. The clay soil couldn't compact as it usually does. The corn got plenty of water and light, fluffy soil. Now, though, things have dried out. The rain isn't reaching up into Colorado, and the corn is thirsty. The beans next to them are stunted and unproductive. The tomatoes seem to be debating whether or not they feel like fruiting.

Last year at this time, I gave up completely. I tossed everything into the compost and moved my beds around. I don't want to give up again this year. I need to find the gardening fountain of youth. Perhaps the garden itself can give me a few tips.

Stepping out of my grumbling, thinking mind for a moment, I turn my inner attention to the garden and open a channel of deeper listening. In my mind's eye, I see holes dug into the corn's soil, and compost nestled around the bases of all my plants. I get a negative gut reaction when I think of planting those seeds waiting patiently at the back door.

For now, I spread compost on the plants and dig little watering holes under the corn. I become obsessed with making more compost, dreaming and praying that it will save the garden. One way to invite transformation into the garden is to focus on the epitome of transformation: compost. I cannot think of any other process in my life that dependably transforms waste into gold. Kitchen waste, chicken poop, grass clippings, cat hair, even dust from the vacuum cleaner bag—they all get dumped into a pile in my garden. This is sprinkled with cottonseed meal, a little soil, and some water. Then it cooks. The result is thick brown soil that revives a hot, tired garden practically overnight.

Making compost is something I can act on, whereas I cannot force weather to cool or clay to become fluffy. I read that small amounts of clay soil can be a helpful addition to the compost pile, as clay encourages the breakdown of organic material into soil. Ah-ha! I've always complained that my soil eats any amendment I give it. I was right. My clay soil is encouraging the breakdown of all the compost and manure and fertilizer I can give it. That is why I have to repeatedly add massive amounts of organic material. I mean ridiculous amounts. *Constantly.*

Now I am impatient for the compost pile to turn into the dark goodness that will save my dying plants. I'm not feeling the natural unfolding of the New Moon; I'm feeling the passionate go-for-it energy of Leo the lion. So I ignore some of my garden's advice and plant seeds. Rain is coming. Surely they will germinate.

Waxing

The last Waxing Moon brought a monsoon flow our way. Tropical moisture sometimes gets pushed up into Colorado, producing severe thunderstorms and an occasional tornado. The first two weeks of July brought a third of our annual rainfall (no tornadoes, fortunately). This Waxing Moon, the rain is back, but it keeps missing my garden. Dark clouds on the horizon, sharp bolts of lightning to the east, even rumbles of thunder—but no rain. I drag the hose around the yard.

Watering by hand offers me insight; I notice things I wouldn't otherwise see. Weeds, brown spots on the corn, extra shoots on the tomato plants, and marble-sized green tomatoes. Maybe the lack of rain is trying to transform me into a gardener who slows down and listens as I water each plant by hand. This Waxing Moon seems to be about allowing what is already there to unfold. I'm always so impatient for new projects, new plants, new growth, but maybe waxing energy isn't always about *more*. Sometimes transformation happens quietly, unseen, silent. While this hidden transformation can be powerful, it can be difficult to wait for.

The seeds I planted at the New Moon didn't germinate. The garden told me they wouldn't, that it wasn't time, despite what I wanted. I need to focus on the quieter, subtler transformations, like compost. Or perhaps on transforming my own impatience!

On one level, I completely trust the unfolding of nature's rhythms. I'm completely opposed to grocery store tomatoes sold in January, unnecessary childbirth inductions, and genetic modification of fish—all examples of our human compulsion to override or ignore nature's laws. This attitude in general has created problems like global climate change, increased rates of cancer, and polluted drinking water. I know this. And yet a part of me still wants what it wants, when it wants it. Like planting seeds when I shouldn't. Sigh.

I read a library book to my children wherein Winnie-the-Pooh and friends visit Rabbit's garden in early summer. The illustrations showed ripe orange pumpkins growing next to snap peas and plump strawberries. Pumpkins aren't ripe in early summer. Peas might be, if we're talking May, but strawberries don't plump up until June. At least not in a garden plot outside of California. This innocent children's book made me mad. It and other books like it cater to the childish idea (which many adults still hold) that we can grow whatever we want whenever we want it, natural rhythms be damned.

But of course, a part of me longs for that perfect Disney garden, too. That longing is why I get mad at my garden in August. My plants shouldn't be stressed! My soil can't be hard packed and dry! Quick, garden, be something you aren't!

As I water and dream of rain, I wonder—do I also expect myself to transform into something I am not and cannot be? Perhaps the garden can teach me something about being easy on myself. Letting go of expectations and judgments, and letting natural rhythms and beauties and gifts unfold on their own. I realize I need this in my garden and my life.

I pick some purslane, an invasive weed, and eat it. The plant is high in vitamin C and Omega-3 fatty acids, and it grows well in my garden in August. Perhaps I need to cultivate that instead of trying to grow chard in this scorching heat. The garden doesn't need transforming—my idea of what the garden should be needs transforming. By changing my expectations, I can accept the garden and my impatience.

Full

Nestling compost around my late-summer-drooping plants wakes them up almost immediately. This makes me wonder what I could nestle around myself to perk me up. The sun is hot, the days a little too bright, and at night the Full Moon spills reflected sun-

light across my bed. In the hot, active yang of summer, I long for
the cool yin of deep darkness: autumn, winter, compost, a dark,
cooling cave.

And yet the high-summer Full Moon works its intense magic
on me. During the day I garden, take the kids on outings, plan
our homeschool year, attend to the neverending flow of house-
work, and otherwise busy myself like a bee in a field of clover. At
night I have trouble sleeping, and the household arises just after
dawn. I am as burned out as the garden soil.

Tomatoes are green still but they weigh down the vines. Zuc-
chinis fatten in quick succession. The corn pushes tassels toward
the blazing sun. The garden, and my life, radiate activity and
ripening and fullness. Yet I resist the intensity. Working with
the compost in its shady corner of the garden provides a bit of
an antidote. Then, as I tuck fluffy dark soil around the plants, I
find myself rejoicing at the ripening fruit instead of fighting the
high season. This is, of course, just what I was impatient for a few
weeks ago: fruits to show for my labor.

The Moon is in Aquarius. Like Leo, this is a masculine, dry,
barren time. It's about making improvements. I contemplate further how maybe my garden needs rethinking. Perhaps the patch
I've plotted out isn't the best spot for annuals like corn and lettuce, since each year I find this time disappointing as everything
fries in its sunny corner of clay soil. I consider putting in fruit
trees and other perennials and creating a different, more yin space
for my vegetables. Letting edible weeds thrive. Letting the garden
show me how to transform it. However, with the heat and the
Moon sign being what they are, I shouldn't act yet. The energy
of the garden confirms this when I tune in and feel its pulse.
The pregnant Moon is time to plan and prepare, like a pregnant
mother before childbirth.

With both of my children, I was eight months pregnant in the
August heat. I loved being pregnant—feeling my baby's move-

ments, announcing love and fecundity with my silhouette, antici-
pating the arrival of a new person. Being hugely pregnant in
August, however, I did not like. I knew that this ephemeral time
would be gone in a blink, so I wrapped my hands across my Full
Moon belly and let gratitude and presence chase away my impatience as best I could.

I let the memory of that pregnant time of waiting, planning,
and preparation guide me now. I let the energy of the garden
be pregnant, ready to transform when the time is right. As with
natural childbirth, the garden follows its own mysterious time. I
have to be both mother and midwife. Patient, supportive, ready
to catch the metamorphosed garden when it is ready to emerge.

I prepare the garden for its next unfolding. I cut down the
orach plants that have gone to seed and bury them. I turn the
compost. I fill a corner of a mostly empty bed with branches that
will be used in a future huglekultur treatment. I water the corn
and tomatoes, but I let the empty beds rest. I envision fruit trees;
it feels right.

Waning

As the Moon turns her dark face toward us once again, I find
myself retreating from garden chores. I leave the compost to do its
thing. I release the temptation to urge the plants along. The buried
orach seeds might germinate for a fall crop, or they might wait
until next spring. The corn might grow ears, and it might not.
The tomatoes may ripen before frost, and they might not. In the
cooling light of the waning Moon, I care less what happens; my
impatience and my resistance are waning.

The Moon is in Virgo: feminine, dry, barren, earthy. Still not
time to plant, nor time to act on new projects. It is time to harvest
what is ripe but not push new sprouts. I am harvesting a new
understanding of transformation. Through chronicling my gardening this month, I've seen how I hold this idea of the perfect

Winnie-the-Pooh garden in my mind, and it stands in the way of other possibilities. At the very least, my expectations drive me into an anxious state I can surely do without. By honoring the energies of the Moon, my climate, and the personality of my particular garden plot, I might create a wholly different garden that is even more perfect than the storybook fantasy.

One never knows where transformation will take us. That's the resistance, the fear of what might happen if we let go of the reins. I have to learn to trust each step and allow the dance to unfold. I've transformed my garden through tools such as huglekultur, inner listening, following the Moon, respecting seasonal flow, and using loads and loads of compost. My garden has, in turn, transformed me by showing me that the great dance will lead me to freedom—and a great garden—if I can learn to follow my gut and trust in Mother Nature.

About the Author

Clea Danaan is the author of The Way of Hen: Zen and the Art of Raising Chickens *(Lyons Press 2011),* Voices of the Earth *(Llewellyn, 2009) and* Sacred Land *(Llewellyn, 2007) as well as numerous articles in almanacs and spiritually minded magazines. She lives in Colorado with her two homeschooled children, a pack of hens, two lovingly neglected cats, and her music therapist husband. Connect with her at CleaDanaan.com, on Facebook, or as GardenWhisperer on Twitter.*

2013 Eclipses—Will They Affect Your Career?

By Alice DeVille

The map of your life known as your natal chart presents a fascinating diagram of the path you are taking to invent your future. Your birth chart comes packed with potential—your career choices, dreams, education, family, partnerships, socializing preferences, soul purposes, and any number of goals that capture your attention during life's journey. All you have to do is go with the flow and let the people, circumstances, and lessons you have chosen unfold. Of course, this process takes years to materialize with a bit of help from the steady influence of transiting planets that travel the skies, making aspects and creating relationships with your natal planets. Along with planetary movement, each year four to six eclipses of the Sun and Moon occur in pairs, creating new conditions in your life if the degree of the eclipse comes in close contact with one of your natal planets, points, or house cusps. While some years won't be exceptionally eventful, you will experience a number of changes when a year's eclipses highlight your chart.

How Eclipses Work

Solar eclipses occur at the time of the New Moon, while lunar eclipses fall during the Full Moon. The solar eclipse New Moon occurs in the same astrological sign that is currently transiting Earth, while the lunar eclipse Full Moon falls in the opposite sign. The house in which the solar eclipse occurs defines the department of life that needs attention and is likely to undergo change. Variables are significant, and it takes professional interpretation to understand the scope of the upcoming changes. The most profound effect takes place when the solar eclipse creates a conjunction, meaning it is right on top of the planet, within 1–5 degrees of that planet's degree. Another intense condition occurs when a lunar eclipse opposes one of your planets and highlights situations that need your attention. If the eclipse is both conjunct to a planet in your chart and opposite another, you might have your work cut out for you! The kind of work depends upon the house and the nature of the planets affected. In this article we focus on examples of how eclipses trigger major career activity.

The 2013 Eclipses and Your Job

A challenging component of chart analysis is taking a look at the level of impact the current eclipses are generating and interpreting the possible outcomes for clients. In 2013, five eclipses occur. Four different astrological signs (two in Scorpio) cover the 2013 eclipse dates as indicated below. Consult with your astrologer to see if your chart has planets or house cusps at these degrees.

April 25, 05° ♏ 51', Partial Lunar Eclipse

May 9, 19° ♉ 33', Annular Solar Eclipse

May 25, 03° ♐ 58' Penumbral Lunar Eclipse

October 18, 25° ♈ 51' Penumbral Lunar Eclipse

November 3, 11° ♏ 16' Total Solar Eclipse

Career information appears in every house in your chart. In varying levels of importance, planets and their aspects describe what fulfills you in your career and work life. In the natural zodiac, solar houses start with Aries on the first house cusp and end with Pisces on the cusp of the twelfth house. In this scheme, the two Scorpio eclipses occur in the natural eighth house, while the Taurus eclipse occurs in the second house, the Sagittarius in the ninth, and the Aries in the first house. Normally houses that relate to your career or job include the second house of income; the fifth house of entrepreneurial undertakings or self-employment; the sixth house of daily work environment; the seventh house of partners and cooperative ventures; the eighth house of new income streams and partnership assets; the ninth house of moving out of the area for a new job or studying advanced subjects to qualify for a new position; the tenth house of ambition, career, and authorities that influence your status; and the eleventh house of employer compensation, which includes salary and benefits package as well as awards. Your individual chart drives the location of eclipses. If you have planets in any of these houses and the eclipses make a strong connection to them, your work life is likely to change.

When Eclipses Come Calling: Case Studies

Recent eclipse activity affected my clients in diverse ways. Be on the lookout for similarities in your own career path.

For nearly two years, Client A had major eclipse hits bouncing back and forth between his sixth house, where Mercury and Uranus were in residence, and his twelfth house. The climate in the workplace was edgy. Disruption became the norm, while erratic activity replaced the steady stream of work, hinting that a

shakeup was in the works. The company relied on funded contracts to guarantee employment for the workforce. Client A had
been instrumental in securing contracts in the past, but the state
of the national economy led to reduced funding. Select employees
experienced layoffs, and a dismal outlook prevailed. When an
eclipse hit sixth house Mercury, a major contract came through
for my client and the race was on to re-hire more staff, including
some of those who had lost their jobs. Within two weeks, another
eclipse exactly opposed Uranus from the twelfth house, and my
client broke his arm (the sixth house also relates to health). He
adjusted to one-handed pecking on his computer in the midst
of a high demand cycle. A few days later—Uranus also being the
bearer of surprising windfalls—the company CEO rewarded him
a new position.

Client B spent several months dealing with temporary bosses
after her much-revered employer retired. A new authority pat-
tern opened up after her tenth house cusp had a direct hit from a
solar eclipse. During the next round of eclipses, Jupiter (expansion, prosperity) in her tenth house had an eclipse conjunction
followed by an opposition eclipse two weeks later from Saturn
in her fourth house (home, family). Finally, after adapting to the
management styles of three other executives, a new candidate
emerged to fill the position. "The boss from Hell" became my
client's "permanent" reward. She soon realized that her polished
skills and open communication style were not attractive to her
new boss, who coveted every bit of information and hoarded it,
gave no direction regarding his expectations, and kept his office
door tightly closed. Within a month, my client lost her job and
was unable to find a new one for nearly a year. Lack of income
forced her to move in with her parents while she continued to
search for employment. A third eclipse brought new options and
a desirable position within two months. Although her salary fell
below the level she desired, her reputation for being a top pro-

ducer brought her new recognition and a hefty bonus within six months.

An example of how an eclipse may influence the decision to retire from the work world took place when Client C experienced an eclipse on Venus and Saturn in her eighth house of investments and assets. A study team examined her company's benefits package to cut operating costs. As a result, management decided to phase out certain benefits within three years, advising employees who were nearing 65 that they could retire early with a buyout package or stay until 65. However, the company stated that they would no longer pay into the pension fund of employees who stayed beyond age 55.

When my client came to me for a consultation, we looked at the big picture—she really wanted to stay in the work world until she was 70 and had no desire to draw Social Security benefits until then, preferring to stay employed. A look at her chart told me the company was not going to stop at the announced benefit cuts and that what they suggested would be a three-year phase-out was likely to occur much sooner. The eclipse pairs operating in her chart occupied the second house of income as well as the eighth house of insurance, funds, and deferred assets. I could see that the Venus/Saturn conjunction in her eighth house was going to get a blast from the opposition of an eclipse six months down the road that would change the dynamics of anything she had been promised. Since she had a ninety-day decision window, my advice was to revamp her resume, start looking for employment in a similar field, and apply for a new position before agreeing to take the early retirement option.

She quickly found a job, which she accepted knowing that she would have a nearly six-month wait before she could actually start work. At the end of the ninety days, Client C gave her company notice that she would be leaving her job in sixty days and was accepting the early retirement package. Within a month after she

left, Client C was happily engaged in a new job, one that would make her eligible for a new retirement package in five years.

Career-related geographical moves show up in your chart when eclipses trigger activity in the third and ninth houses. Long-distance moves come about when planets in these houses make close contact with eclipses via conjunctions or oppositions. During a recent eclipse cycle, Client D contacted me from her high-level military post in Europe for advice on applying for a less demanding military position on the West Coast of the United States. She had also been house hunting during trips back to the states. Her current job as a top aide to a high-ranking person on this strategically located foreign base was two years from completion. A family emergency arose involving the health of a terminally ill adult child with a baby. These complicated circumstances would lead to hardship if the situation were unattended. While the client was taking leave periodically to resolve emerging matters, the declining health of her daughter called for immediate assistance and could not be delayed while she completed her two-year tour of duty. Eclipses on the nodes in each house and on Mercury (contracts, agreements) in the ninth house conjunct the North Node (direction in life) brought the matter to the attention of military officials, who ruled expeditiously on the favored outcome. Within a few months, my client successfully relocated back to the States with a new job and a new home much closer to her family.

Boredom is another reason why career and job change occurs. Over time the lack of passion for work creeps in until a catalyst stimulates a move. Eclipses can play that role, as they did in the case of Client E, who was grateful to have income after a corporate acquisition shifted his responsibilities. Still, he felt that his most productive years were behind him. He went to work every day but slid into a downward spiral without realizing his condition or that he had options. Paper pushing became a way of life. He missed the people-to-people contact he formerly had as a leader of a complex project. When he consulted with me, it was clear that eclipses through his eleventh house of goals on his natal Sun and Saturn conjunction opposed to Mars in his fifth house of personal and creative enterprise were manifesting awareness. I asked about his short- and long-term career goals and the questions triggered a big "ah ha" reaction. He had lost sight of these goals. He admitted that nothing he did at work gave him much of a sense of accomplishment, nor did he feel in tune with the organization's philosophy and mission. The eclipses were just getting started making aspects not only in the fifth and eleventh houses, but also to his money houses in challenging aspect to natal planets in residence. Key eclipses affected his chart for nearly two years. During that time, he worked with a proficient headhunter and landed a coveted position as division director with a mid-size electronics company.

. . . .

From this article you have seen how eclipses in key houses are instrumental in patterns of career change. Consult your own natal chart to see see how the 2013 eclipses will influence your work life.

Resources

All reference material in this article comes from my personal consulting/client files; I changed a few facts about clients' circumstances to protect identity.

DeVille, Alice. "Astrology in the Workplace." *Llewellyn's 2002 Sun Sign Book.* St. Paul, MN: Llewellyn, 2002.

———. "Catalysts for Career Change." *Llewellyn's 2002 Sun Sign Book.* St. Paul, MN: Llewellyn, 2003.

Pottenger, Rique. *The American Ephemeris for the 21st Century.* San Diego, CA: ASC Publications, 1996

About the Author

In addition to being an internationally known astrologer, consultant and writer, Alice DeVille works as an executive coach meeting the needs of clients in the corporate, government and small business worlds. Alice specializes in business advice and counsel, career and change management, real estate, relationships, and training. She has developed and presented more than a hundred and fifty workshops and seminars related to her fields of expertise. The Star IQ, Astral Hearts, Llewellyn, Meta Arts, Inner Self, ShareItLiveIt, Twitter, and numerous websites and publications feature her articles. Quotes from her work on relationships appear in books, publications, training materials, calendars, planners, audio tapes and Oprah's website. Alice is available for writing books and articles for publishers, newspapers, or magazines and for conducting workshops and radio or TV interviews. Contact Alice at DeVilleAA@aol.com.

Waxing Moon Yardwork

By Elizabeth Barrette

The energy of the Moon creates a kind of mystical tide as it waxes and wanes. During the waxing Moon, this energy promotes initiation and growth. During the waning Moon, it facilitates reduction and banishment. The new and full phases provide turning points between the tides.

Your lawn and garden can benefit from these effects. Simply suit the tasks you choose for yardwork to the current phase of the Moon. You can find the phases for the year listed in this almanac. Now let's explore some activities that harness the power of the waxing Moon.

Initiation Processes

Initiation processes mark the beginning of something new. Start these when you see the first crescent of the waxing Moon, or shortly thereafter. They benefit from the fresh, new energy of this phase, which lasts for a few days.

Shopping in catalogs is one of the few yard and garden tasks that you can do during the dormant season. In some areas, such as the southern parts of the United States, this works best in late autumn. In other areas, such as the north where the ground freezes solid, you should do catalog shopping in winter. Know your local planting season. Also, look in the catalogs; most of them suggest the best time to order seeds and live plants.

Buying these things counts as starting a project because it is the first step in growing your garden or lawn. You can do it even before the ground is ready to be worked. For an extra boost, leave your catalogs in a window to absorb the light of the waxing Moon before your order.

Starting seeds will put your garden into the active phase. Sprouting seeds indoors is a task belonging in late winter or early spring. Check references for frost dates and soil temperatures for your area. Then factor in the types of vegetables, herbs, flowers, or other plants that you wish to grow. Each kind of plant takes a certain amount of time to germinate and sprout, and then grow to suitable transplant size. Make sure you have the right kind of potting medium and growth lamps too. Use these points of information to decide when to start your seeds.

Similarly, planting seeds in the ground is an initiation process that uses much of the same information. Do the ground preparation during the waning Moon, and then sow the seeds themselves during the waxing Moon. Look in the weekly almanac section to find the best dates for sowing your seeds.

Setting up a new bed or garden gives you a whole fresh space in which to work. A *bed* is small and often raised above the surrounding ground level. It can thus be assembled in a short time. A *garden* is often larger and is usually level with the ground. You may need to spread garden preparation over different phases. For instance, you might define and edge the garden to start it on a waxing Moon. Then you could remove or kill off existing sod during a waning Moon.

In this case, the blessing of the Moon's phase falls not on a living thing but on a container: the bed or garden. The phase assists you in completing your project successfully and aids the space in producing robust and healthy plants. To help capture the energy of the Moon, consider using a lunar decoration or a white boundary marker.

Creating new hardscaping features is a different type of beginning than live plants. Hardscaping comprises all the nonliving things that give shape and interest to a garden: walkways, benches, fountains, walls, fences, etc. When you begin a new project like this on the waxing Moon, you have plenty of time to complete it during the phase—and the energy helps keep it intact so that it will last for a long time without needing as much maintenance over the years.

This is another good opportunity to harness lunar energy in decorative motifs. Moon shapes may be stamped into wet concrete or painted onto fences. Features such as fountains may represent the Moon, the Sun, deities related to flowers or other gardening influences, and so on.

Growth Processes

Growth processes activate the life force and strive toward maturity. They benefit most from the middle part of the waxing phase. It lasts the longest, over a week. In addition to plants, growth processes affect other living creatures. For instance, if you want to attract more friends, try holding a cookout during this phase of the Moon.

Transplanting seedlings requires a delicate touch. Some types of plant dislike being moved and respond by "sulking" for days or weeks before they resume growth. They may even die. Other types of plant are more resilient to transplanting. However, young seedlings of any kind need extra care. Performing this task on a waxing Moon encourages the seedlings to root themselves quickly in the soil of their new home, so that they can soon send out fresh green leaves.

Harden off seedlings raised indoors by taking them out for short periods before planting in-ground. This gets them used to the outdoor temperatures, lighting, and air movement. Make sure that the outdoor soil is fluffy and moist, ready to receive the seedlings. Handle seedlings carefully and do not leave roots exposed to air for long. Once they are planted, water them generously.

Feeding plants helps them to grow bigger and stronger. The best fertilizer to use during a waxing Moon is a foliar spray, which the plants absorb through their leaves. Spray the plants thoroughly so that all surfaces of the leaves are moistened. It's best to do this in the evening, in order to avoid the risk of sunburn through the droplets on the leaves. You may also use other liquid fertilizers that can be sprayed or poured on the ground for immediate uptake by the roots. The Moon's energy helps pump the fresh nutrients through the plants to generate new growth.

Pruning for density is a technique that applies to certain types of plants. When making a hedge, you want the bush to put out many small twigs. Pruning the tips makes this happen. Similarly, pinching back herbs will make them shorter and leafier. Certain flowers will also produce more blooms if pinched back to encourage side shoots. All of these activities benefit from the waxing Moon, as it helps stimulate the plants to produce new growth rather than stay smaller. Look for nodes on the stems where shoots could appear, usually at or near places where leaves attach. Prune or pinch just beyond those spots.

Watering the lawn or garden stimulates growth by allowing plants to take up nutrients through their roots along with the water. It is best to water plants in the evening or during the overnight. This mimics the fall of dew and minimizes waste from evaporation. It also prevents burning of the leaves as sun moves through water droplets, acting like tiny lenses—a key risk of daytime watering. Plus your yard gains more benefit from the energy of the waxing Moon as the light shines down on the water.

It is better to water plants deeply and infrequently rather than shallowly and often. Give them a thorough soaking twice during the waxing phase, once at the beginning and once at the end. Wait out the waning phase, then repeat. (Use a watering can to perk up any plants that wilt unbearably in the meantime.) This encourages your grass and flowers to put down deep roots, reducing the need for supplemental water.

Expansion and Maintenance Processes

Expansion and maintenance processes consist of building on what you already have. This may be enlargements of an existing structure or upkeep to keep something in good condition. Such processes benefit from the waxing Moon, especially the few days toward the end of the phase, when the Moon is nearly full.

Dividing and moving mature plants is an expansion process akin to the growth process of transplanting. By cutting into an old stand of plants such as daylilies or top onions, the individual plants can be rejuvenated and given room to grow more. This lets you spread the plants out over a wider area. The Moon's energy helps divided plants recover faster and fill in their new space.

Laying sod in a yard is another example of moving mature plants, whether it's done with plugs or whole sheets of grass. Sod gives you a functional yard much faster than one started from seeds. Here the waxing Moon aids the grass in attaching its roots to the new soil, and in spreading quickly to cover any gaps. Both grass and other types of mature transplant will need extra water for a while, until they are fully established in their new location.

Grafting is an expansion process. It entails cutting a small sample of one plant—such as a twig, or even just a single strong bud—and carefully attaching it to a different compatible plant. This is most often done to propagate named cultivars of roses or fruit trees, which must be reproduced by vegetative cloning so that they remain true to type. The tricky part is getting the graft to "take" properly so that the donor material merges with the host plant. The waxing Moon helps the grafted tissues to join, heal, and eventually expand into what will become the functional top part of the plant.

Painting is an important maintenance task for many hardscaping features. This may include such items as statuary, a picnic table, a garden shed, or even the lining of a pond made from concrete. Generally you need to start by removing any old paint and cleaning the surface carefully. Let it dry. Then put the new coat of paint on. The energy of the waxing Moon helps the paint to bond with the underlying surface. It also encourages the paint to last for a long time without fading, cracking, or flaking. You may even find that things like bugs or leaves are less likely to fall into the wet paint to blemish or weaken it.

Mulching paths or driveways involves putting down a layer of material that you want to remain intact. This intention distinguishes a maintenance task from soil amendments (best done during the waning Moon), which are intended to break down. Here you want your bark chips, gravel, or other media to maintain its integrity and stay where you put it. Doing this task on a waxing Moon means it will last longer so that you won't have to redo it again soon.

. . . .

When planning your garden tasks, pay attention to the phases of the Moon. There is always something that you can be doing. Here we've explored some possibilities for waxing Moon yardwork. Look at the broad categories listed thus far—initiation processes, growth processes, and expansion and maintenance processes—then think about what you could do with those in your particular yard. It helps to observe your yard not just by daylight, when it's easy to see small details, but also by moonlight, when the subtle energies become clearer. This patient course of observation draws your attention where it needs to go as the Moon moves through the phases.

About the Author

Elizabeth Barrette has been involved with the Pagan community for more than twenty-two years. She served as Managing Editor of PanGaia for eight years and Dean of Studies at the Grey School of Wizardry for four years. She has written columns on beginning and intermediate Pagan practice, Pagan culture, and Pagan leadership. Her book Composing Magic: How to Create Magical Spells, Rituals, Blessings, Chants, and Prayers *explains how to combine writing and spirituality. She lives in central Illinois where she has done much networking with Pagans in her area, such as coffeehouse meetings and open sabbats. Her other public activities feature Pagan picnics and science fiction conventions. She enjoys magical crafts, historic religions, and gardening for wildlife. Her other writing fields include speculative fiction, gender studies, and social and environmental issues. One of her Pagan science fiction poems, "Fallen Gardens," was nominated for the Rhysling Award in 2010. Visit her blog, The Wordsmith's Forge, at http://ysabetwordsmith.livejournal.com.*

Straw Bales for Growing Herbs

By Charlie Rainbow Wolf

Straw has long been used as a suitable mulch and ingredient in compost for the home gardener. Recently there has been a growing trend to plant directly in the bales. This method of gardening is cultivating favor for many reasons.

Straw bale gardening is not dependent on soil types. The bales can even be placed on gravel or concrete, making a garden very accessible to those who have limited space. The bales have to be conditioned before planting, but most who advocate this method of gardening will agree that conditioning a bale is easier than trying to correct very acidic or alkaline soil.

This method also provides instant raised beds. While many raised beds take time and effort to create, a bale creates a raised bed immediately, with the added advantage of being easily moved before planting should it be decided that its location is less than desirable. And bales are easier to tend, because their height makes for less stooping for the gardener.

Another convenience of bales is the temporary nature of the gardens. Great labyrinths and other patterns can be created. They can be used as border to create a cold frame too. At the end of the season, the straw is broken down to mulch the ground and winter it over. The following year, new bales can be placed on top of the mulch, or the mulch can be removed and other things planted, should a bale garden no longer be appropriate.

There is very little weeding involved when using this technique. Any weeds that do form can be removed easily without the backbreaking bending that often accompanies traditional gardening methods. Sometimes grass will grow through the bales, but this is rarely invasive, and a quick haircut with a pair of scissors will usually do the trick.

First Steps

Straw, rather than hay, should be used. Straw and hay have very different compositions and will behave in very different ways. In a pinch, hay can be used and the plants will grow, but hay contains more seed and seems to be less durable than straw. Hay may be less expensive, though, or it may be easily obtained free of charge if a farmer happens to have some bales that have gone off. Adapting to the available resources is always a good idea.

If straw can be acquired from multiple sources, a bit of comparison may be wise. Bales can vary in price, size, and quality. A fresh, tightly bound bale is the best for gardening. Synthetic twine may not be as environmentally friendly as regular twine, but it is more resistant to rot, and therefore lasts longer. Sometimes wet bales can be purchased at a discount, and these are great for gardening.

Once the bales have been acquired, they need to be placed where the herbs are to be grown. The temporary nature of this type of gardening once again proves advantageous, since one bale can be put here and another there, making the most of the available light and prevailing weather conditions. Place the bales with the twine parallel to the ground and the straw running up and down for best results.

After placing the bales, it is time to condition them. The first step is to give them a good soaking with the hose—or pray for a *lot* of rain! Three days of heavy watering, both morning and night, is recommended. The bales need to be wet to start the decomposition that is going to nurture the planted herbs.

The next step is to apply something to help with the break down of the straw. Most who use this method for growing recommend ammonium nitrate, but that is often hard to obtain. Ammonium sulfate is more readily available and will work just as well. Uric acid works too, for those who are into a truly organic gardening method. Sprinkle about a half cup of the substance on the bales once a day, and continue to water twice a day. This should be repeated for at least five days before cutting back to a quarter cup of the powder for another five days.

After ten days, discontinue using the ammonium and start adding a plant food. A pellet food with a ratio of 10 percent nitrogen (N), 10 percent phosphate (P), and 10 percent potash (K) should be used. This will usually be labeled 10-10-10 fertizlier. Again, sometimes this is hard to obtain, but anything close to this ratio will be acceptable. For those who desire a chemical-free garden, this fertilizer can be made with compost teas and other more natural ingredients. For the novice, a commercially made food is usually the best method. Nitrogen, phosphate, and potash are all naturally occurring ingredients.

Different people recommend different procedures at this point. Some will suggest to plant the bales now, while others will suggest to dress the top of the bales with a thin layer of topsoil. Personal experience has proven that it may be too soon to plant the bales now, and the ammonium and fertilizer could burn the tender young plants. Resting the bales for at least another five days while still keeping them well watered morning and night is my recommendation.

Planting

The plants can now be added to the bales. There are many types of annual herbs and flowers that lend themselves to this type of gardening. Plants with fairly shallow root systems and compact growing habits should be chosen. It stands to reason that, because there is little to anchor the roots into the bales, top-heavy plants do not make good candidates for this type of gardening. Should a larger plant be desired, it will need to be staked in order to not pull itself out of the bale with its own weight.

Careful planning is needed when choosing which herbs to put into the bales. It is desirable for the bale garden to look well considered and aesthetically pleasing, as well as to be an efficient growing medium. The mature plants are going to want to fill the bales but not be overcrowded. Remember, the plants are going to be competing for water and nutrients, and they must be nurtured carefully in order to grow and thrive.

One method that I have successfully used to create different elevations among the herbs in the straw is to place wooden trellises at the back of the bales. Larger plants and those that climb can be anchored or assisted onto the trellises, making a nice background for the shorter plants. Nasturtiums and sweet peas have been successfully grown in this manner, as have mangetout and members of the squash family.

Vines also look very nice planted in the straw bales and cascading down over them in waves onto the ground. This is particularly effective if vertical designs have been built with the bales, such as pyramids. The cascading vines and flowers cover the straw and bring a soft, flowing feel to the rigid corners of the bales.

When choosing plants for the bale garden, consider what size they are going to be at maturity, their lighting needs, their feeding requirements, and their growth habit. Group plants with similar needs together. This makes tending for them easier in the long run. Place tall plants at the back of the bale garden to form a nice backdrop, trellising or staking them as necessary to give them the support they will need as they mature. Place cascading plants at the front to gracefully grow over the straw and soften the edges. Plant other herbs in the middle of the bales, as fillers.

Most annual herbs that can be obtained from garden centers are suitable for this type of gardening Parsley, basil, cilantro, fennel, dill, catnip, and mint are all appropriate for straw bales. Place the taller plants at the back, and be ready to stake or anchor them when they start to get a bit top heavy. Pinching out the tips to encourage bushiness is also a good idea. Mints will go a bit rampant, so don't plant them too close to something that is more delicate, or the mint will smother it! Mints are good in a garden though, for they help repel some of the undesirable insects. Catnip will also deter bugs, as will nasturtiums, marigolds, and bee balm. Marigolds and nasturtiums can even be planted into the sides of the bales, to help them look less stark. Try to think outside the box and let unusual plant placement inspire a creative and different overall look.

Care and Disposal

Remember that the bale garden is going to need a considerable amount of water. There is nothing in the straw that will hold the water, and it must be constantly replenished. I recommend a thorough watering early in the morning every day. Remember, it is impossible to overwater a bale garden, for the excess water will just run through the bale. For this reason, bales prove very advantageous when wet early spring weather makes the ground too soft to plant; bales are never too soggy for planting.

Once the frosts arrive and the herbs have started to die for the winter, the bales can either be left in place over the winter, or they can be broken down and used as a straw mulch. For those who do not want to break their bales down for mulch or compost, it may be possible to save your bales and use them for a second season. Some sources advocate this, some do not. The advantage is that there is no financial outlay for new bales, and the bales are already seasoned. The disadvantage is that the bales are likely to be very loose by now, and they may not hold the new plants tightly. Also, many smart bugs will overwinter in the bales, creating more of a pest problem the next year. I leave it up to you which path to take.

Straw bale gardening is both rewarding and easy when it is done correctly. As with most things, there are advantages and disadvantages. The bales need more care and attention when it comes to watering and feeding, but they reward that with less weeding, less stooping and bending for the gardener, and no soil preparation nor permanent impact on the land. Many people say that once they tried straw bale gardening, they could never return to tilling the land again.

About the Author

Charlie Rainbow Wolf is of Cherokee and English heritage and has studied the mysteries of both cultures. A published author and recorded singer/songwriter, Rainbow is happiest when she is creating something. She is a practitioner of shamanic healing, crystal therapy, and meditation as medicine. She is a member of the ATA, certified as a professional reader by the TCBA, works as an intuitive adviser for a prestigious international company, and is the Dean of Faculty and a teacher at the Grey School of Wizardry. Rainbow has a flair for recycling, and she is keenly interested in organic gardening and cooking. She feeds her creative muse with writing, pottery, knitting, and other inspired activities. She lives in the Midwest with her husband and special-needs Great Danes.

Farmers' Market Preserving

By Laura Frerichs & Adam Cullip, Loon Organics Farm

We are organic vegetable farmers in Hutchinson, Minnesota, where we operate a Community Supported Agriculture (CSA) program and also sell at a large farmers' market on Saturday mornings. We do our fair share of food preservation during the summer months and offer preserving shares to our CSA members and farmers' market customers. Freezing and/or canning even just a few items for the winter months takes a little bit of time in the summer, but it pays big dividends in the winter when you have great-tasting summer produce to eat! Preserving vegetables is also very economical, especially if you buy your produce at the peak of the season, when local prices are typically lower and the flavor of locally grown fruits and veggies are much better than anything you can buy at the grocery store. Ask your favorite farmers' market vendor if they offer a discount if you buy larger quantities of produce for preserving or if they have extra produce for canning/freezing. At the peak of the season, farmers often have produce with some cosmetic imperfections that make it less desirable to sell retail, but these imperfections make excellent food for preserving. Those ugly tomatoes taste like heaven in February! Here are simple instructions for preserving basil in the form of pesto, cooking greens, salsa, and tomatoes.

Basil for Pesto

Pesto freezes beautifully for the winter months when basil is expensive and of poor quality in the grocery store. To make a great batch of pesto, look at your local farmers' market for basil bunches or loose basil with bright green leaves, a fragrant smell, and no wilted or blackened leaves. If you love pesto and want a full winter's supply, buy 2 pounds of basil for making into pesto.

Pesto

3 cups packed fresh basil (remove any tough main stems)
2–3 cloves garlic
1/3 cup nuts
1/3 cup olive oil
1/3 cup Parmesan (optional)
Splash of lemon juice
Pinch of salt and pepper

Puree together in a blender or food processor until it becomes uniform. Makes six to eight servings. This recipe can easily be doubled or tripled for freezing.

Freezing

Make pesto as usual, but leave out the cheese or use the finely grated Parmesan that comes in a can. Good-quality Parmesan doesn't always freeze and re-heat well; you can add fresh cheese to your pesto mixture when you re-heat it. You also have the option to leave out the nuts in case you want just a basil, olive oil, and garlic mixture to add to soups and sauces. Put your pesto mixture in ice cube trays so that they freeze into individual, smaller-sized cubes. Once the pesto cubes are frozen (after about 12 hours), pop them out of the trays and put them in larger freezer bags for bulk storage. When you want to add pesto or basil to a recipe this winter, you can take out the number of servings you want and add them to your dish during the cooking process.

Greens: Kale, Swiss Chard, and Collards

Kale, swiss chard, and collard greens are great sources of vitamins A and C, some B vitamins, folic acid, calcium, iron, and magnesium. They also freeze and dehydrate very well. When shopping at the farmers' market for greens to freeze, look for crisp leaves and good color. Avoid wilted, spotted, or yellow spots/edges on the leaves. A bunch of greens (around ¾–1 pound) will shrink in volume and cook down considerably, so even several bunches, once cooked or deyhdrated, will fit in a quart-sized freezer bag. We freeze about a bushel of greens to get us through the winter months, and this fills up several gallon-sized freezer bags.

Freezing

De-stem at base of leaves, wash, and roughly chop. You can also freeze whole leaves, if you prefer. Drop leaves in boiling water for 2–3 minutes, just until they turn bright green. Remove from boiling water with a slotted spoon (or immerse the greens in the boiling water using a strainer for easy removal). Dunk greens in a bath of cold water with ice in your kitchen sink to stop the cooking process. After a few minutes of cooling, squeeze excess water out of greens. Pack cooked greens in freezer bags or freezer containers and store in freezer.

To use your frozen greens in cooked dishes, it is best to take them directly out of the freezer and reheat them immediately or just add to your soup, stew, or sauce to cook. If you let the greens defrost for a few hours first and then add them to dishes or cook them, they can turn mushy. Greens straight out of the freezer can also be added to your winter smoothies for a little dose of much-needed nutrients and chlorophyll.

Dehydrating

Dehydrated greens are a wonderful addition to soups, sauces, stews, quiches, and casseroles. You can dehydrate using any dehydrator or your oven set on low (90 degrees).

Wash and de-stem the leaves, and roughly chop or let the leaves remain whole. If using a dehydrator, set the leaves out on one layer in the dehydrating trays and follow the dehydrator's instructions. If you are using the oven, place leaves (de-stemmed) in a single layer on a cookie sheet, place in 90-degree oven, and flip leaves every couple hours until leaves have dried and become slightly brittle (but not burnt!). As soon as leaves in the oven or dehydrator are slightly brittle, remove them to prevent burning or over-drying. Let the leaves cool on the counter for a few hours before putting them in bags or mason jars for storage. Store in a cool, dry place out of the sun, such as a cupboard.

Salsa

Homemade salsa is a real treat! Salsa ingredients will be plentiful in your local farmers' market at the peak of the summer tomato and pepper season. Look for farmers selling half bushels (20 pounds) or bushels (40 pounds) of "canning tomatoes," which are less expensive in bulk. Red, ripe tomatoes are the best to use—either romas or slicing tomatoes. Yellow tomatoes and other pretty colors of tomato are great for fresh salsa, but these often have a lower acidity than the red varieties and therefore are not as safe for canning. If tomatoes have slight blemishes or cracks, just cut away the damaged areas and use the rest of the tomato. Peppers should be firm and crisp; if there are small blemishes on the peppers, simply cut those areas out before using for salsa.

If you are canning salsa, you will have to add additional acid (bottled lemon or lime juice or vinegar with 5% acidity), cook the salsa down, and then pack your canning jars with the hot salsa mixture. The recipe below is our favorite canned salsa recipe because roasting the tomatoes helps to drain off some of the tomato liquid before you boil it all together. This then reduces your boiling time. Salsa can also be frozen with good results— cook salsa before freezing for better texture.

Be careful when handling hot peppers! The juice from hot peppers can literally burn your hands, so wear gloves when preparing them. Avoid touching your face and eyes when cutting the hot peppers. The hot peppers we use in our salsa are habaneros (small, crinkled orange ones—very hot!), jalapeño (small, pointed, green or black in color—medium hotness), and Hungarian Hot Wax (long, yellow/orange/red in color—medium hotness). You can use any variety or combination of hot peppers to reach your desired level of heat.

Roasted Tomato Salsa

This is a relatively mild salsa. If you want a spicier salsa, just add additional hot peppers or some cayenne powder to the mixture.

   20 lbs. red slicing or roma tomatoes. roasted*
   6 medium/large onions
   2 ½ bulbs garlic
   6 sweet bell peppers, assorted colors
   3 jalapeño peppers
   2 habanero peppers
   1–2 bunches cilantro (1/2–1 pound total)

---

* If you prefer to not have the tomato skins in your salsa, you can pass your roasted tomatoes through a food mill OR dip the raw, whole tomatoes in boiling water for 30 seconds to peel off skins before roasting. We throw in the tomatoes with their skins on since everything will be pureed together.

2½ T salt

4 T bottled lime or lemon juice (or 5% acidity vinegar)

1. Roast the tomatoes with olive oil and salt at 400 degrees for an hour. Start by de-coring and quartering the tomatoes, then mound them in roasting pans (make sure to put them in pans with sides so that the juice doesn't run all over your oven) and drizzle with olive oil and salt. Stir the tomatoes every 15 minutes and as the tomatoes begin to cook they will release juices. Strain the juice off the tomatoes when they are done cooking (save that juice for soups or broths!).

2. De-seed the bell peppers and hot peppers. Peel the onions and garlic, and chop onions into quarters. Wash and dry the cilantro; cut off ½ inch of the cilantro stems. Add onions, garlic, peppers, cilantro, salt and lime/lemon juice to a food processor and process until ingredients are finely chopped.

3. Combine chopped ingredients with the roasted tomatoes in a big stock pot. Stir frequently over high heat until mixture begins to boil, then reduce heat and simmer for 10 minutes, stirring occasionally.

4. Ladle salsa into hot, sterilized pint jars, leaving ½ inch headspace. Adjust lids and process in a boiling water bath for 15 minutes. If you want to freeze salsa, just combine ingredients, cook down, and put in freezer jars (preferably wide mouth jars or plastic containers), leaving an inch or two at the top of the jar for the salsa to expand. Salsa can be frozen for up to six months.

Tomato Preservation

Tomatoes are one of the most frequently preserved vegetables, and they can either be canned using the hot-water bath method or a pressure canner. Tomatoes also freeze quite well. Canned and frozen tomatoes work best in cooked dishes, such as soups, sauces, stews, chilis, casseroles, etc. When buying tomatoes for preserving, look for farmers selling ½ bushels (20 pounds) or full bushels (40 pounds) of "canning tomatoes". Red, ripe tomatoes are the best to use—either the roma variety or any red, round slicing tomatoes. Yellow tomatoes and other colors of tomato can also be used, but often they contain less acid and are therefore not as safe for canning. Save your yellow and multi-colored tomatoes for freezing. If tomatoes have slight blemishes or cracks, just cut away the damaged areas and use the rest of the tomato. As long as the tomato is grown in season and picked ripe, it should have great flavor even if it has slight blemishes.

Freezing

De-core tomatoes, leave whole or quarter, and then pack a quart-sized freezer bag made of rigid plastic, Tupperware, or glass wide-mouth quart jars. We prefer freezing tomatoes raw in plastic freezer bags, and one or two quart-sized bag of tomatoes works well for a batch of soup or sauce. Obviously, freezing the tomatoes raw with their skin on is very fast, and this works fine for your everyday sauces, stews, and chilis, as long as you don't mind the tomato skins. Some people prefer to de-skin the tomatoes before freezing and even cooking them down a little first to get rid of some of the juice. To de-skin your tomatoes, cut a small X on the bottom (blossom-end) of the tomato and dip the tomato in boiling water for 30 seconds. Remove the tomato from boiling water with a slotted spoon and submerge it in ice water to cool. The tomato skin should easily peel off. De-core the tomatoes and either pack raw or quarter them and cook them down in a big stock pot to your desired consistency.

When you are ready to use your tomatoes in a dish, just take out how many bags, jars, or containers of tomatoes you would like and add them to your dish to re-heat, thaw, and cook down. Do not thaw tomatoes before cooking—there is no need, and doing so will affect the texture of the tomatoes.

Another option is to make your favorite tomato soup, sauce, stew, or broth and freeze that in rigid containers. This will provide a ready-made base that already has herbs, garlic, onions, etc. added into it.

Canning

Since tomatoes are a high-acid food, they can be safely canned either with a pressure canner or using the hot water bath method. If you use a pressure canner, you must specifically buy a true pressure canner that comes with weights and instructions for canning different food items. Regardless of

2012 © Richard Nelson. Image from BigStockPhoto.com

method, you should add 2 T of bottled lemon juice or 4 T of 5% acidity vinegar to each quart jar of tomatoes to ensure safe and proper acidity. Acid should be added directly to the jars before filling with your tomatoes. For pint jars, use 1 T bottled lemon juice or 2 T of 5% acidity vinegar. We don't feel that the added acid affects the flavor, but you may choose to add sugar to offset the acid taste, if you are concerned.

Sterilize your glass canning jars and put your lemon juice or vinegar in the bottom of the jar. Wash tomatoes and de-skin if desired. Core and quarter tomatoes, then pack them into the sterilized jars. Press tomatoes down with a spoon or spatula to compact and slide a rubber spatula down the sides of the canning jar to remove air bubbles. Leave about 1 inch of headspace at the top of the jar so that there is room for liquid to expand during the canning process. Wipe the rim of the jar with a clean cloth or paper towel. Apply the two-piece canning lid, making sure not to over-tighten the lid.

For a hot water bath, process pint jars for 40 minutes and quart jars for 50 minutes in boiling water that covers the tops of the jar by 1 or 2 inches. When using a hot water bath, jars can be removed at the end of their processing time.*

For a pressure canner, follow the manufacturer's instructions for the canning of tomatoes. Many pressure canners recommend 25 minutes at 10 pounds of pressure. If you are using a pressure canner, let the canner de-pressurize for several hours before removing jars.

After processing with either method, place jars on a folded towel to cool. Be sure jars aren't touching each other so that air can circulate properly around the jars. As the jars cool, the lids will seal (if they havn't already), and you may hear a pop. Do not tighten or touch the lids until jars have cooled and sealed. If jars have cooled and not sealed, you may either process them again with a fresh lid or refrigerate the contents and use within a week.

Screw bands are not needed on stored jars. They can be removed easily after jars are cooled. The screw bands can be used again in future canning projects if they are thoroughly washed. Self-sealing lids are one-time use only and cannot be used again to safely can foods.

About the Author
Loon Organics is co-owned and operated by Laura Frerichs and Adam Cullip. 2012 was our eighth season of independently farming, growing around 8 acres of certified organic vegetables and herbs at our 40-acre organic farm just west of Hutchinson, MN. We provide for a 150-member CSA (community supported agriculture, or farm share), local retailers, restaurants, and the Mill City Farmers' Market in Minneapolis.

---

* For complete and detailed instructions about hot water bath canning, see the University of Minnesota's Extension page "Canning Tomatoes": http://www1. extension.umn.edu/food-safety/preserving/tomatoes-salsa/canning-tomatoes/

The Fragrant Garden

By Janice Sharkey

Our sense of smell is an essential human instinct. We all react in different ways to aromas, but it makes sense to include in our gardens some of the plants with pleasurable fragrance. Aromatic plants can turn a good-looking garden into an unforgettable one.

Our senses can be bombarded by visual shape and color and react to touch, while that invisible sense, smell, is often overlooked. Scent is subtle. Its power all too often reaches us subliminally. To embrace scent, you need to slow down and follow your nose. This might mean brushing past a lavender path that releases aroma into the air, or it could mean crushing leaves of thyme underfoot that send scent up to your nasal hairs. As humans, our brain's olfactory system connects with our emotions, linking scent and feelings. Lavender is a good example of an emotionally balancing oil used in aromatherapy, but it can be just as effective inhaled direct from the plant in our garden. Humans link smells with memories and associations, so scent can be used for nostalgia and happiness. Sometimes our sense of smell is there to protect us, which is why we react to obnoxious whiffs from toxic sources. Aroma is also the bringer of sensual pleasure. Aromas can store lots of pheromones, sending signals to the opposite sex. Plants do not waft wonderful scent for us humans, however; they do it for survival reasons. Plants predominantly use scent to attract pollinators for the purpose of seed fertilization and the continuation of their species.

Aromatic essential oils that are taken from certain flowers, fruits, leaves, and roots contain liquids indispensable to medicine and to the food and cosmetic industries. There are about 300 essential oils that make up an extremely effective medical system. In food and drink, essential oils are used to give natural flavor and aroma and to act as a preservative. The perfume and cosmetic industries use aroma in mood- and emotion-enhancing capacities. In fact, aromas used as insect repellents or disinfectants have been around for a very long time. In medieval times, women scattered lavender and made pot pourri to hang over doorways to keep away unwanted vermin.

One question that springs to mind is why some plants are fragrant are others are not. Flowers are fragrant to attract pollinators. Inside the flower are the plants' reproductive organs, the fertilization of which is dependent on getting pollen brought in by insects. Bees are visual animals, targeting flowers by how they look rather than scent. Thus the level of scent depends upon the type of pollinator the plant needs to attract. Plants meant for moths and butterflies usually have the strongest scent, because they have to attract insects that fly over distances. Some flowers open to receive pollinators only at night, such as evening primrose and woodland tobacco, so they use scent to attract their pollinators in the absence of light.

Aroma can also act to protect a plant, as from drought or predators. Many aromatic foliar plants have leaves that exude oils to prevent them from wilting out in dry conditions, which is why so many Mediterranean herbs have an abundance of aromatic foliage: rosemary, lavender, and sage to name but a few. In the case of thyme, the oils are stored near to the surface and are released when the leaves are warmed by the Sun or touched by contact. Lots of plants, such as spurges or rockroses, create a smell to ward off would-be predators that seek to eat the plant. Garden plants like chrysanthemums give off odors that repel harmful insects.

What this means for us gardeners is we can protect some plants just by placing them next to others. You can disguise one plant with the other's scent, or use one type of plant as a sacrifice to spare another, e.g., an artemisia to attract bugs away from your beans.

The Fragrant Garden

Every gardener appreciates smells or scents in different ways, and what is nectar to one may be unpleasant to another. Learning to mix scents can be fun, but you may find that you do not enjoy some of the mixtures—perhaps the strong smell of the curry plant will clash with the subtle sweetness of the lavender. Through planning your garden design, you can choose when and how aroma will be released. It is possible to have a scented garden year-round and, depending upon where you position your plants, have them waft wonderful fragrance only when you are there. Remember, some scents exude only at certain times of the day, and others only when you touch them, so take these factors into consideration. There are fragrant plants in all shapes and sizes such as trees; wall shrubs; climbers; carpeting plants, like mountain gold; or ground cover, like chamomile and thyme.

A sheltered and sunny site is the ideal place for fragrant plants. Draw up a plan and mark out where the sunlight will be during the time you are most likely to be enjoying the scent. Many scents are stronger in the early evening after the heat of the day. "Smell-me" plants whose fragrance is carried on the air are mainly from the flowers, sometimes from leaves like curry plant. The strongest "smell-me" plants waft their fragrance onto the air, e.g., judd viburnum and yellow azalea. The less strong "smell-me" types need to be approached by the nose, e.g., Reeves skimmia and hardy blue ceanothus. You should try to have access to these plants, either within nose or hand reach when walking or sitting.

"Touch me" plants, as the name suggests, contain fragrance in their leaves and release it with a gentle touch or brush of the fingers. Examples are rosemary, lemon verbena, and scented geraniums. "Crush me" plants are those whose leaves have to be bruised between the fingers in order to release their fragrance. Examples are Mexican orange, bay laurel, and American wintergreen.

Companion Planting

Planting certain species next to each other can benefit more susceptible plants, either by masking the sweet scent from predators or luring them away to hardier specimens. French marigolds are an old faithful companion plant, as their scent disguises that of beans, thus protecting them from attack. Poached egg plant is great at attracting hoverflies and so keeps down aphids. The fragrant flower garden is a natural companion to the vegetable garden, because its scent disguises the smell of vegetable, thus protecting them from critters.

Having fragrant herbs such as lavender, oregano, and sage helps to make the garden smell good but also increases biodiversity and attracts pollinators like bees. Some plants can be sacrificial plants or act like a magnet for bugs to save the plant you really want to see succeed, such as sacrificing a basil plant to keep the nearby tomatoes thriving.

As the science of scent analysis improves, a more complex and fascinating picture is emerging. When certain plants are eaten by insects, they have been found to emit a chemical to attract other insects; this second round of insects eats the first kind! Cabbages that are infested with cabbage white butterfly caterpillars attract a parasitic wasp that attacks the caterpillar. Other plants that are under insect attack generate a chemical to warn neighboring plants, which then produce certain substances to make themselves less palatable to the offending bugs. This could be good news for encouraging organic methods and letting nature find her own way of dealing with imbalance rather than relying on chemical pesticides and fungicides.

Aromatic Lawn

An alterative to grass is to plant a chamomile lawn. In very dry situations, wild or creeping thyme might survive better. Thyme has the added advantage of producing masses of mauve, purple, white, or pink flowers that are great for attracting bees. Why not opt for a patchwork quilt effect with varying colors? Chamomile is part of the daisy family and has relaxing aromatic feathery leaves. The best variety for lawns is the non-flowering form 'Treneague', which concentrates on lush leaf growth. Occasional trimming with shears is all that is needed to keep it looking good.

Other aromatic lawn options include pennyroyal with its mint scent, New Zealand burr, or wild white clover, which is low maintenance and fixes its own nitrogen into soil. If your garden is cool and shady, you might plant earthy-scented mosses, which are wonderfully soft on your feet.

The Moveable Scented Garden

Portable perfume offers the flexibility of choice, so opting for growing scented plants in containers has real advantages. You can design pot themes for every season; when the plants start to look jaded, just move them into the background and bring on the next seasonal display. Containers can be adapted to suit your garden no matter what size, and you can enjoy a constantly changing feast for the senses—especially the aroma in the air.

Pots also allow you to have plants in places you might not otherwise be able to. Ideal places to have scent are around doorways, windowsills, and seats, where the aroma will tempt you to rest and savor the smells. During summer, put fragrant flowers by open windows so their perfume fills the house. Heat from conservatories will encourage aromas to release into the air. Having "inside-outside" tender exotic plants, such as lemon verbena, gives you the flexibility of enjoying them indoors during wintertime; come spring, the potted plants can be moved to the summer patio.

Scented Bulbs

If you have a large enough container, you could plant a pot of layered bulbs and get bursts of scented color wherever you want them. The lowest bulbs work their way around those that are higher up to create a wonderful display. Plant the largest first, such as lilies, hyacinthes, or tulips. Follow with a layer of medium-sized bulbs, such as tete a tete daffodil, which will show first in early spring. Bulbs should be covered with soil up to three times their height. Ensure your pot has good drainage holes and a layer of stones in the base. Ideally, lift the pot off the ground.

Seasonal Aromas

Scented lemon yellow cowslips planted in a window box with contrasting purple-yellow heartsease will give an enchanting but easy display in spring.

High summer offers an abundance of choice, but my favorites are angel's trumphets with its scented trumpets that are exotic and dramatic—watch out with this plant, however, as all parts of it are poisonous. One scented climber that offers good coverage if mixed with honeysuckle is jasmine.

In the fall and throughout wintertime, go for the evergreen Christmas box, which offers winter foliage and flowers and can be planted in sunlight or shade.

. . . .

Scent is that extra invisible ingredient and should never be overlooked if you want a garden to be fully alive. Aroma sends coded messages to us humans to brighten our mood. To flora and fauna, scent acts as a defense mechanism and a vital source of attraction to lure pollinators to fertilize our flowers. We are rewarded as we sit back and savor that aroma. Whether we crush, brush, or just allow our noses to inhale, we are therapeutically intoxicated by aromas that offer pleasure in their perfume.

Resources

Brickell, Christopher. *The Royal Horticultural Society Encyclopedia of Gardening*. London: Dorling Kindersley, 1994.

Colborn, Nigel. *The Garden Floor*. North Pomfret, VT: Trafalgar Square, 2000.

Fisher, Sue. *Scented Containers*. London: Ward Lock, 1999.

Flowerdew, Bob. *The No-Work Garden*. San Diego, CA: Laurel Glen, 2002.

Worwood, Valerie Ann. *The Fragrant Pharmacy*. London: Macmillan, 1990.

About the Author

Janice Sharkey is a freelance writer and organic lunar gardener. She is working on creating a permaculture garden in her own backyard. Her other interests include urban community gardens and rescuing old buildings. She lives in Scotland with her husband and teenage daughter, Rose.

GET MORE AT LLEWELLYN.COM

Visit us online to browse hundreds of our books and decks, plus
sign up to receive our e-newsletters and exclusive online offers.

- **Free tarot readings • Spell-a-Day • Moon phases**
- **Recipes, spells, and tips • Blogs • Encyclopedia**
- **Author interviews, articles, and upcoming events**

GET SOCIAL WITH LLEWELLYN

 Find us on
Facebook

www.Facebook.com/LlewellynBooks

Follow us on

www.Twitter.com/Llewellynbooks

GET BOOKS AT LLEWELLYN

LLEWELLYN ORDERING INFORMATION

 Order online: Visit our website at www.llewellyn.com to select your books
and place an order on our secure server.

 Order by phone:
- Call toll free within the U.S. at 1-877-NEW-WRLD (1-877-639-9753)
- Call toll free within Canada at 1-866-NEW-WRLD (1-866-639-9753)
- We accept VISA, MasterCard, and American Express

 Order by mail:
Send the full price of your order (MN residents add 6.875% sales tax) in U.S. funds,
plus postage and handling to: Llewellyn Worldwide, 2143 Wooddale Drive
Woodbury, MN 55125-2989

POSTAGE AND HANDLING
STANDARD (U.S. & Canada):
(Please allow 12 business days)
$25.00 and under, add $4.00.
$25.01 and over, FREE SHIPPING.

INTERNATIONAL ORDERS (airmail only):
$16.00 for one book, plus $3.00 for
each additional book.

Visit us online for more shipping options.
Prices subject to change.

FREE CATALOG!

To order, call
1-877-
NEW-WRLD
ext. 8236
or visit our
website